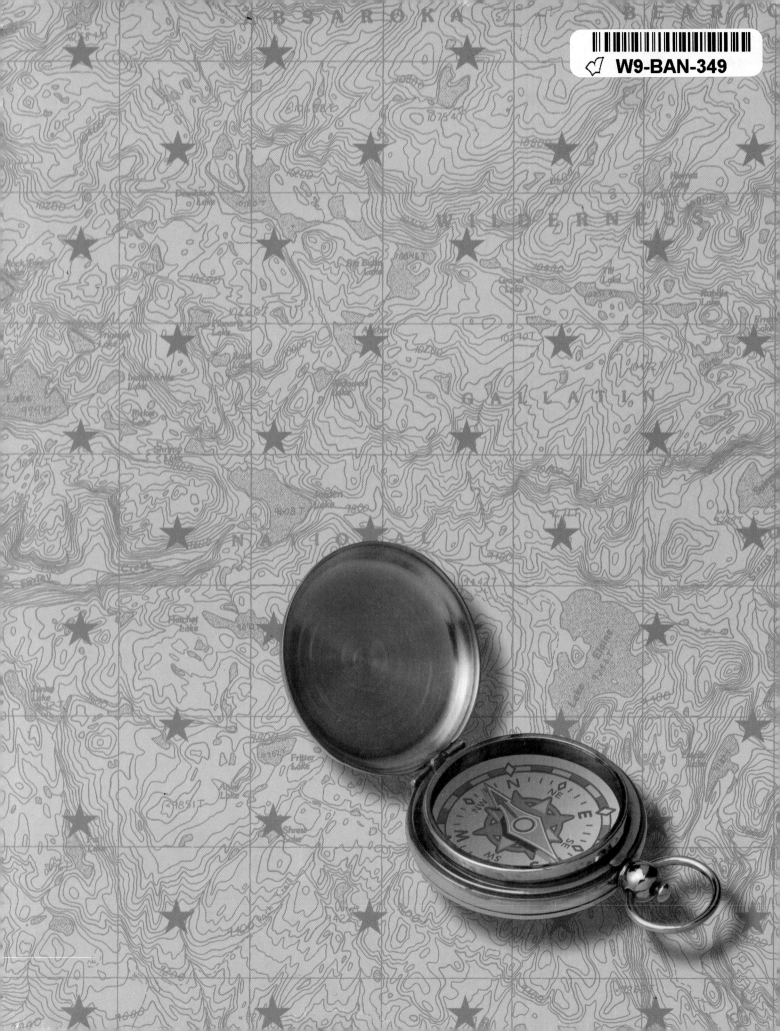

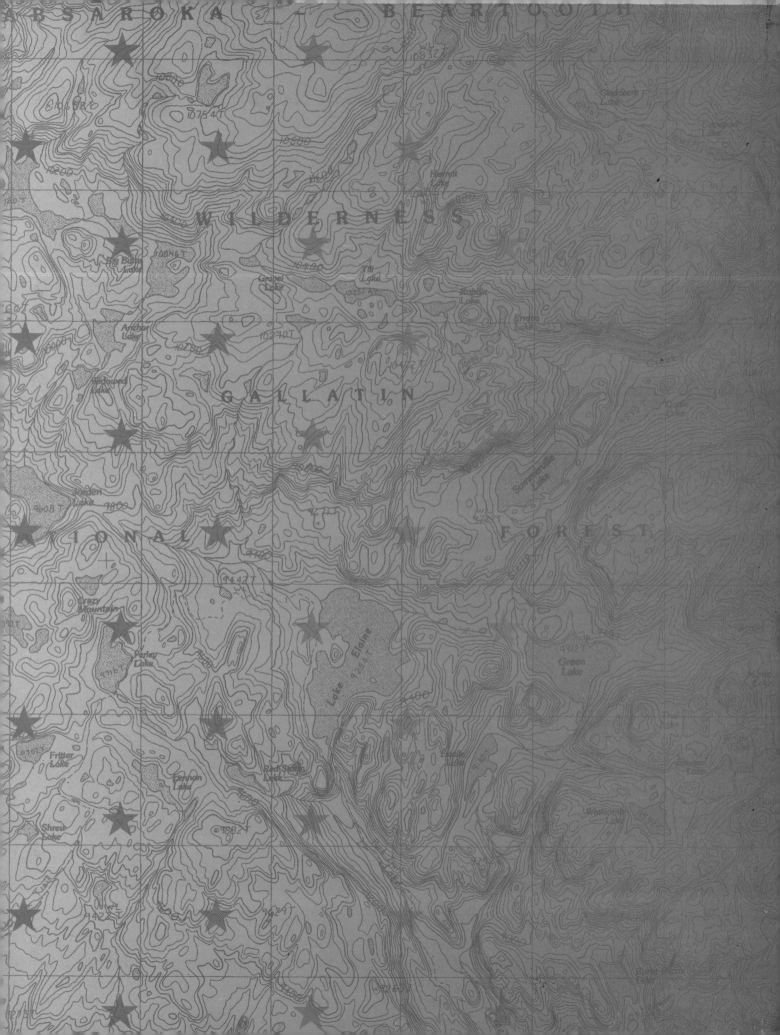

HOUGHTON MIFFLIN
SOCIAL STUDIES

★ COMMUNITIES ★

Visit **Education Place**®
www.eduplace.com/kids

 HOUGHTON MIFFLIN   BOSTON

★ AUTHORS ★

Senior Author
Dr. Herman J. Viola
Curator Emeritus
Smithsonian Institution

Dr. Cheryl Jennings
Project Director
Florida Institute of
Education
University of North
Florida

Dr. Sarah Witham Bednarz
Associate Professor,
Geography
Texas A&M University

Dr. Mark C. Schug
Professor and Director
Center for Economic
Education
University of Wisconsin,
Milwaukee

Dr. Carlos E. Cortés
Professor Emeritus, History
University of California,
Riverside

Dr. Charles S. White
Associate Professor
School of Education
Boston University

Consulting Authors
Dr. Dolores Beltran
Assistant Professor
Curriculum Instruction
California State University, Los Angeles
(Support for English Language Learners)

Dr. MaryEllen Vogt
Co-Director
California State University Center
for the Advancement of Reading
(Reading in the Content Area)

The United States has honored the Louisiana Purchase and the Lewis and Clark expedition in a new nickel series. The first nickel of the series features a rendition of the Jefferson Peace Medal. Thomas Jefferson commissioned this medal for Lewis and Clark's historic trip, which began in 1804.

HOUGHTON MIFFLIN
SOCIAL STUDIES

★ COMMUNITIES ★

 HOUGHTON MIFFLIN   BOSTON

Consultants

Lucien Ellington
UC Professor of Education,
    Asia Program Co-Director
University of Tennessee,
Chattanooga

Thelma Wills Foote
Associate Professor
UC, Irvine

Charles C. Haynes
Senior Scholar
First Amendment Center

Douglas Monroy
Professor of History
The Colorado College

Lynette K. Oshima
Assistant Professor
Department of Language,
    Literacy and Sociocultural
    Studies and Social Studies
    Program Coordinator
University of New Mexico

Jeffrey Strickland
Assistant Professor, History
University of Texas Pan
    American

Clifford E. Trafzer
Professor of History and
    American Indian Studies
UC, Riverside

Teacher Reviewers

Stacy Acker
Copopa Elementary
Columbia Station, OH

Kerrie Bandyk
Southeast Academic Center
Grand Rapids, MI

Julie Bauer
Mandela Elementary
East St. Louis, IL

Rosie Becerra-Davies
Montebello Intermediate
Montebello, CA

Cris Ferguson
Casillas Elementary
Chula Vista, CA

Nancy Hassard
Ryerson Middle School
Ringwood, NJ

Lynda Lemon-Rush
Cedargrove Elementary
Covina, CA

Karen Pratt
Fulford Elementary
North Miami Beach, FL

Stephanie Raker
Chestnut Ridge Elementary
Rochester, NY

Lorrie Soria
St. Augustine School
Oakland, CA

Sandra Stroud-Pennington
Winnona Park Elementary
Decatur, GA

Melissa Wamboldt
Mary M. Bethune Elementary
Hollywood, FL

Peggy Yelverton
Lockmar Elementary
Palm Bay, FL

Printed in the U.S.A.

ISBN: 0-618-42361-3

456789-VH-13 12 11 10 09 08 07 06 05

Contents

Bringing the world to your classroom!

vii

References

Citizenship Handbook

Resources

Extend Lessons

Connect the core lesson to an important concept and dig into it. Extend your social studies knowledge!

More biographies at
www.eduplace.com/kids/hmss05/

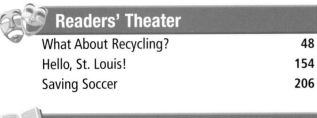
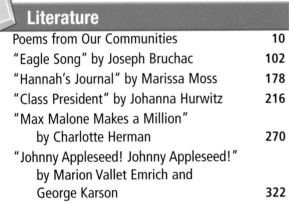

Skill Lessons

Take a step-by-step approach to learning and practicing key social studies skills.

Map and Globe Skills

Chart and Graph Skills

Study Skills

Reading and Thinking Skills

Citizenship Skills

Reading Skills/Graphic Organizer

Visual Learning

Become skilled at reading visuals. Graphs, maps, and timelines help you put all of the information together.

Diagrams and Infographics

xvii

About Your Textbook

➊ How It's Organized

Units The major sections of your book are units.

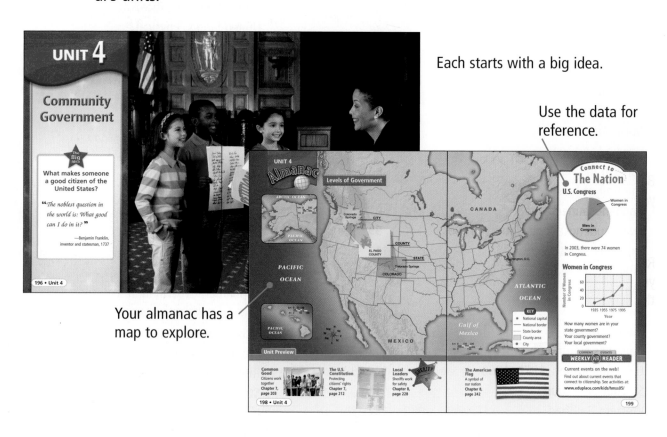

Each starts with a big idea.

Use the data for reference.

Your almanac has a map to explore.

Get ready for reading.

Chapters Units are divided into chapters, and each opens with a vocabulary preview.

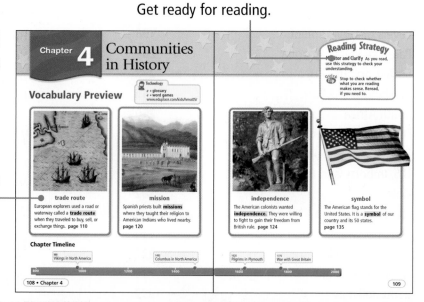

Four important concepts get you started.

② Core and Extend

Lessons The lessons in your book have two parts: core and extend.

Core Lessons
Lessons bring social studies to life and help you meet your state's standards.

Core Lesson **2**

Extend Lessons
Go deeper into an important topic.

Extend

Primary Sources

Core Lesson

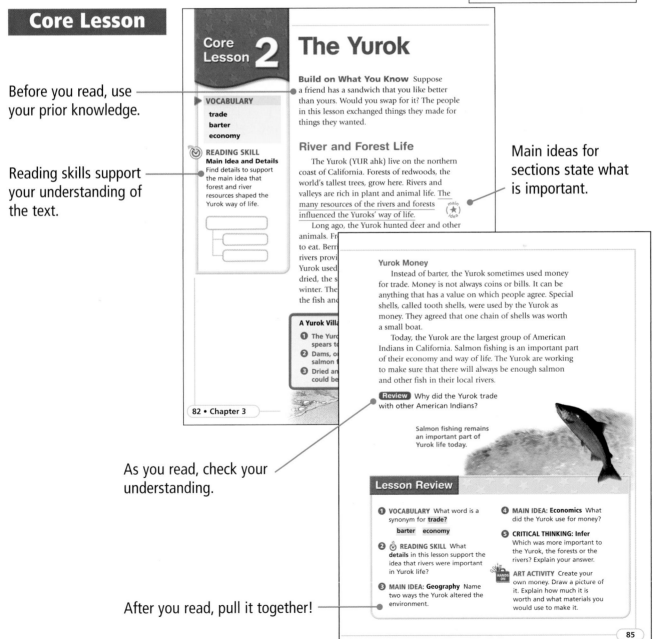

Before you read, use your prior knowledge.

Reading skills support your understanding of the text.

Core Lesson **2**

The Yurok

Build on What You Know Suppose a friend has a sandwich that you like better than yours. Would you swap for it? The people in this lesson exchanged things they made for things they wanted.

VOCABULARY
trade
barter
economy

READING SKILL
Main Idea and Details Find details to support the main idea that forest and river resources shaped the Yurok way of life.

River and Forest Life

The Yurok (YUR ahk) live on the northern coast of California. Forests of redwoods, the world's tallest trees, grow here. Rivers and valleys are rich in plant and animal life. The many resources of the rivers and forests influenced the Yuroks' way of life.

Long ago, the Yurok hunted deer and other animals. Fr... to eat. Berr... rivers provi... Yurok used... dried, the s... winter. The... the fish and...

A Yurok Villa...
1 The Yuro... spears to...
2 Dams, o... salmon...
3 Dried an... could be...

82 • Chapter 3

Main ideas for sections state what is important.

Yurok Money

Instead of barter, the Yurok sometimes used money for trade. Money is not always coins or bills. It can be anything that has a value on which people agree. Special shells, called tooth shells, were used by the Yurok as money. They agreed that one chain of shells was worth a small boat.

Today, the Yurok are the largest group of American Indians in California. Salmon fishing is an important part of their economy and way of life. The Yurok are working to make sure that there will always be enough salmon and other fish in their local rivers.

Review Why did the Yurok trade with other American Indians?

As you read, check your understanding.

Salmon fishing remains an important part of Yurok life today.

Lesson Review

1 **VOCABULARY** What word is a synonym for **trade?**
    barter   economy

2 **READING SKILL** What **details** in this lesson support the idea that rivers were important in Yurok life?

3 **MAIN IDEA: Geography** Name two ways the Yurok altered the environment.

4 **MAIN IDEA: Economics** What did the Yurok use for money?

5 **CRITICAL THINKING: Infer** Which was more important to the Yurok, the forests or the rivers? Explain your answer.

ART ACTIVITY Create your own money. Draw a picture of it. Explain how much it is worth and what materials you would use to make it.

85

After you read, pull it together!

Extend Lesson   Learn more about an important topic from each core lesson.

Look closely. Learn more about economics.

Dig in and extend your knowledge.

Look for biographies, readers' theater, geography, literature—and more.

Write, talk, draw, and debate!

3 Skills

Skill Building Learn map, graph, and study skills, as well as citizenship skills for life.

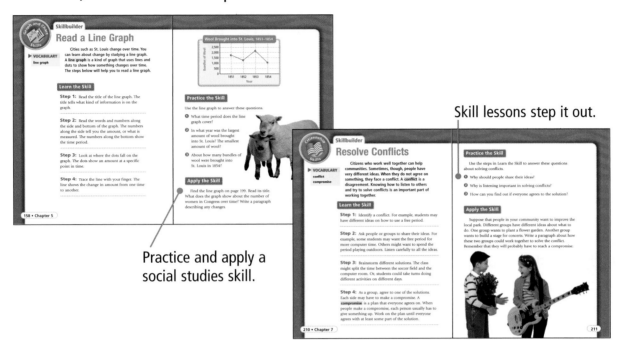

Skill lessons step it out.

Practice and apply a social studies skill.

4 References

Citizenship Handbook
The back of your book includes sections you'll refer to again and again.

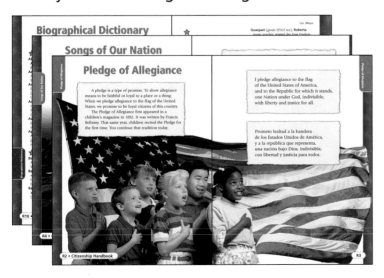

Resources
Look for atlas maps, a glossary of social studies terms, and an index.

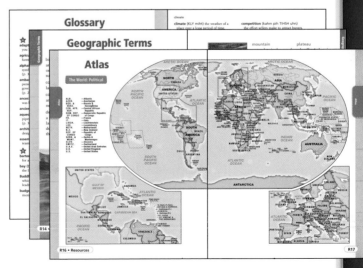

Reading Social Studies

Your book includes many features to help you be a successful reader. Here's what you will find:

VOCABULARY SUPPORT

Every chapter and lesson helps you with social studies terms. Your vocabulary will get stronger, lesson to lesson.

Preview
Get a jump start on four important words from the chapter.

Vocabulary Practice
Reuse words in the reviews, skills, and extends. Show that you know your vocabulary.

READING STRATEGIES

Look for the reading strategy and quick tip at the beginning of each chapter.

Predict and Infer
Before you read, think about what you'll learn.

Monitor and Clarify
Check your understanding. Could you explain what you just read to someone else?

Question
Stop and ask yourself questions. Did you understand what you read?

Summarize
After you read, think about the most important ideas of the lesson.

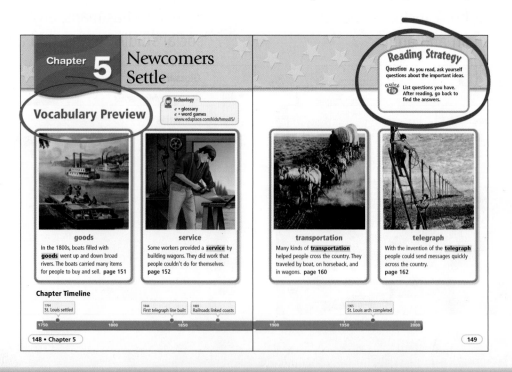

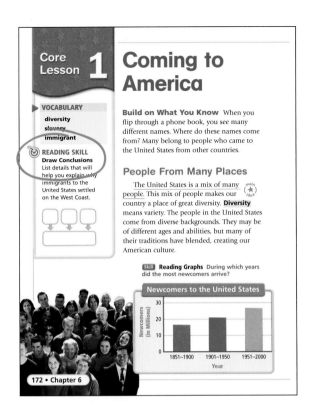

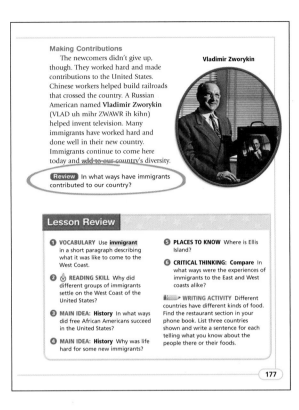

READING SKILLS

As you read, organize the information. These reading skills will help you:

Sequence

Cause and Effect

Compare and Contrast

Problem and Solution

Draw Conclusions

Predict Outcomes

Categorize (or) Classify

Main Idea and Details

COMPREHENSION SUPPORT

Build on What You Know
Check your prior knowledge. You may already know a lot!

Review Questions
Connect with the text. Did you understand what you just read?

Social Studies:
Why It Matters

Learning social studies will help you know how to get along better in your everyday life, and it will give you confidence when you make important choices in your future.

WHEN I
- decide where to live
- travel
- look for places on a map—

I'll use the geography information I've learned in social studies.

WHEN I
- choose a job
- make a budget
- decide which product to buy—

I'll use economic information.

WHEN I

▶ hear the story of a person from the past
▶ read books and visit museums
▶ look closely at the world around me—

I'll use what I've learned about history.

WHEN I

▶ go to a neighborhood meeting
▶ decide who to vote for
▶ get a driver's license—

I can use what I've learned about citizenship.

Town Meeting Tonight

UNIT 1

Community and Geography

The Big Idea

What does community mean to you?

"The great city is that which has the greatest man or woman; If it be a few ragged huts, it is still the greatest city in the whole world."

—Walt Whitman,
from "Song of the Broad-Axe," 1856

ARCTIC OCEAN

km 0   300
mi 0   300

ALASKA

PACIFIC OCEAN

PACIFIC OCEAN

Seattle
WASHINGTON

OREGON

IDAHO

MONTANA

NORTH DAKOTA

MINNESOTA

Minneapolis

SOUTH DAKOTA

WYOMING

IOWA

NEVADA

San Francisco

UTAH

NEBRASKA

COLORADO

KANSAS

MISSOURI

CALIFORNIA

Los Angeles

ARIZONA

NEW MEXICO

OKLAHOMA

ARKANSAS

TEXAS

km 0   50 100
mi 0   50 100

HAWAII

PACIFIC OCEAN

M E X I C O

Unit Preview

Urban Communities
Cities grow
Chapter 1, page 16

Bodies of Water
People use water in different ways
Chapter 2, page 28

Natural Resources
People care for our land
Chapter 2, page 44

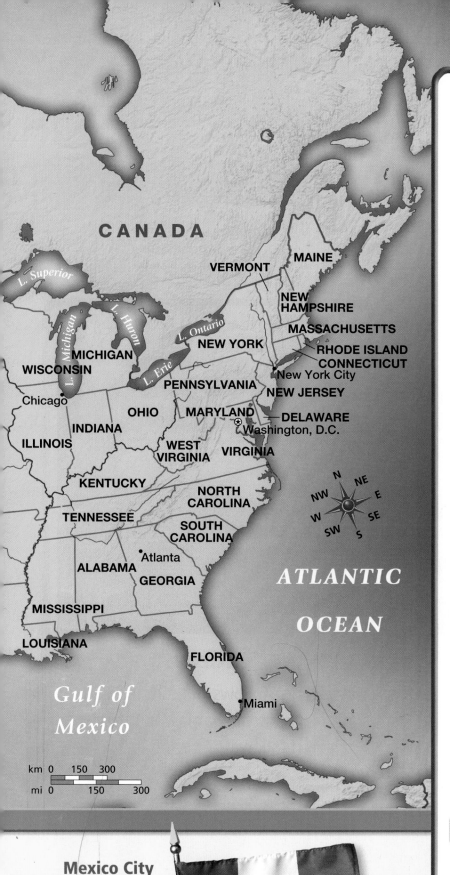

CANADA

L. Superior

L. Michigan

L. Huron

L. Ontario

L. Erie

MICHIGAN
WISCONSIN

Chicago

VERMONT

MAINE

NEW
HAMPSHIRE

MASSACHUSETTS

NEW YORK

RHODE ISLAND
CONNECTICUT

New York City

PENNSYLVANIA

NEW JERSEY

OHIO

MARYLAND

DELAWARE

INDIANA

Washington, D.C.

ILLINOIS

WEST
VIRGINIA

VIRGINIA

KENTUCKY

TENNESSEE

NORTH
CAROLINA

SOUTH
CAROLINA

ALABAMA

Atlanta

GEORGIA

MISSISSIPPI

LOUISIANA

FLORIDA

Gulf of
Mexico

Miami

ATLANTIC

OCEAN

N
NW NE
W   E
SW SE
S

km 0   150   300
mi 0   150   300

Mexico City
A city changes
**Chapter 2,
page 54**

Connect to
The Nation

U.S. Temperatures

134°F
Death Valley,
California

−80°F
Prospect Creek,
Alaska

These are the hottest and coldest temperatures ever recorded in the United States.

U.S. Heights

Highest Place: Denali
(Mt. McKinley), Alaska
20,320 ft.

Sea Level
0 ft.

Lowest Place:
Death Valley,
California
−282 ft.

Death Valley has both the hottest temperature and the lowest height in the United States.

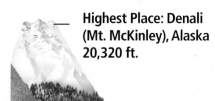
3

Chapter 1

The Places We Live

Vocabulary Preview

Technology

e • **glossary**
e • **word games**
www.eduplace.com/kids/hmss05/

community

Most people live in a **community.** There are many kinds of communities in which people live, work, study, play, and help one another. **page 6**

citizen

A **citizen** follows the rules and laws of the country. What law are these children following? **page 8**

Reading Strategy

Summarize As you read, use this strategy to focus on important ideas.

Quick Tip Review the main ideas first. Then look for details to support each main idea.

urban area

Many people live and work in cities. Another name for a large city is an **urban area.**

page 17

suburb

A **suburb** is a community near a city. Cities usually have several suburbs around them.

page 18

READING SKILL

Main Idea and Details
As you read, fill in the chart with details about a community.

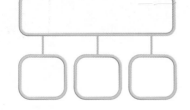

What Is a Community?

Build on What You Know Where do you live? Maybe you live in a large city. Maybe your home is in a small town. What makes it a good place to live?

People Together

People who live and work together can do things one person cannot do alone. Working with others is an important part of being in a community. A **community** is a place where people live, work, and play together.

main idea

Think about a school. The teachers, students, and principal help each other to learn. A community is like that. People in a community help one another.

In small towns, students might ride a bus to school.

Small Town

Communities and Their People

All communities are the same in some ways. That is because people in big cities and small towns need the same things. They need places to live. They need food to eat and water to drink. People want good jobs and good schools. They also want friends and family to laugh with and to help each other.

Many kinds of people live in a community. Some live in families with children. People young and old are often neighbors. Some might come from other countries.

Review In what ways are communities alike?

Places to play and work make living in big and small towns exciting.

Big City

Wearing a seat belt helps keep you safe. It also may be the law in your community.

BUCKLE UP
IT'S OUR LAW

Laws and Communities

People need ways to get along with each other. One way is to have laws. A **law** is a rule that tells people how to behave in their communities. Laws can help people live together safely and treat each other fairly.

Think of laws that you follow. In many communities, you are obeying a law when you wear a seat belt. That law helps keep people safe.

Following rules and laws is part of being a citizen. A **citizen** is an official member of a community, state, or country. Citizens can help their communities in important ways. In the United States, citizens choose people to be their leaders. The leaders make laws with the help of citizens. One law says that people born in the United States are citizens. Another law says that other people can become citizens, too.

main idea

Your Community

Think about your community. What laws does it have? Maybe there is a law about waiting for the walk light before crossing the street. That law lets people who are driving and walking share the street safely. There might also be a law against littering, to keep your community clean.

Your community is different from any other. What makes it special to you?

Review Why do communities have laws?

Community Laws
This traffic officer helps drivers on busy streets.

Lesson Review

① VOCABULARY Give two examples of ways in which a **citizen** can help his or her **community.**

② READING SKILL Use **details** from your chart to write a description of your community.

③ MAIN IDEA: Geography In what ways are communities different?

④ MAIN IDEA: Citizenship Why are laws important to follow?

⑤ CRITICAL THINKING: Compare and Contrast In what ways are the rules in your school like the laws in your community?

WRITING ACTIVITY Suppose that you are in charge of a community clean-up day. Write a short speech about what you would do. Include ways you would get citizens and leaders involved.

Poems from Our COMMUNITIES

Communities in the United States come in all shapes and sizes. In the following two poems, the people live in different communities, but they share much in common.

Walking Home from School
by Ann Whitford Paul

Grandpa Stokes calls out from
his porch,
"Your backpack looks
mighty full."
"Just like always," I say.

Mrs. Sanchez, working
in her garden, says,
"Take a flower to your mother."
I pick my favorite daffodil.

Mrs. Carter climbs into her van.
"I forgot something for supper."
I laugh and think, Again!

Julie Kim is on the telephone.
She gives me the thumbs-up sign.
That means her boyfriend's calling.

Mr. Potner hammers at his workbench.
"How's it going, Lauren?"
He asks the same thing every day.

On my street as far as I can see
I know everyone.
Everyone knows me.

Neighborhood of Sun

I live in San Francisco
in the Mission District
Neighborhood of sun
of colors and flavors

Avocadoes and mangoes
papayas and watermelons
Here my friend Tomás
laughs louder with the sun

Here in my neighborhood
you can taste
a soup of languages
in the wind

Chinese in the restaurant
Arabic in the grocery store
and everywhere
English and Spanish

Here in my barrio
the Mission District
the sun always shines
just like in El Salvador

Barrio lleno de sol

Vivo en San Francisco
en el Distrito de la Misión
Barrio lleno de sol
de colores y sabores

Aguacates y mangos
papayas y sandías
Aquí mi amigo Tomás
con el sol se ríe más

Aquí en mi barrio
se puede saborear
una sopa de lenguas
en el viento

Chino en el restaurante
árabe en la tienda de abarrotes
y por dondequiera
inglés y español

Aquí en mi barrio
el Distrito de la Misión
siempre hace mucho sol
igual que en El Salvador

by Jorge Argueta

Activities

1. **DRAW YOUR OWN** Make a poster showing what makes the community you live in special to you.

2. **WRITE ABOUT IT** Write a poem about your community. Tell about the people and things you see every day.

Review Map Skills

Different kinds of maps show different information. They usually have parts that are the same, though. The parts of a map help you understand the information on the map.

Learn the Skill

Step 1: Read the map title, or name of the map. The **map title** tells you what is shown on the map.

Step 2: Look at the map key. The **map key** tells what the colors, pictures, and lines on a map mean.

Step 3: Find the compass rose on the map. The **compass rose** shows the four main directions. These are north (N), south (S), east (E), and west (W). Often, the compass rose also shows the directions that fall between the main directions. They are northeast (NE), northwest (NW), southeast (SE), and southwest (SW).

The United States

Practice the Skill

Use the map to answer these questions.

1. Using the map key, tell what the thick gray line means.

2. What direction is between north and west?

3. Use the compass rose to tell where Florida is in the United States.

Apply the Skill

Use the map above and on pages 2–3 to answer these questions.

1. In what ways are the two maps different?

2. What country is north of the United States?

3. Is New York City northwest or northeast of Atlanta?

Kinds of Communities

VOCABULARY

population
urban area
suburb
rural area

READING SKILL
Compare and Contrast
As you read, list the ways that urban and suburban communities are alike and different.

Build on What You Know Think about the town or city where you live. Is it busy or quiet, small or large? What words would you use to tell about your community?

The Places People Live

New York City is our largest city. Its population is bigger than any other city in the country. **Population** is the number of people who live in an area. In big cities such as New York, many people live close together.

Large cities have many stores and many different jobs for people to do. Smaller communities have fewer people and fewer stores. Communities come in different sizes. (★) main idea

Atlanta Many people live in cities such as Atlanta.

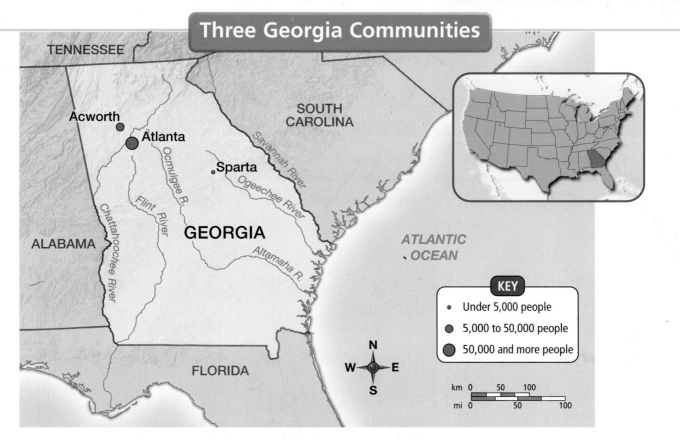

Three Georgia Communities

TENNESSEE

Acworth

Atlanta

SOUTH CAROLINA

Sparta

Ocmulgee R.

Savannah River

Ogeechee River

Flint River

ALABAMA

GEORGIA

Altamaha R.

Chattahoochee River

ATLANTIC OCEAN

FLORIDA

N
W — E
S

KEY
- Under 5,000 people
- 5,000 to 50,000 people
- 50,000 and more people

km 0   50   100
mi 0   50   100

Georgia Large and small communities can be found in Georgia.

Skill **Reading Maps** How many people live in Sparta?

An Urban Community

Many people live and work in urban areas. An **urban area** is another name for city land and spaces. The city of Atlanta is an urban area in Georgia. Find Atlanta on the map above. More than 400,000 people live there.

Companies large and small have offices or shops in Atlanta. They need thousands of workers. Many people live in Atlanta to be near those jobs. Cars, buses, and trains carry workers to their jobs.

Work is not all that brings people to big cities like Atlanta. Urban places buzz with things to do. In Atlanta, families often visit the zoo. Some enjoy the city's museums. Other people go to hear music or to see a baseball game.

Review Why does Atlanta have a large population?

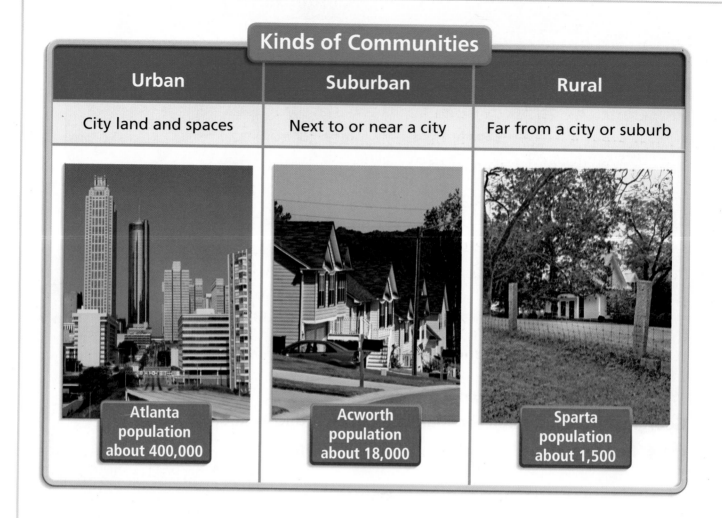

Kinds of Communities

Urban	Suburban	Rural
City land and spaces	Next to or near a city	Far from a city or suburb
Atlanta population about 400,000	Acworth population about 18,000	Sparta population about 1,500

Suburban and Rural Communities

People who want to live near a city, but not in one, might live in a suburb. A **suburb** is a community next to or close to a city. Millions of people live in Atlanta's suburbs. Many travel to Atlanta each day to work. In some ways, suburbs are like urban areas. They have schools, grocery stores, and banks just like cities. Suburbs are not as crowded, though. Acworth (AK wurth), Georgia, is a suburb about 35 miles from Atlanta. It has a population of about 18,000 people.

People in Acworth live in houses and apartments. The suburb has three elementary schools. It also has a lake and many parks for people to enjoy.

A Rural Community

Travel far enough from a city and its suburbs and you may see small communities. Often they are surrounded by farms or open land. You have come to a rural area. A **rural area** is far from a city. Rural areas have fewer people than suburban areas, and more open spaces. Sparta, Georgia, is a rural area. About 1,500 people live there.

Sparta does not have many stores to shop in. People go to other towns to buy some of the things they want. Some people who live in Sparta work there. Some are teachers. Others have jobs fixing roads. Many others have jobs in larger communities.

Review In what ways are suburban and rural areas alike and different?

Farmers in Georgia's rural areas grow many peaches. Georgia is the third largest peach-growing state.

Lesson Review

1 **VOCABULARY** Use **suburb** in a sentence about Acworth.

2 **READING SKILL** Use your chart to **compare** and **contrast** a city and a suburb.

3 **MAIN IDEA: Geography** In what ways is Atlanta like many other urban areas?

4 **MAIN IDEA: Economics** Where do some people who live in rural areas work?

5 **CRITICAL THINKING: Predict** In what ways might Sparta change if large companies built offices there?

HANDS ON **DRAWING ACTIVITY** Draw a picture of a main street in your town. Is it busy or quiet?

Our Largest City

It's tall. It's crowded. It glitters with lights at night. People call it the Big Apple. What is it?

It is New York City. This city has the largest **population** in our country. Over eight million people live there. Millions more visit the city every year. All around the city, buses, subways, bikes, and cars carry people where they want to go.

New York has some of the tallest buildings, or skyscrapers, in the world. Some are apartment buildings. Others are offices where people work.

New York also has plenty of places to play. There are more than 1,500 parks and playgrounds.

New York City

Parks for People

When Central Park was built, workers planted more than 270,000 trees and bushes. People today bike, play ball, watch birds, and picnic in the park's woods and fields.

Activities

1. **TALK ABOUT IT** Talk about ways people in a crowded place can get along with each other.

2. **WRITE ABOUT IT** New York's nickname is the Big Apple. Write your own slogan for the city and tell why you chose it.

Visual Summary

1–3. Write a description of each item named below.

Community

_____
_____
_____
_____
_____

Rules and laws

_____
_____
_____
_____
_____

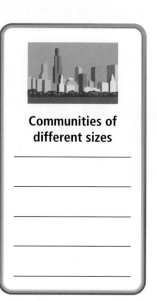

Communities of different sizes

_____
_____
_____
_____
_____

Facts and Main Ideas

✓ **TEST PREP** Answer each question below.

4. **Culture** What do people in every community need?

5. **Citizenship** In what ways can citizens help their community?

6. **Geography** What kind of community has the most people?

7. **Geography** What kind of community is far from a city?

8. **Government** In what ways do laws help a community?

Vocabulary

✓ **TEST PREP** Choose the correct word from the list below to complete each sentence.

citizen, p. 8
population, p. 16
suburb, p. 18

9. Sparta, Georgia, has a _____ of 1,500 people.

10. A _____ can be like a city, but it is less crowded.

11. In our country, a _____ can help leaders make laws.

Apply Skills

✅ TEST PREP Review Map Skills

Study the map of Illinois below. Then use your map skills to answer each question.

12. In what part of Illinois is Chicago?

    A. the southwest

    B. the northwest

    C. the northeast

    D. the southeast

13. What does the map key show?

    A. lakes

    B. cities

    C. rivers

    D. other states

Critical Thinking

✅ TEST PREP Write a short paragraph to answer each question below. Use details to support your response.

14. **Compare** In what ways is your class a community?

15. **Predict Outcomes** If citizens want their community to be safe and clean, what kinds of laws might they have?

Activities

Art Activity Draw a picture of your favorite building in your community.

Writing Activity Write a description of an activity people might do for fun in a city or a rural area. Tell why the activity would be fun.

Technology

Writing Process Tips

Get help with your description at **www.eduplace.com/kids/hmss05/**

Chapter 2

Our Land and Resources

Vocabulary Preview

Technology
e • **glossary**
e • **word games**
www.eduplace.com/kids/hmss05/

climate

The **climate,** or the weather over a period of time, is different in various parts of the United States. Climates may be warm or cold, wet or dry.
page 30

desert

A **desert** is often hot during the day and cooler at night. Deserts are dry and have fewer plants than wetter places.
page 37

Reading Strategy

Predict and Infer Use this strategy as you read the lessons in this chapter.

 Quick Tip Look at the pictures in a lesson to predict what it will be about.

natural resources

Water and plants are found in nature. People depend on these **natural resources** to live.
page 44

pollution

Some big cities have a large amount of **pollution.** Traffic fumes and smoke from businesses can dirty the air, soil, and water.
page 56

Earth's Land and Water

VOCABULARY

landform
erosion
geography
climate

READING SKILL

Main Idea and Details
As you read, list details that tell how different landforms affect the communities near them.

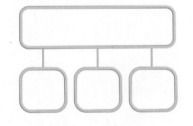

Build on What You Know Riding a bike down a hill is easy. Going up is harder. You pedal hard going up hills. On a bike, you can tell when the land slopes up and down.

Looking at Landforms

The hill that you worked so hard to climb is a type of landform. A **landform** is a shape or feature of the earth's surface. Think of how the earth is shaped where you live. Erosion helped form the landforms you see. **Erosion** is the way wind and water wear away the land, bit by bit.

When you think about landforms and erosion, you are thinking about geography. **Geography** is the study of people, places, and the earth.

Earth This photograph from space shows part of North America.

Living on the Land

People live in many different places on the earth. Landforms affect where people build communities. People often live where the land is level, or flat. There they can farm and travel easily. These are two reasons why many people also live on plains. A plain is a large area of flat or gently rolling land.

main idea ★

Because people often build communities where they can farm, many people live in valleys. A valley is the land between mountains or hills. The rich soil at the bottom of valleys can be good for farming.

Fewer communities are high in the mountains. Mountains can be rugged and have steep slopes. Food can be hard to grow on the high slopes.

Review Why might people live on plains?

Three Landforms

plain	a large area of land that is flat or almost flat	
plateau	an area of high land that often has steep sides and can be flat or hilly on top	
hill	a raised mass of land, smaller than a mountain	

Salt Water, Fresh Water

Water also affects where people build communities. Earth has two kinds of water: fresh and salt. People need fresh water to drink. We cannot drink salt water found in oceans, but it can be used for travel and fishing. <u>Many cities and towns are near oceans, rivers, or lakes.</u>

main idea

Rivers and lakes hold much of the earth's fresh water. Rivers are bodies of water that flow downhill. Lakes are large bodies of standing water, surrounded by land.

The world's oceans are salt water. Oceans cover more than two-thirds of the earth. Parts of oceans have names. A gulf is a large section of ocean partly surrounded by land. A bay is also partly surrounded by land, but is usually smaller than a gulf.

Bodies of Water Streams and rivers flow downstream to the ocean.
Skill **Reading Visuals** What parts of a river are shown?

source of river

stream

lake

river

delta

wetland

bay

Living Near Water

People in communities around the world use bodies of water in many ways. Many cities and towns build ports on rivers, lakes, or oceans. A port is a place where ships and boats can dock. People can earn a living at ports. Fishers catch fish to sell. Other people might work on the ships and boats that come and go.

Businesses also use water. They make drinks, prepare food, or water crops with fresh water. Some businesses build dams on rivers to create electricity. Others may use the oceans to ship things all over the world.

People also use water to have fun. In communities near water, people can swim or sail. In the winter, if the water freezes, people can ice skate.

Review Why are many communities near water?

waterfall

gulf

ocean

Lake Baikal in Russia is the world's deepest lake.

The Nile, a river in Africa, is the world's longest river.

St. Petersburg
63° F

Anchorage
12° F

Winter climates near St. Petersburg, Florida, and Anchorage, Alaska, are very different.

Skill **Reading Visuals** What clues about the climate do you see in each photograph?

Weather and Climate

What is the weather like today? Is it rainy or windy? Weather is what the air is like at a certain place and time. Weather affects people at work and play. For example, on snowy days, people may stay home until snowplows clear the roads.

In places where the climate is hot, snow may not fall in winter. **Climate** is the weather of a place over a long period of time. Climates can be warm or cold, wet or dry. They may change from season to season. Climates are also affected by water and landforms. For example, the cool water in an ocean tends to cool nearby air in the summer. The climate high in mountains is cooler than in the valleys below.

Climate Makes a Difference

Climate affects how people live. It affects their choice of shelter, food, and clothing. When it is winter in a cold climate, people wear coats and hats outdoors. In hot climates, people may cool their homes and businesses year-round.

Climate also affects the plants that grow and the animals that live in an area. Some plants, such as cactus, grow well in areas with little rain. Other plants grow only in wet climates. Certain animals, such as some kinds of horned lizards, live only in a hot climate. Animals such as moose, elk, and bears need cooler climates.

Review In what ways does climate affect people's lives?

Horned lizards live in the southwestern United States.

Lesson Review

1 VOCABULARY Write a paragraph that tells about the kind of **climate** you live in.

2 READING SKILL List at least three examples of how landforms affect communities.

3 MAIN IDEA: Geography List two ways that communities use bodies of water.

4 MAIN IDEA: Geography Why are ports good places for people to find jobs?

5 CRITICAL THINKING: Compare and Contrast In what ways might living near a river be similar to living on a plain? What would be different?

WRITING ACTIVITY Write a paragraph about the landforms or water you see in your community. Describe how people use them.

Geography

Erosion Shapes the Land

Arches National Park, Utah

Glacier Bay National Park, Alaska

Rocks split. Riverbanks tumble down. All over the earth the forces of **erosion** are at work, changing the land.

Wind is one force of erosion. It can reshape sand dunes on a beach. Over time, it can eat away at the **landforms** in deserts or other dry places.

Glaciers also cause erosion. A glacier is a frozen river of ice. It moves slowly down a slope or valley. Some glaciers spread out across the land. Over thousands of years, they grind and flatten the earth.

Water can also change the shape of the earth. Waves from the sea crash into sea cliffs and shores. Water flowing in rivers can lift and move earth from the river's bottom and its banks.

Over time, the Colorado River has cut through the rocky land around it. This helped create Marble Canyon in Arizona.

Activities

1. **TALK ABOUT IT** What three forces of erosion are shown? Talk about how they are different.

2. **WRITE ABOUT IT** Look carefully at the picture on this page. Write a paragraph describing what the land may have looked like before erosion.

Skillbuilder

Read a Climate Map

▶ **VOCABULARY**

climate map

If you were moving to a new place, you might want to know what the weather is like during different seasons. To find out, you could read a climate map. A **climate map** shows the weather of an area over a long period of time.

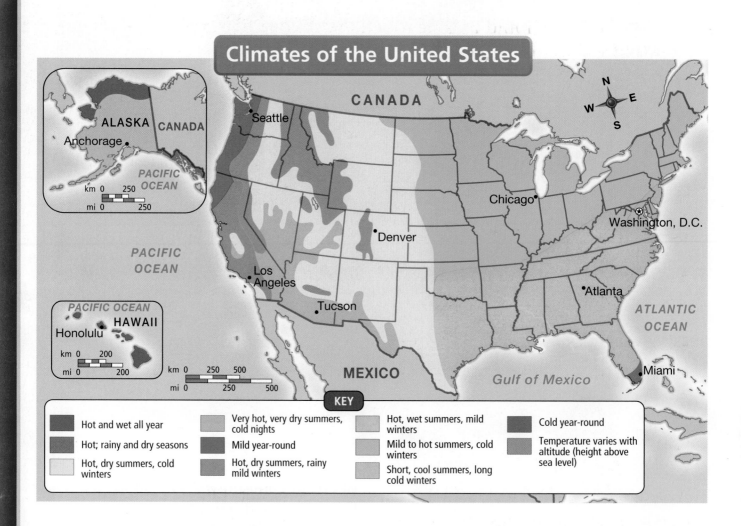

Climates of the United States

CANADA

Seattle

ALASKA CANADA

Anchorage

PACIFIC OCEAN

km 0   250
mi 0   250

Chicago

Denver

Washington, D.C.

PACIFIC OCEAN

Los Angeles

Atlanta

ATLANTIC OCEAN

PACIFIC OCEAN

HAWAII

Honolulu

Tucson

km 0   200
mi 0   200

km 0   250   500
mi 0   250   500

MEXICO

Gulf of Mexico

Miami

KEY

- Hot and wet all year
- Hot; rainy and dry seasons
- Hot, dry summers, cold winters
- Very hot, very dry summers, cold nights
- Mild year-round
- Hot, dry summers, rainy mild winters
- Hot, wet summers, mild winters
- Mild to hot summers, cold winters
- Short, cool summers, long cold winters
- Cold year-round
- Temperature varies with altitude (height above sea level)

Learn the Skill

Step 1: Read the map title to find what kind of information is on the map.

Step 2: Study the map key. Each color stands for a different climate on the map.

Step 3: You should be able to tell the climate for each colored area on the map. Check the map key for help.

Practice the Skill

Use the climate map to answer the questions below.

1. What are the winters like in Seattle?

2. Which cities are in areas with summers that are both hot and wet?

3. If you wanted to live in an area with a dry climate, which city might you choose?

Apply the Skill

Ask three other students what climate they would like to live in and why. Then find a city on the map that has the best climate for each student. Share with the class the most popular cities and climates.

Our Country's Geography

VOCABULARY

coast
desert
region

READING SKILL
Categorize Place
each landform and
body of water in the
right category: West,
Central, East.

West	Central	East

Build on What You Know When you look outside, what kinds of landforms do you see? Children in another part of the country see different landforms.

Traveling West to East

The United States has many types of landforms and bodies of water. The map on the next page shows the location of plains and plateaus, lakes and rivers. A location is where a place is on the earth.

Look on the map to find where the land and the Pacific Ocean meet. This is the West Coast. A **coast** is the land next to the ocean. Mountain ranges, or long rows of mountains, are located along the West Coast. These are the Coast Ranges. Find the Sierra Nevada mountains. Between these two ranges lies the Central Valley.

Sierra Nevada This mountain range is about 400 miles long.

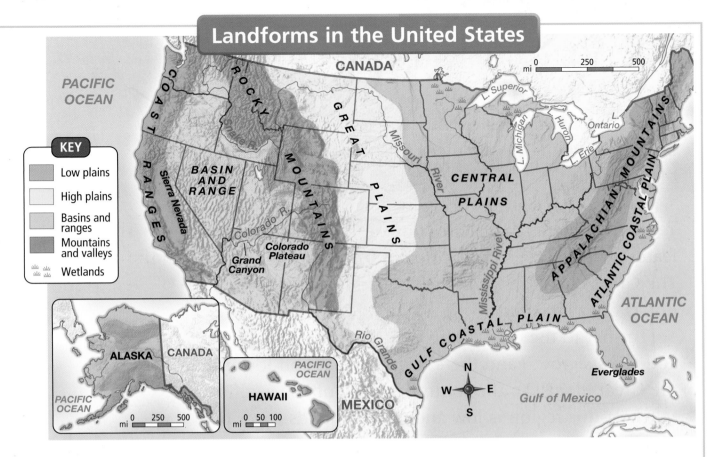

Landforms in the United States

KEY
- Low plains
- High plains
- Basins and ranges
- Mountains and valleys
- Wetlands

Skill **Reading Maps** What landforms are in Alaska?

Dry Land, Sharp Peaks

East of the Sierra Nevada is the Basin and Range. Low, flat areas of desert and mountains cover this part of the country. A **desert** is a dry area where little rain falls and few plants grow. In summer, deserts can be hot during the day and cooler at night. The hottest place in the country, Death Valley, is in the Basin and Range.

Move southeast on the map to find the Colorado Plateau. Here are mountains and canyons. A canyon is a V-shaped valley made by a river. Find the Grand Canyon. In some places it is more than a mile deep. The Rocky Mountains, the largest mountain range in the country, are east of the Grand Canyon.

Review Name three landforms in the western part of our country.

The Central United States

East of the Rocky Mountains lies the central part of the United States. Here the land flattens out. Rivers, lakes, and plains are the main features of the central part of the country.

The Great Plains are a vast region of grasslands. A **region** is an area that shares one or more features. Those features make one region different from another region. The Great Plains are gently rolling and dry, but they are not as dry as a desert.

Farther to the east, in the Central Plains, tall grasses, and forests grow. Land there is mostly flat and lower than the Great Plains. To the south lies the Gulf Coastal Plain. Much of this region is low and flat. Wetlands cover part of the plain.

Great Plains Hay, cut and rolled, lies on a field in Colorado.

Gulf Coastal Plain Wetlands in Louisiana are a feature of this region.

A Mighty River and Great Lakes

On the map, find where the Mississippi River enters the Gulf of Mexico. The river flows south for more than 2,000 miles to its mouth. The Mississippi is a major shipping route. Many barges travel up and down the river. They carry things such as corn and coal from port to port.

Look all the way north on the map. You will see five huge lakes. These are the Great Lakes. Together, the lakes form the earth's largest body of fresh water.

Review In what way is the central part of the country different from the western part?

Mississippi River Barges move along the river in Illinois.

Great Lakes The five lakes are located between Canada and the United States.

Appalachians The highest peaks are less than 7,000 feet above the sea.

Atlantic Coastal Plain This flat wetland in South Carolina is a salt marsh.

Eastern Mountains and Plains

The final region of the country is located east of the plains and the Great Lakes. Mountains, hills, plains, and rivers are the main features of this region. The Appalachian (ap uh LAY chee uhn) Mountains run from Maine to Georgia. They are not as high as the Rocky Mountains. Millions of years of erosion have made these mountain peaks low and rounded.

main ★ idea

East of the Appalachian Mountains is the Atlantic Coastal Plain. Parts of the plain are good for farming. Beaches and wetlands lie along the coast. This region spreads from Massachusetts down to Florida.

Wetlands and Ocean

Using the map on page 37, find a peninsula in the south. A peninsula is land nearly surrounded by water. On Florida's southern end are the Everglades. They are vast wetlands. East of the Everglades is the second largest ocean in the world, the Atlantic Ocean.

The Atlantic and Pacific oceans mark the coasts of the United States. Many landforms shape the country between them. In the West are mountain, desert, and plateau regions. The central United States has plains, rivers, and lakes. The East is a region of low mountains, coastal plains, and wetlands.

Florida The Florida peninsula is about 400 miles long.

Review Describe some of the main features of the eastern part of the country.

Lesson Review

1 **VOCABULARY** Write a sentence using **coast** and **region.**

2 **READING SKILL** Refer to your chart. In which **category** did you place wetlands? Why?

3 **MAIN IDEA: Geography** Write one or two sentences describing a landform you might find in the western United States.

4 **MAIN IDEA: Geography** Compare the Appalachian Mountains to the Rocky Mountains.

5 **CRITICAL THINKING: Infer** If you decided to walk from the West Coast to the East Coast, which parts of the country might be the hardest to pass through? Why?

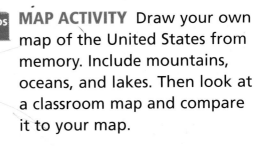

MAP ACTIVITY Draw your own map of the United States from memory. Include mountains, oceans, and lakes. Then look at a classroom map and compare it to your map.

Protecting the Land

Stand in the stillness of a forest. Hear the birds call through a wetland. Forests and wetlands are some of the special places in our country. We enjoy them today because people in the past worked to protect them.

John Muir
(1838–1914)

As a young boy, John Muir (myur) explored the forest and countryside near his home. In college, one of his favorite subjects was botany, or the study of plants. This led him to travel through Wisconsin, Iowa, and parts of Canada to learn more about plants.

Later, Muir took long journeys through other parts of our country. He lived for several years in the Yosemite Valley in California. He wrote about Yosemite's plants and amazing landforms. He wrote articles about the need to care for and protect the valley. In 1890, United States leaders made Yosemite a national park.

Marjory Stoneman Douglas
(1890–1998)

Like John Muir, Marjory Stoneman Douglas loved the land around her. She moved to Florida as a young woman and worked as a newspaper reporter. She began writing about the Everglades and the alligators, pelicans, and panthers there.

In a book, Douglas explained that the Everglades are like a big river. People began to understand the **region** better. The government made part of the Everglades a national park in 1947.

Douglas worked late into her life teaching people about the Everglades. She became known as the "Grandmother of the Glades."

Activities

1. **THINK ABOUT IT** In what ways did John Muir and Marjory Stoneman Douglas show they were **caring** for the land?

2. **PRESENT IT** Think about an outdoor place you love in your community. Write and present a short description of its plants, animals, or landforms.

Technology Read more biographies at Education Place. www.eduplace.com/kids/hmss/

Communities and Resources

VOCABULARY

environment
natural resources
renewable resources
nonrenewable resources

READING SKILL
Draw Conclusions
List what you learn about natural resources. Then reach a conclusion about how people should use them.

Build on What You Know What are the clothes you wear made of? Your shirt or pants might be made of cotton. Cotton is one of the many things from nature that people use.

Natural Resources

When you play outside, the sun warms you and the air around you. Air is part of your environment. The **environment** is the water, soil, air, and living things around you.

Plants are part of the environment. The fresh water in lakes and rivers is part of the environment, too. Plants and fresh water are natural resources. **Natural resources** are things found in nature that are useful to people. People use natural resources every day.

main idea

Natural Resources A farmer uses a tractor to gather crops from the land.

Three Kinds of Resources

Some natural resources are renewable. **Renewable resources** are resources that can be replaced. The vegetables you eat are renewable resources that grow from seeds. Farmers use seeds to plant new fields of vegetables.

Other natural resources are nonrenewable. **Nonrenewable resources** cannot be replaced. Oil is an example. People drill wells to get oil from the earth. They use oil for things such as fuel for their cars. Once used, oil is gone forever.

A third kind of natural resource is a flow resource. Sun and wind are examples. Flow resources are renewable, but they cannot be used all the time. People can only use them when they happen. When there is no wind, people can't use it.

Review What is the difference between renewable and nonrenewable resources?

Renewable Wheat for cereal is a renewable resource.

Nonrenewable Gasoline can be used only once.

Flow Wind power makes the electricity for this lamp.

Oroville Dam This dam in California is more than 700 feet high.
Skill Reading Visuals
In what ways did the dam change the river?

Communities Use Resources

Communities use their resources in different ways. Miami, Florida, has warm beaches and a sunny climate. These are two natural resources that draw many people to Miami. People often live where there are natural resources they can use.

main idea ⭐

When people use natural resources, they change the environment. The state of California built the Oroville Dam to block the water of the Feather River and make a large lake. People use water from the lake to make electricity. They also use it for drinking and to water their crops. However, the new lake destroyed places where river fish and wildlife lived. When people decide to change the environment, they must also think about the effects of the changes.

Electricity travels from tower to tower along wires.

Conserving Natural Resources

Many of the resources people depend on are nonrenewable. If they are used carelessly, they will run out quickly. However, people can use nonrenewable resources wisely. Communities can conserve, or save, renewable resources, too. One way to do that is to recycle. Recycling means reusing things that have been thrown away. Can you think of something that you can recycle today?

In this lesson you have learned that people depend on natural resources. Some natural resources can be replaced, but others cannot. People often live near natural resources they can use. When people use resources wisely, they help to conserve them.

Review Why should people conserve the resources in their communities?

Lesson Review

1 **VOCABULARY** Write one or two sentences describing the **environment** of your school playground.

2 **READING SKILL** Use the information on your chart to draw a **conclusion** about renewable resources.

3 **MAIN IDEA: Geography** Give an example of one renewable and one nonrenewable resource.

4 **MAIN IDEA: Geography** Why do people often settle near natural resources?

5 **CRITICAL THINKING: Cause and Effect** How might a community be affected if all or most of its resources were nonrenewable?

WRITING ACTIVITY Town leaders are asking your community to save water. Write a list of steps you would take to conserve water.

Readers' Theater

What About Recycling?

Whose job is it to care? A group of third-graders decides that it is everyone's job to care for the **environment.**

Ms. Pierce

Mr. Kato

Characters

Narrator

Rafael: student

Katie: student

Misa: student

Teddy: student

Ms. Pierce: principal

Mr. Kato: teacher

Ms. Schultz: teacher

Narrator: It's a warm fall day at Northfield School. During lunch recess, four students are playing freeze tag on the playground. The principal and two teachers are standing nearby.

Rafael: Watch out, Katie! You're about to step on that juice can!

Katie: Thanks. I didn't see it. I'll toss it in the trash.

Misa: At my cousin's school, they don't throw cans out.

Teddy: What? They just leave them lying around?

Misa: No! They recycle them.

Katie: That's what we do at home. We put used bottles and cans in a special bin. We have a bin for paper, too.

Misa: Exactly. Every week a truck comes by and collects it all.

Rafael

Katie

Teddy: Where does it go?

Katie: To a recycling factory. The stuff gets mashed up and they use it to make new glass, metal, and paper.

Teddy: That makes sense.

Misa: Recycling paper saves trees. You don't have to cut so many down if you use paper again.

Teddy: So why don't we recycle here at school?

Rafael: Let's ask Ms. Pierce. She's right over there.

Katie: Ms. Pierce, we have a question. Could our school recycle?

Ms. Pierce: Funny you should ask. We were just talking about that at a teachers' meeting.

Mr. Kato: Do you think students would separate paper and recycle it in bins?

Katie and Misa: Of course!

Ms. Schultz: Some of us have concerns, though. Bins might be too expensive for the school right now.

Teddy: We could use old boxes instead.

Mr. Kato: Good idea, Teddy.

Ms. Schultz: Yes, and there are other things to think about if we start recycling.

Katie: Like what?

Ms. Schultz: It can cost money for workers to pick up and sort bottles and cans. It's not cheap.

Mr. Kato

Teddy

Mr. Kato: True, but recycling saves energy. It takes less energy to use metal from cans than to dig for new metal.

Ms. Pierce: Plus, the more people recycle, the less they throw out. That saves space in landfills, where garbage gets dumped. They're getting filled up.

Bottles

Katie: So let's stop filling them up.

Rafael: I think we should waste less and recycle more.

Ms. Pierce: Sounds like a good motto. Would you students like to be on a school recycling committee?

Cans

All students: Yes!

Ms. Pierce: Teachers and students can work together to set up a paper recycling program.

Ms. Schultz: We can start by learning more about recycling.

Newspapers

Rafael: We could make posters and put them up around the school.

Misa: Let's ask the art teacher for some poster paper.

Katie: Great idea—as long as it's recycled poster paper!

Activities

1. **TALK ABOUT IT** What are the pros and cons of recycling? Are there others you can think of? Discuss your ideas with classmates.

2. **WRITE YOUR OWN** Write a short Readers' Theater about protecting the environment in your community.

Map and Globe Skills

Use a Map Grid

► VOCABULARY

map grid

One easy way to find a place on a map is to use a map grid. A **map grid** is a set of straight lines that cross to form squares of equal size.

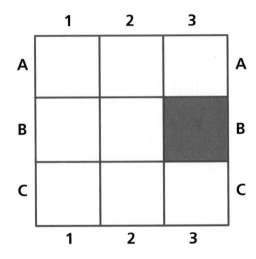

Learn the Skill

Step 1: Boxes that go from left to right form rows. Each row is labeled with a letter. Boxes that go from top to bottom form columns. Each column is labeled with a number. Every box has a letter-number name.

Step 2: Look at the red box. Move your finger to the right edge of the grid. The box is in Row B.

Step 3: Trace your finger along the column up to the top of the map. The red box is also in Column 3. This box is B-3.

Downtown Miami, Florida

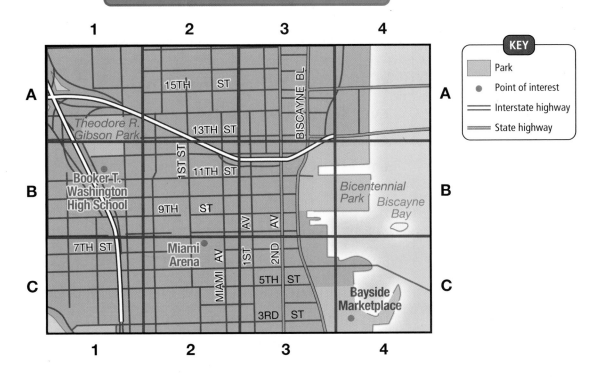

Practice the Skill

Use the grid labels and boxes to answer the questions below.

1 Which point of interest is in B-1?

2 Where can you find the Miami Arena?

3 Which column has no parks?

Apply the Skill

Draw a map grid of your classroom. Label the rows and columns. Include three objects such as the board, your teacher's desk, and your desk. Exchange maps with a classmate. Find the grid box and letter-number name for each object on your classmate's map.

WORLD CONNECTION
Mexico City

VOCABULARY

capital

canal

pollution

READING SKILL

Sequence As you read, write the events that took place in Mexico City over time. Be sure to put the events in order.

Build on What You Know Have you ever wanted to travel to another country? The country of Mexico is located to the south of the United States.

The Capital of Mexico

Mexico and the United States are neighbors. Look on the map below. Find Mexico City. It is the capital of Mexico. A **capital** is a city where a country's laws are made. Mexico City is located in the mountains. The air is often cool and dry, but summer days can be hot.

Skill **Reading Maps** What bodies of water border Mexico?

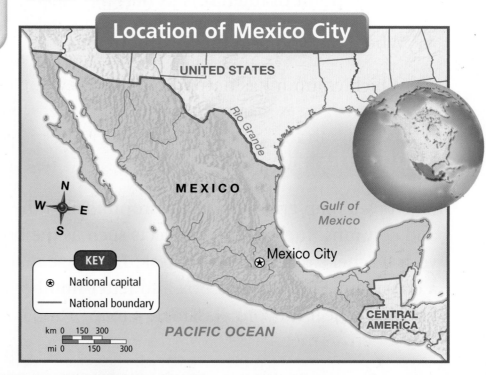

Location of Mexico City

UNITED STATES

Rio Grande

MEXICO

Gulf of Mexico

Mexico City

KEY

⊛ National capital

— National boundary

km 0   150   300

mi 0   150   300

PACIFIC OCEAN

CENTRAL AMERICA

Tenochtitlán This painting shows what the city might have looked like 500 years ago.

Mexico City's Past

Mexico City is very old. <u>The people who have lived there have slowly changed its environment.</u> Long ago, the city was once on an island in a lake.

main idea (★)

Almost 700 years ago, Aztec Indians settled on the island. Over time, they built a city we call Tenochtitlán (teh nawch tee TLAHN). The Aztecs made many changes to the land and water around them. They dug canals and built gardens. A **canal** is a waterway made by people.

Then, almost 500 years ago, people from Spain came to the area. They were looking for gold. The Spanish built a new city on the island. This became Mexico City. The Spanish wanted land, not water. They began to drain the lake. More people moved to Mexico City. They built buildings where the lake once was.

Review In what ways did the Aztecs change their environment?

Mexico City Today, nearly 20 million people live in the city. **Skill** **Reading Visuals** In what ways is Mexico City today different from Tenochtitlán?

The Mexican flag

Mexico City Today

Mexico City is now one of the largest cities in the world. Millions of people live and work there. People in the city enjoy concerts, museums, markets, and parks filled with trees.

As the city has grown, it has spread. Newer buildings now stand on the nearby mountains. Cars, trucks, and buses crowd Mexico City's streets.

When cities grow, they can create pollution. **Pollution** is anything that dirties the air, soil, or water. Fumes from traffic and smoke from businesses can cause air pollution. Like other large cities in the world, Mexico City has air pollution. The mountains around the city block the wind so it cannot blow the polluted air away.

Mexico City Looks Ahead

People in Mexico City are working to clean their environment. Some buses and trains now use cleaner fuel. City leaders shut down some businesses that made the air dirty. Leaders also made rules about which cars can drive in the city on which days. These steps have helped improve the city's air.

People have changed the land, water, and air of Mexico City. The Aztecs were the first to build a city on an island there. Later, the Spanish also made changes to the water and land around the city. Today, people are working to make Mexico City's environment cleaner.

People gather at a plaza, or public square, in Mexico City.

Review What is air pollution, and what are people in Mexico City doing to clean it up?

Lesson Review

1 **VOCABULARY** Use **capital** and **canal** in a sentence about Mexico City.

2 **READING SKILL** How did Tenochtitlán develop into Mexico City? Use information from your chart to list the events in order.

3 **MAIN IDEA: Geography** Why is Mexico City no longer on an island in a lake?

4 **MAIN IDEA: Geography** In what ways are people today affecting the environment of Mexico City?

5 **CRITICAL THINKING: Generalize** In what ways could Mexico City's steps to reduce air pollution be used by other cities with air pollution?

WRITING ACTIVITY Suppose you were able to visit Mexico City. List the things you might see there.

The City on the Lake

The Aztec farmer in Tenochtitlán takes a long look at his work. He remembers all the hard work he did when he planted the seedlings with his digging stick. Now corn, pumpkins, beans, and tomatoes grow in his garden. The city around him is full of green gardens like his.

Natural resources and technology helped the Aztecs turn their island into a big city. Trees from the mountains provided wood for building. The Aztecs used technology to build channels, which carried fresh water to the city from springs nearby. They built more and more **canals** as their city grew. People used canoes to glide through the canals to get to their gardens.

Some Mexican farmers continue to farm as the Aztecs did 500 years ago.

Activities

1. **EXPLORE IT** Put yourself in the picture and talk about what it would be like to live in a city of gardens and canals.

2. **COMPARE IT** Compare and contrast Aztec canals to the roads used today. Or compare and contrast tools. Create a chart to show what is alike and what is different.

59

Skillbuilder

Use Parts of a Source

If you wanted to use a book to find out more about a subject, how would you do it? Knowing the parts of a book, or source, will help. Books are organized to make finding information easy.

► **VOCABULARY**

table of
  contents

glossary

index

Learn the Skill

Step 1: A **table of contents** lists sections of the book, such as chapters. It also tells on which page each section begins. You usually find the table of contents at the beginning of a book.

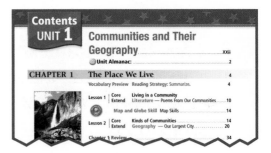

Step 2: A **glossary** is an alphabetical list of words and their meanings. A glossary is usually found near the end of a book.

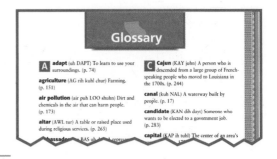

Step 3: An **index** is an alphabetical list that includes each subject mentioned in the book. It also gives the page numbers where each subject is found. An index is usually at the end of a book.

Practice the Skill

Use the parts of this book to answer the questions.

1 On which page does Unit 4 of this book begin?

2 What would be the quickest way to find all the pages that mention John Muir?

3 What is the definition of population?

Apply the Skill

Choose a question about a country that interests you. At your library, find different books on this country. Use each book's table of contents and index to find the information you need to answer your question.

Visual Summary

1–4. Write a description of each item named below.

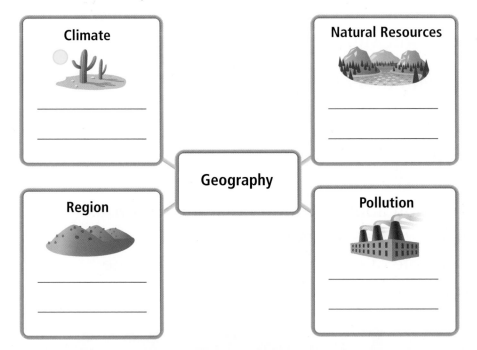

Climate

Natural Resources

Geography

Region

Pollution

Facts and Main Ideas

✓ **TEST PREP** Answer each question below.

5. **Geography** Why are communities often located near water?

6. **Geography** Name four types of landforms.

7. **Geography** In what ways did the Oroville Dam change the environment?

8. **Geography** What are people in Mexico City doing to improve their environment?

Vocabulary

✓ **TEST PREP** Choose the correct word from the list below to complete each sentence.

geography, p. 26
environment, p. 44
pollution, p. 56

9. Water, air, and plants are part of the _____.

10. Some _____ can be caused by cars and the gas they use.

11. The study of where people live and why they live there is called _____.

TEST PREP **Use a Map Grid** Study the map of Colorado below. Use what you have learned about map grids to answer each question.

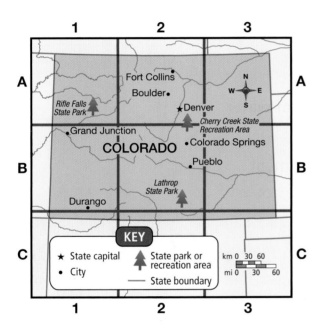

12. What is in grid box B-2?

A. Denver

B. Durango

C. Lathrop State Park

D. Rifle Falls State Park

13. What grid box is Colorado Springs in?

A. A-2

B. B-2

C. C-1

D. C-3

TEST PREP Write a short paragraph to answer each question below. Use details to support your response.

14. **Draw Conclusions** What changes to the environment have taken place in your community?

15. **Analyze** In what ways does the climate in your region affect the way you dress in winter and summer?

Activities

Music Activity Find a song that tells about the geography of the United States or some part of it. Listen to it and add words of your own.

Writing Activity Write a personal narrative telling about an experience you had outdoors. Tell what environment you were in.

Technology
Writing Process Tips
Get help with your narrative at
www.eduplace.com/kids/hmss05/

My Community Handbook
GEOGRAPHY

Geography Where You Live

Take a look around your community. What landforms or bodies of water do you see? How are people using the land? Is anyone planting a garden or building a road? Geography affects your life every day!

Geography Highlights

- **Landforms and bodies of water**
- **Weather and climate**
- **People and the environment**
- **Natural resources and conservation**

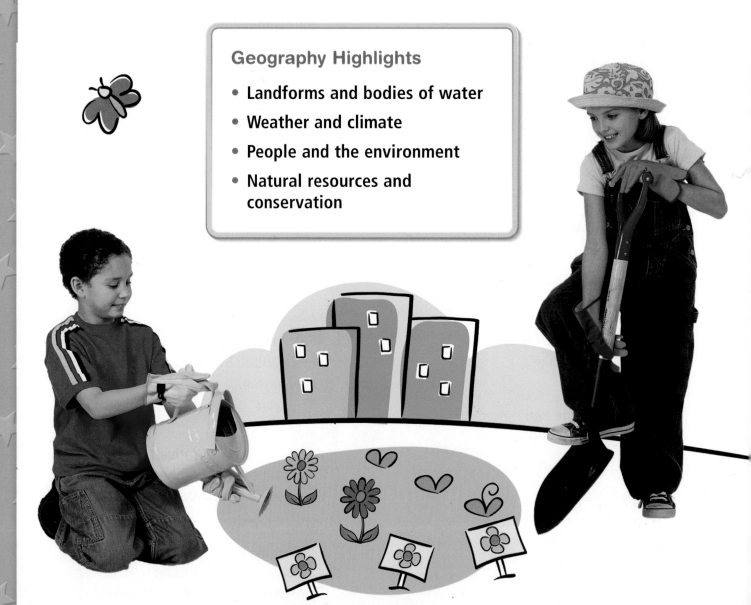

High mountains

Windmills

Desert plants

Find Out!

Windmills in the California desert make electricity.

Explore the geography of your community.

✅ **Start with maps.**
Check the U.S. Geographic Society on line. Or look for landform maps of your community at your library.

✅ **Visit or call the Chamber of Commerce.**
Are there plans for your community that might affect where people live and work?

✅ **Check the weather.**
The National Weather Service has a website to help you get started.

✅ **Are there conservation projects going on?**
The websites of environmental groups might have details.

Use your community handbook to keep track of information you find.

Vocabulary and Main Ideas

✔️ **TEST PREP** Write a sentence to answer each question.

1. What are some reasons that people live in a **community?**

2. In what ways does **climate** affect a community?

3. What landforms are in the western **region** of the United States?

4. Why do people often build communities where there are many **natural resources?**

Critical Thinking

✔️ **TEST PREP** Write a short answer for each question. Use details to support your answer.

5. **Compare** In what ways might living near the Mississippi River be similar to living near one of the Great Lakes?

6. **Summarize** Describe your community's climate.

Apply Skills

✔️ **TEST PREP** Use the map of Miami below and what you have learned about map grids to answer each question.

7. Which place is in B-3?

8. In which box is the Frederick Douglass Elementary School located?

   A. A-1

   B. B-1

   C. C-2

   D. C-4

Unit Activity

Map a Community

- Think of different kinds of communities. Choose one.

- Make a list of features that might be part of that community, such as buildings, landforms, or parks.

- Create and label a map of a community that shows the features on your list.

At the Library

You may find this book at your school or public library.

From Dawn till Dusk
by Natalie Kinsey-Warnock

The writer recalls the hard work and fun of growing up on a farm.

Connect to Your Community

Create a bulletin board about a natural resource in your community or state.

- Find two articles about a natural resource.

- Write three sentences summarizing each article.

- Draw a picture to go with each summary. Post your summaries.

 Technology
Weekly Reader online offers social studies articles. Go to:
www.eduplace.com/kids/hmss/

Read About It

Look in your classroom for these Social Studies Independent Books.

UNIT 2

America's Early Communities

The Big Idea

Were people long ago like you?

"*There are no unknown words . . . or sayings in new languages that have not already been said by the ancestors.*"

—Senusret II, Egyptian king, 2150 B.C.E.

Almanac

North America, 1750s

NORTH

AMERICA

Columbia R.

Missouri River

Platte River

Colorado River

Arkansas River

YUROK

NAVAJO

Rio Grande

Mississippi River

PACIFIC

OCEAN

Gulf of Mexico

km 0 150 300
mi 0 150 300

Unit Preview

1400   1500   1600   1700

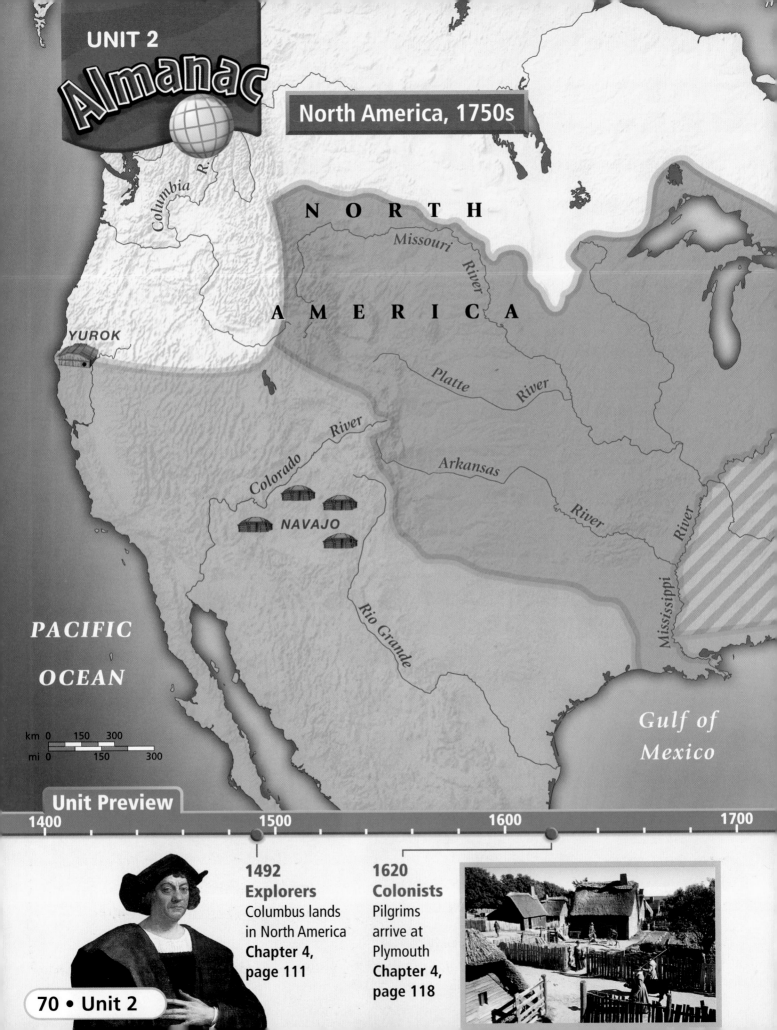

**1492
Explorers**
Columbus lands
in North America
**Chapter 4,
page 111**

**1620
Colonists**
Pilgrims
arrive at
Plymouth
**Chapter 4,
page 118**

U.S. Population, 1750–1800

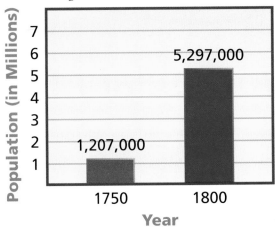

Population (in Millions)

7
6
5
4
3
2
1

5,297,000

1,207,000

1750   1800

Year

U.S. Population, 1950–2000

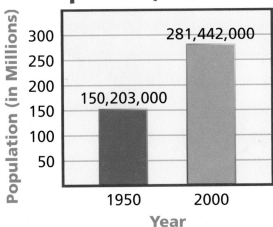

Population (in Millions)

300
250
200
150
100
50

281,442,000

150,203,000

1950   2000

Year

Look at the bar graphs. Do you think the population will increase or decrease by 2050?

CURRENT   EVENTS

WEEKLY WR READER

Current events on the web!

Read social studies articles at:

www.eduplace.com/kids/hmss/

St. Lawrence River

HAUDENOSAUNEE

Ohio River

CHEROKEE

ATLANTIC

OCEAN

N
NW NE
W   E
SW SE
S

KEY

- British
- French
- Spanish
- Disputed
- YUROK American Indians

1800   1900

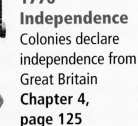

1776
Independence
Colonies declare independence from Great Britain
Chapter 4, page 125

1867
Canada
Canadians gain independence
Chapter 4, page 133

Old and New Communities

Vocabulary Preview

Technology

e • **glossary**
e • **word games**
www.eduplace.com/kids/hmss05/

ceremony

Navajos may hold a **ceremony** as part of their religion. This event may include singing and sand painting.
page 77

economy

What makes an **economy?** Money is part of it. For some people long ago, shells, not dollars, were money.
page 84

Reading Strategy

Question As you read this chapter, ask yourself questions to check your understanding.

Quick Tip What do you want to know more about? Write your questions as you read.

tradition

People share a **tradition** they care about. American Indian nations today pass along beliefs and special celebrations.
page 91

government

The Haudenosaunee were made up of several nations. To make laws and keep order, they founded one **government.**
page 98

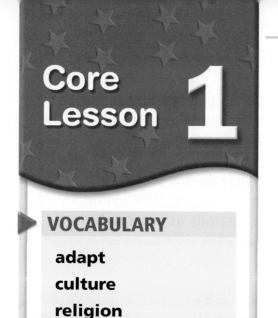

VOCABULARY

adapt

culture

religion

ceremony

 **READING SKILL**

Problem and Solution
The Navajo faced the problem of learning to live in the desert. List some of the solutions they found.

The Navajo

Build on What You Know Think of a group of people who lived in the past. Does that group exist today? The people you will read about in this lesson do.

Living in the Desert

The Navajo (NAHV ah hoh) are Native Americans. Nearly 300,000 Navajo live in the southwestern United States today. Their land of deserts and mountains covers parts of Arizona, New Mexico, and Utah.

People who study American Indians think that the Navajo came from forests far to the north. Many Navajo believe that they came from another world long ago. They see the world around them as holy, or sacred.

Navajo Land Long ago, the Navajo made their home in the Southwest. Many Navajo continue to live there today.

Adapting to the Desert

Living in a desert takes special skill. The Navajo learned to use the desert's natural resources. They adapted to their land. To **adapt** means to change the way you live to fit a new place. Some Navajo say that spirits helped them adapt. Scientists, however, think that the Navajo learned some skills from other American Indians. They also tried new ideas of their own.

The Navajo learned to farm and hunt in the desert. They grew corn, squash, and beans. With little rain, the people planted seeds deeply to reach water underground. They gathered plants and nuts to eat. The Navajo also hunted deer and other animals for meat and skins.

In time, the Navajo began to herd sheep and goats. Using sheep's wool, they wove warm blankets. These blankets are known for their unique patterns and designs.

Review What skills did the Navajo learn in order to live in the desert?

Skill **Reading Maps** In which state is the largest area of Navajo land?

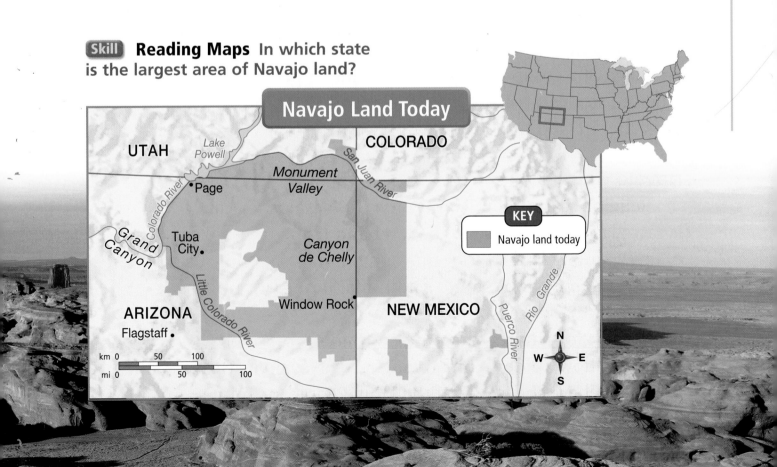

Navajo Land Today

UTAH

Lake Powell

COLORADO

Colorado River

•Page

Monument Valley

San Juan River

Grand Canyon

Tuba City.

Canyon de Chelly

KEY

Navajo land today

Little Colorado River

Window Rock•

NEW MEXICO

Puerco River

Rio Grande

ARIZONA

Flagstaff.

km 0   50   100

mi 0   50   100

N W E S

By teaching children respect for nature, Navajo families help their culture to continue. This family enjoys a hike in the Arizona desert.

The Navajo Today

The Navajo taught their children what they learned in the desert. In this way, Navajo culture continues today. **Culture** is the way of life, or the beliefs, ideas, and language of a group of people. It includes a people's religion, stories, arts, and even their food. **Religion** is the belief in God or gods.

main idea

Navajo Culture

Religion is central to Navajo life. To Navajos, nature is sacred. They feel close to the land and living things. For example, many thank the plants and animals that they use for food. Some Navajo build traditional homes, or hogans, facing east to show respect for the sunrise.

Respect for nature is found in Navajo stories. One story tells how Spider Woman taught the Navajo to weave. Navajos believe she is one of the Holy People, or spirits.

Holding Ceremonies

To ask the Holy People for help, Navajos may hold a ceremony. A **ceremony** is a formal act or event that celebrates a people's beliefs. Some Navajo ceremonies may include sand paintings. These are sacred pictures made with colored sand and other materials.

Today Navajos live in many parts of the United States as well as on Navajo land. Many are farmers and sheep ranchers. Others are engineers, miners, and teachers.

Review In what ways does Navajo culture continue today?

This Navajo engineer uses a machine to test for water.

Lesson Review

1 VOCABULARY Use **adapt** in a short paragraph describing Navajo life in the desert.

2 READING SKILL Using your chart, describe one **solution** the Navajo found to the **problem** of living in the desert.

3 MAIN IDEA: Geography What natural resources did the Navajo learn to use in the desert?

4 MAIN IDEA: Culture In what ways do the Navajo show their respect for nature?

5 CRITICAL THINKING: Cause and Effect Why might it be difficult to grow food in a desert?

HANDS ON

ART ACTIVITY Make a booklet of drawings or pictures with captions that tell about your family's culture. Include details such as language, foods, or family stories.

NAVAJO Sand Painting

The medicine man's helper leans over the earth. He takes a pinch of colored sand from a small leather pouch as the medicine man directs him. The helper lets the sand trickle down his fingers. Grain by grain, line by line, a sand painting takes shape.

The purpose of a sand painting is to bring the Holy People together with the Navajo. Sand paintings are used to treat the ill. The Navajo believe that the sand painting **ceremony** brings power to cure the patient.

When the sand painting is done, the medicine man checks it. Each line and color must be in the right place.

Navajo Holy People

The figures of the Holy People are created in layers. This makes them stand out.

Preparing to Work

The helper takes careful measurements before he begins. The figures must be the right size and in the right place.

Making the Painting

Sand paintings may contain many colors, but white, blue, yellow, and black are always included.

Activities

1. **THINK ABOUT IT** Why is it important for the figures in the painting to be right?

2. **WRITE ABOUT IT** Write a poem about sand painting. What might the helper see and hear as he paints with sand?

Technology Go to Education Place for more primary sources. www.eduplace.com/kids/hmss05/

Study Skills

Skillbuilder

Choose the Right Source

▶ **VOCABULARY**

reference book

Internet

You just learned about the Navajo. What if you still have questions? Different sources of information can help you answer your questions.

Learn the Skill

Step 1: Write down your question.

Step 2: Look at different sources of information. Which will best answer your question?

- A **reference book** contains facts on different subjects. You might use a reference book, such as an encyclopedia, to get an idea about a topic.

- Use magazines and newspapers to find out about recent events. These sources also have information about many different subjects.

- The **Internet** is a large system of computers. It allows people to communicate and find information on almost any subject.

Step 3: Choose the kind of source that will best answer your question.

Reference books

Internet

Newspaper

Practice the Skill

Think about different sources of information. Then answer the questions below.

1 Which source of information might you use to find out about Navajo life in the past?

2 What sources would you use to find out about local events in the Navajo nation?

3 What would be the best sources of information about events in the Navajo community in the last few days?

Apply the Skill

Think of a question about the Navajo that you would like to have answered. Then look for the right source to help you answer your question.

The Yurok

VOCABULARY

trade

barter

economy

READING SKILL

Main Idea and Details
Find details to support the main idea that forest and river resources shaped the Yurok way of life.

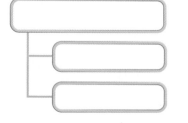

Build on What You Know Suppose a friend has a sandwich that you like better than yours. Would you swap for it? The people in this lesson exchanged things they made for things they wanted.

River and Forest Life

The Yurok (YUR ahk) live on the northern coast of California. Forests of redwoods, the world's tallest trees, grow here. Rivers and valleys are rich in plant and animal life. The many resources of the rivers and forests influenced the Yuroks' way of life.

main idea

Long ago, the Yurok hunted deer and other animals. From oak trees, they gathered acorns to eat. Berries and seeds were easy to find. The rivers provided salmon. To catch them, the Yurok used nets and spears. Smoked and dried, the salmon could be stored for the winter. The entire Yurok community shared the fish and other food.

A Yurok Village

❶ The Yurok used nets or spears to catch salmon.

❷ Dams, or weirs, trapped salmon for easy catching.

❸ Dried and smoked salmon could be stored.

Daily Life

The Yurok built their houses partly underground. They used redwood planks for the walls. For doors, houses had a small round hole. The Yurok also made baskets instead of clay pots. To cook, they put food and water in a basket. Then they added hot rocks to boil the water.

Changing Their Environment

Like the Navajo, the Yurok felt that nature was sacred. When they changed the land, they did so with great care. For example, though their dams helped them catch fish easily, they did not catch more fish than they could use. When they cleared trees and bushes, the open spaces gave forest plants, such as oaks, more light and room to grow.

Review In what ways did the Yurok change their environment?

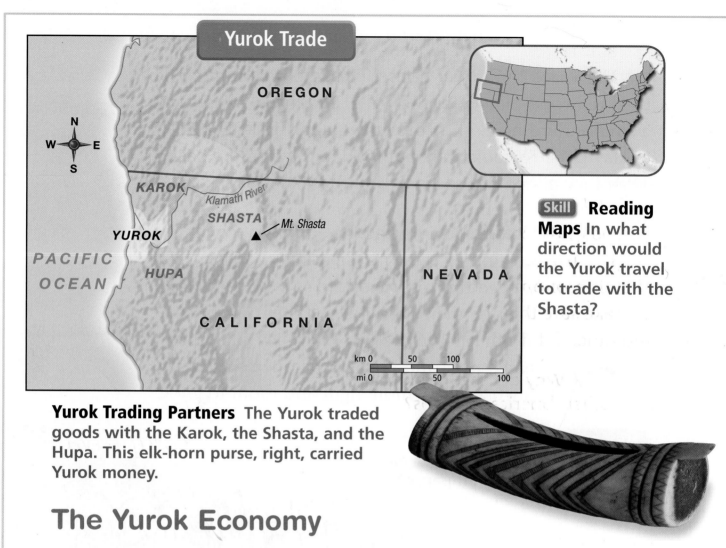

Yurok Trade

OREGON

KAROK
Klamath River
SHASTA
▲ Mt. Shasta
YUROK

PACIFIC
OCEAN

HUPA

NEVADA

CALIFORNIA

km 0   50   100
mi 0   50   100

Skill Reading Maps In what direction would the Yurok travel to trade with the Shasta?

Yurok Trading Partners The Yurok traded goods with the Karok, the Shasta, and the Hupa. This elk-horn purse, right, carried Yurok money.

The Yurok Economy

The Yurok were a giving people. If someone was hungry, the Yurok would give food. They valued those who shared.

The Yurok sometimes traded things, such as canoes, with other American Indians. To **trade** means to exchange things with someone else. One kind of trade is barter. When you **barter,** you trade one item for another. The Yurok bartered with other Indians for things they could not make or find in their own environment.

The Yurok economy was based on trade and the natural resources of their land. An **economy** is the way that people choose to make, buy, sell, and use things. The Yurok economy depended on the people's skill in using their resources and bartering for things they wanted. Some Yurok grew quite wealthy.

main ★ idea

Yurok Money

Instead of barter, the Yurok sometimes used money for trade. Money is not always coins or bills. It can be anything that has a value on which people agree. Special shells, called tooth shells, were used by the Yurok as money. They agreed that one chain of shells was worth a small boat.

Today, the Yurok are the largest group of American Indians in California. Salmon fishing is an important part of their economy and way of life. The Yurok are working to make sure that there will always be enough salmon and other fish in their local rivers.

Review Why did the Yurok trade with other American Indians?

Salmon fishing remains an important part of Yurok life today.

Lesson Review

1 VOCABULARY What word is a synonym for **trade?**

   barter **economy**

2 READING SKILL What **details** in this lesson support the idea that rivers were important in Yurok life?

3 MAIN IDEA: Geography Name two ways the Yurok altered the environment.

4 MAIN IDEA: Economics What did the Yurok use for money?

5 CRITICAL THINKING: Infer Which was more important to the Yurok, the forests or the rivers? Explain your answer.

HANDS ON

ART ACTIVITY Create your own money. Draw a picture of it. Explain how much it is worth and what materials you would use to make it.

Economics

Yurok Money

Tooth shells are not actually teeth. Why were these unusual shells so valuable? They look like long, smooth teeth, but tooth shells come from shellfish that live in deep water along the Pacific coast. The Yurok used long strings of these shells as money.

With strings of tooth shells, the Yurok bought things they needed. They bought items from one another and from other American Indians. Find the price in tooth shells for a canoe. Compare it to the price for a Yurok house.

▲ **Redwood House**
The Yurok built their houses with redwood planks.

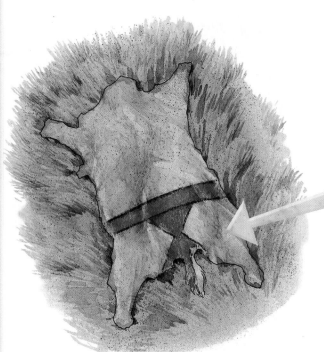

▲ **Deerskin Blanket**
The Yurok traded deerskins. This one is painted on the soft underside of the skin.

Using Yurok Money

Item to Buy	Price in Tooth-shell Strings
Painted deerskin blanket	1 string
Canoe	2 strings
Redwood house	5 strings
White deerskin	10 strings

Tooth-shell String

Each string of shells was about 27 inches long.

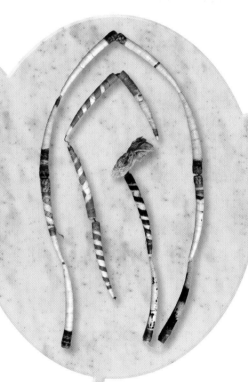

White Deerskin

To own a pure white deerskin was a sign of great wealth.

Canoe

The Yurok hollowed out redwood logs to make canoes.

Activities

1. **TALK ABOUT IT** Look at the chart. Which item did the Yurok value most? Why might that item have been so valuable?

2. **CHART IT** If you could use something besides paper dollars and metal coins for money, what would you use? Create a chart showing the value of your "money" and what it might buy.

The Cherokee

Build on What You Know Today, many people heat their homes in winter and cool them in summer. It wasn't always like this. People years ago lived in different houses at different seasons.

Living in the Southeast

Long ago, the Cherokee Indians lived in the southeastern United States. The Appalachian Mountains and valleys were their home. The Cherokee depended on forests, rivers, and rich soil to survive.

The Cherokee hunted, fished, gathered fruit and nuts, and farmed. They grew corn, beans, squash, pumpkins, and sunflowers. The moist, warm climate allowed many Cherokee to plant two corn crops each year. The rich soil of the piedmont (PEED mahnt) also helped grow crops. The **piedmont** is gently rolling land at the base of mountains. It is formed by rich, fine soil washed down from mountains over many years.

VOCABULARY

piedmont
history
tradition

READING SKILL

Sequence As you read the second section, list in order the events that happened.

Cherokee Houses and Towns

The Cherokee built towns along rivers and streams. Some towns had more than a hundred houses. Cherokee families usually had two homes. In summer, they lived in large houses made of posts. These houses had peaked roofs. Their winter homes were smaller, round, and built for warmth.

Tall walls made of logs circled most towns. In the town center stood a large round building. Here religious ceremonies took place. At times, there was dancing. At other times, people talked about crops, village rules, or other matters.

Sharing stories about their history was an important part of life. **History** is the record of past events. In the early 1800s, a Cherokee named **Sequoyah** (sih KWOY uh) invented a way to write the Cherokee language. As a result, many Cherokee learned to read and write in their own language.

Review What resources did the Cherokee use for food?

Cherokee Houses Many Cherokee families built two homes. They used renewable resources such as twigs, grasses, and mud.

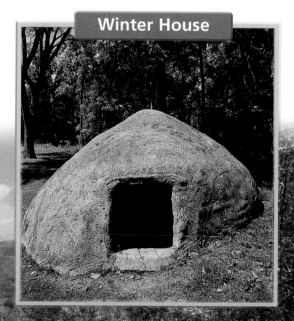

Winter House

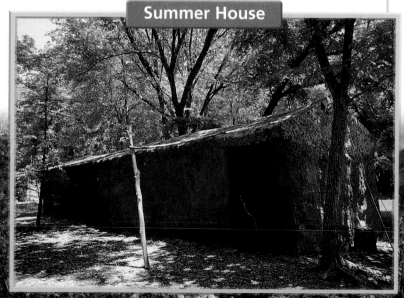

Summer House

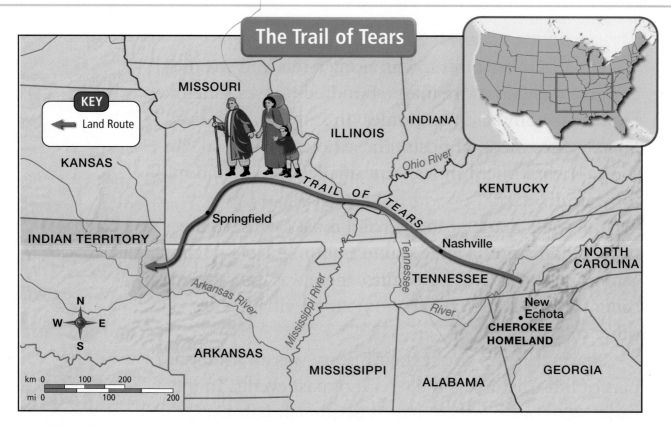

The Trail of Tears

KEY
← Land Route

MISSOURI

INDIANA

ILLINOIS

Ohio River

KANSAS

KENTUCKY

TRAIL OF TEARS

Springfield

INDIAN TERRITORY

Nashville

NORTH
CAROLINA

N
W   E
S

Arkansas River

Mississippi River

Tennessee River

TENNESSEE

New
Echota
CHEROKEE
HOMELAND

ARKANSAS

MISSISSIPPI

ALABAMA

GEORGIA

km 0   100   200
mi 0   100   200

In 1838, the American government forced thousands of
Cherokee men, women, and children to leave their homes.

Skill **Reading Maps** What does the arrow on the map show?

Cherokee History

The Cherokee lived in the South for thousands
of years. The coming of Europeans changed their
way of life. At times, the Cherokee and the settlers
got along peacefully. At other times, they did not.

main idea

By the 1820s, the Cherokee were trading with
the settlers. They started a newspaper. However,
settlers wanted Cherokee land. They fought the
Cherokee over land and other resources.

In the 1830s, the United States forced most
of the Cherokee to leave their homes. They
traveled hundreds of miles west to what is
now Oklahoma. Four thousand Cherokee
died. This event is called the Trail of Tears.

Cherokee children
continue to learn
about their history.

The Cherokee Today

Today, the Cherokee live in Oklahoma, North Carolina, and other parts of the country. They value their history and are proud of their traditions. A **tradition** is a culture's special way of doing something. Cherokee traditions include special foods, dances, and crafts. Wilma Mankiller is one Cherokee who continued the Cherokee tradition of having strong leaders.

Review Why did the Cherokee move to Oklahoma?

Wilma Mankiller In 1985, she became the first woman leader of the Cherokee Nation.

Lesson Review

1. **VOCABULARY** Write a sentence telling what you might grow on the **piedmont.**

2. **READING SKILL** Use your chart to tell the **sequence** in which the following events occurred: the Trail of Tears, Cherokee start a newspaper, Europeans arrive.

3. **MAIN IDEA: Geography** Describe the Cherokee's land in the South and how they used it.

4. **MAIN IDEA: History** In what ways did the coming of European settlers affect Cherokee history?

5. **CRITICAL THINKING: Generalize** In what ways do you think the coming of European settlers affected other American Indians?

WRITING ACTIVITY The Cherokee have many traditions, such as sharing stories. Write a short paragraph about a tradition that your family has.

91

SEQUOYAH

GWY
CHEROKEE
VOL. I.
NEW ECH

After twelve long years, Sequoyah reached his goal. He created his own system of letters so that there could be books in his Cherokee language.

For so long, Sequoyah had been interested in "talking leaves," which is what he called the pages of books. He knew that books and written words were powerful ways to learn and to give information. But there were no written words for the language the Cherokee people spoke.

In 1821, Sequoyah finished 86 letters based on spoken sounds. Within a few months, thousands of Cherokee could read and write in their own language. Many Cherokee use Sequoyah's writing system today.

Did You Know?

Giant sequoia trees are named after the Cherokee leader. These trees are the largest living things on Earth.

Look closely.

Sequoyah's letters spell out the title of this newspaper. What is the title of the paper?

Activities

1. **TALK ABOUT IT** In what ways do you think Sequoyah's writing system changed the lives of the Cherokee people?

2. **MAKE YOUR OWN** Create your own alphabet. Translate a poem or song into your writing system.

Technology For more biographies, go to Education Place. www.eduplace.com/kids/hmss05/

◀ Writing System

Sequoyah's system, or alphabet, was called a syllabary. His daughter was one of the first people to use it.

Reading and Thinking Skills

Identify Cause and Effect

▶ **VOCABULARY**

cause

effect

When you study history, you study events in the past. To learn why the events happened, you need to look at causes and effects. A **cause** is something that makes an event happen. An **effect** is what happens.

Learn the Skill

Step 1: Look for clue words that tell whether something is a cause or an effect. One clue word that helps identify a cause is *because*. Clue words that help identify an effect are *so, after that,* and *as a result.*

Step 2: Identify the cause. Look for something that makes something else happen. This is the cause.

Step 3: Identify the effect. An effect is what happens as a result of a cause.

Cause and Effect

Cause		Effect
Sequoyah wanted to find a way to write down the Cherokee language.		As a result, he invented a way to write Cherokee.

Practice the Skill

Read the paragraph below. Look for clue words that tell you whether something is a cause or an effect. Record the information in a chart.

> Sequoyah wanted to find a way for the Cherokee to have their own written language. Because of this, he created a writing system called a syllabary. Sequoyah then taught others how to read and write in Cherokee. As a result, some Cherokee published books and newspapers in their own language.

Apply the Skill

Look back at Lesson 3. Look for three or four causes or effects related to the Cherokee. Write a paragraph that shows how one cause led to an effect. Try to use clue words.

Haudenosaunee

Build on What You Know Sometimes it's good to do things on your own. At other times, it's helpful to team up with people. Then you can work together.

Life in the Forests

Winters are cold and snowy in the northeastern forests. American Indians, the Haudenosaunee (haw deh noh SAW nee), lived there long ago. The Haudenosaunee planned ahead for the long winters. In the summer, women grew crops such as corn, beans, and squash. Then they stored part of the harvest to eat during the winter. Men hunted deer, bear, and beaver for meat. The skins were used for clothing. The Haudenosaunee depended on the resources of the forest for food, clothing, and shelter.

▶ **VOCABULARY**

government

constitution

READING SKILL
Draw Conclusions
Note details in the second section about Haudenosaunee life before and after the Peacemaker came. Then draw a conclusion telling why the nations united.

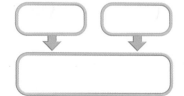

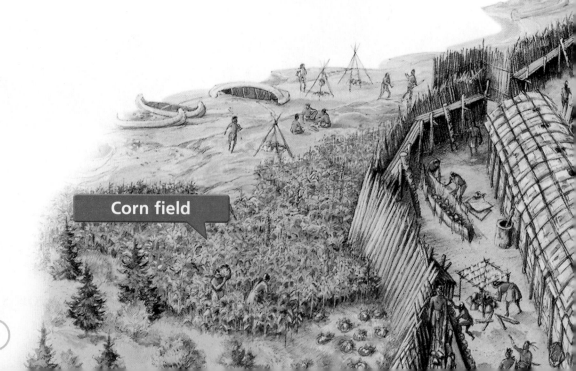

Corn field

Longhouses

Haudenosaunee means "people of the longhouse." The Haudenosaunee built long, narrow houses, much like apartment buildings. They used wooden posts, bark, and animal hides. Six to ten families lived together in a longhouse. Each family had its own space, but shared a fire with the family across the hall.

The families who lived in each longhouse belonged to the same clan, or extended family. They were all related to each other. The oldest woman of the clan was the clan mother, or leader of the longhouse.

Review What did the Haudenosaunee do to prepare for the winter?

Some towns were surrounded by tall fences. Made from posts, the fences kept out wild animals and protected the people.

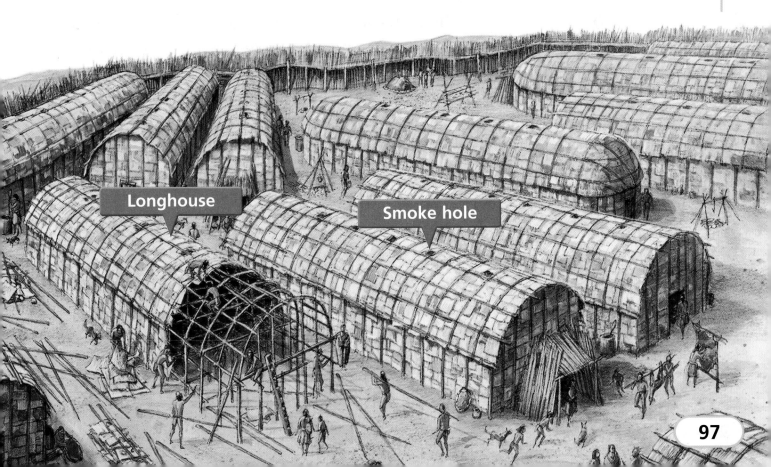

Longhouse

Smoke hole

A New Government

There were many Haudenosaunee nations. They often fought about who could hunt or farm in certain areas. Fighting led to more fighting. Many people died in these battles. Then came a big change. The people tell how a holy man, known as the Peacemaker, visited them. He told them to live together in peace.

Hiawatha

A leader named Hiawatha (hy uh WAHTH uh) listened. Hiawatha agreed with the Peacemaker and helped him spread his message. Five nations agreed to unite in peace. As the story is told, the Peacemaker asked them to bury their weapons. Then he planted a pine tree. He called it the Tree of Peace. It would remind the nations of their promise to stop fighting each other.

The Haudenosaunee Unite

The Peacemaker and Hiawatha helped the Haudenosaunee form a new government. A **government** is an organization that makes laws and keeps order. It helps settle arguments about the laws. Haudenosaunee government is sometimes called the Iroquois League. (The name "Iroquois" was given by the French.)

main idea

Usually, each Haudenosaunee nation ruled itself. However, for big questions about war, peace, and trade, the five nations worked together. Fifty leaders from all five nations met for the Grand Council. They gathered near what is now Syracuse, New York. There they discussed problems and made decisions together.

Review What was the purpose of the Haudenosaunee government?

Haudenosaunee Government

The pattern on this wampum belt shows the unity of the five nations. The four white squares stand for four of the nations. The tree in the center stands for the Onondaga nation and the Tree of Peace.

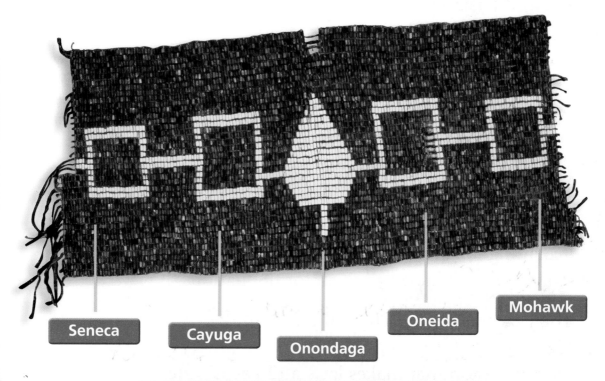

Seneca

Cayuga

Onondaga

Oneida

Mohawk

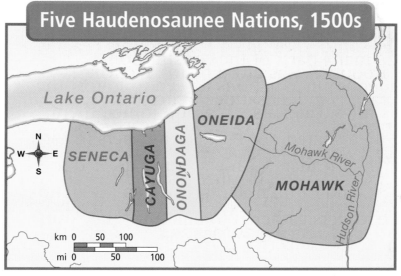

Five Haudenosaunee Nations, 1500s

Compare the map of the five Haudenosaunee nations to the wampum belt. What do they have in common?

Grand Council, 1871

Grand Council, 1988

Government Haudenosaunee leaders (above left) hold wampum belts. Today, leaders from the six nations continue to meet in council and to govern the Haudenosaunee.

The Constitution

According to Haudenosaunee tradition, the Peacemaker set out a constitution for the nations. A **constitution** is the basic laws and ideas that a government and its people follow. The Haudenosaunee constitution was not written down at first. It was oral, or spoken aloud. To keep a record, the people made belts out of wampum, or shell beads. The beads in the belt helped them remember the many parts of the constitution.

Five Haudenosaunee nations agreed to follow the constitution's rules. Later a sixth group joined them. Women and men shared power. Clan mothers in each nation chose their leaders. Leaders were expected to be patient, honest, and calm, not angry. When the nations disagreed, the leaders gathered to talk until they came to a decision.

main idea

The Haudenosaunee Today

Today, thousands of Haudenosaunee live in New York, Wisconsin, and Oklahoma. They also live in Canada. In both the United States and Canada, a Haudenosaunee government acts for the people. Just as it did long ago, their government works hard to protect Haudenosaunee land and tradition.

Review What does the Haudenosaunee government do today?

A Haudenosaunee boy learns from his grandfather.

Lesson Review

1 VOCABULARY In what ways do rules or laws made by a **government** help people live together?

2 READING SKILL Complete your chart. **Draw a conclusion** telling why you think the five nations chose to unite.

3 MAIN IDEA: Geography On what resources did the Haudenosaunee depend for food and clothing?

4 MAIN IDEA: Government Who took part in the government of the five nations?

5 CRITICAL THINKING: Compare In what ways are the Haudenosaunee government of the past and present alike?

WRITING ACTIVITY Write a short poem telling how the Haudenosaunee united.

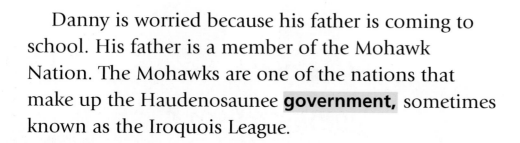

Eagle Song

by Joseph Bruchac

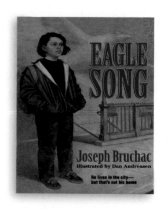

Danny is worried because his father is coming to school. His father is a member of the Mohawk Nation. The Mohawks are one of the nations that make up the Haudenosaunee **government,** sometimes known as the Iroquois League.

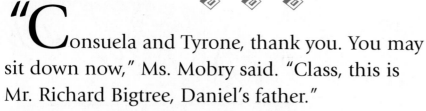

"Consuela and Tyrone, thank you. You may sit down now," Ms. Mobry said. "Class, this is Mr. Richard Bigtree, Daniel's father."

Richard Bigtree flashed a smile at his son and then looked out around the class as he took something out of his bag.

"Who knows what this is?"

Danny knew what it was: a wampum belt. His father had made it, copying the design of the ancient Hiawatha Belt. On the belt in purple and white beads were the shapes of a tall tree and four squares, symbols of the founding of the Great League of Peace.

"Is it a headband?" someone said from the back of the room.

Danny's father shook his head.

"Is it a belt?" Consuela said.

"That's good," said Danny's father. "But what kind of belt is it?"

A boy named Kofi raised his hand on the other side of the room. Danny's father nodded to him.

"I know," Kofi said. "It's a wampum belt. I saw one at the museum last week."

"That's right," Danny's father said. "It's a wampum belt. To us it is like a book because it tells a story. Would you like to hear that story?"

"Yes," everyone said.

And Danny listened again as his father told the story of the coming of peace, the story of Aionwahta.

Danny's father finished his story and looked at the classroom. No one moved or said a word. He smiled.

"Has anyone ever seen that pine tree anywhere?"

No one answered him. Then he held up his hard hat, and some of the kids laughed.

"It's on your hat," said a boy in the front row. Danny was surprised. The boy, whose name was Tim, was never the first to answer any question. Tim looked back at Danny and grinned.

Richard Bigtree nodded his head.

"One of the first flags that the United States used had a pine tree on it. The founders of this country, Benjamin Franklin in particular, knew about the Iroquois League. Old Ben Franklin said that the colonists ought to band together like the Iroquois nations did. A lot of people

who study how governments are made now think that the United States Constitution is partially modeled after the Iroquois. Any of you got a quarter?"

Everyone in the class began searching their pockets. Danny, though, had been waiting for this moment. He had the quarter ready in his hand.

"Here, Dad," Danny said, tossing the quarter to him.

Richard Bigtree reached out one big hand and caught the quarter without even looking at it. He held it up.

"You see what's on one side of this? It's an eagle, just like the one on my hat. Just like the one on top of that big pine tree. What's it holding?"

Brad raised his hand. "I know," he said. "It's holding thirteen arrows. They stand for the thirteen colonies."

"Just like our Iroquois eagle that holds five arrows standing for the five Iroquois nations."

"Awesome," Brad said.

Ms. Mobry stood and held her hands up, palms toward the class.

The class exploded into applause and Danny's father smiled back at them. He looked at Danny and winked.

Danny winked back. It was great that his father had come to school.

Activities

1. **TALK ABOUT IT** What objects does Mr. Bigtree show to the students as he tells them about the Iroquois?

2. **DRAW YOUR OWN** Draw a symbol that is special to you. Write a description of the symbol and explain why it is important to you.

Review and Test Prep

Visual Summary

1–4. ✏️ Write a description of each item named below.

Navajo culture

_____
_____
_____
_____

Yurok use of
natural resources

_____
_____
_____
_____

Cherokee writing

_____
_____
_____
_____

Haudenosaunee
government

_____
_____
_____
_____

Facts and Main Ideas

✔️ **TEST PREP** Answer each question below.

5. **Culture** What are two things that are part of Navajo culture?

6. **Economics** What did the Yurok use for money?

7. **Geography** Why did Cherokee families usually have two homes?

8. **Government** What was the Haudenosaunee constitution?

Vocabulary

✔️ **TEST PREP** Choose the correct word from the list below to complete each sentence.

culture, p. 76
economy, p. 84
government, p. 98

9. Five Haudenosaunee nations formed a _____.

10. Natural resources often shape a people's _____, or way of life.

11. Trade with other groups was part of the Yurok _____.

Apply Skills

 TEST PREP **Identify Cause and Effect** Use the organizer below and what you have learned about cause and effect to answer each question.

A man known as the Peacemaker told the Haudenosaunee to stop fighting and live together in peace.	As a result, five Haudenosaunee nations agreed to stop fighting.

12. What caused the Haudenosaunee to stop fighting?

13. What clue words tell you that something is an effect?

  A. The Peacemaker

  B. Haudenosaunee nations

  C. as a result

  D. together in peace

Critical Thinking

 TEST PREP Write a short paragraph to answer each question below. Use details to support your response.

14. **Compare and Contrast** In what ways did the Navajo and the Yurok learn to use natural resources?

15. **Infer** In what ways might growing two corn crops a year have helped the Cherokee?

16. **Draw Conclusions** How might forming a government have helped the Haudenosaunee to stop fighting one another?

Activities

Research Activity Use library resources to find out about the first people to live where your community is today. Write a paragraph about their history.

Writing Activity Write a report about an American Indian nation that lives near your community.

 Technology
Writing Process Tips
Get help with your report at
www.eduplace.com/kids/hmss05/

Communities in History

Vocabulary Preview

Technology
e • **glossary**
e • **word games**
www.eduplace.com/kids/hmss/

trade route

European explorers used a road or waterway called a **trade route** when they traveled to buy, sell, or exchange things. **page 110**

mission

Spanish priests built **missions** where they taught their religion to American Indians who lived nearby. **page 120**

Chapter Timeline

About 980
Vikings in North America

1492
Columbus in North America

| 800 | 1000 | 1200 | 1400 |

Reading Strategy

Monitor and Clarify As you read, use this strategy to check your understanding.

Quick Tip Stop to check whether what you are reading makes sense. Reread, if you need to.

independence

The American colonists wanted **independence.** They were willing to fight to gain their freedom from British rule. **page 124**

symbol

The American flag stands for the United States. It is a **symbol** of our country and its 50 states. **page 135**

1620
Pilgrims in Plymouth

1775
War with Great Britain

1600　　　　1800　　　　2000

Explorers Arrive

VOCABULARY

trade route

explorer

◎ **READING SKILL**
Categorize Chart details you learn about explorers from Spain and France into two categories.

Spain	France

800   1200   1600   2000

900–1608

Build on What You Know Think of a place you have never visited. The people in this lesson had never been to North America. They knew little or nothing about it before they came.

Exploring the Americas

The first Europeans to visit North America arrived more than 1,000 years ago. Known as the Vikings, they sailed here from northern Europe. Hundreds of years later, other Europeans followed them. They were looking for Asia.

In the 1400s, some European countries grew rich through trade with Asia. Trade routes by sea and land were long and difficult. A **trade route** is a road or waterway that people travel to buy, sell, or exchange goods.

Christopher Columbus He left Spain with a crew and three ships in August of 1492.

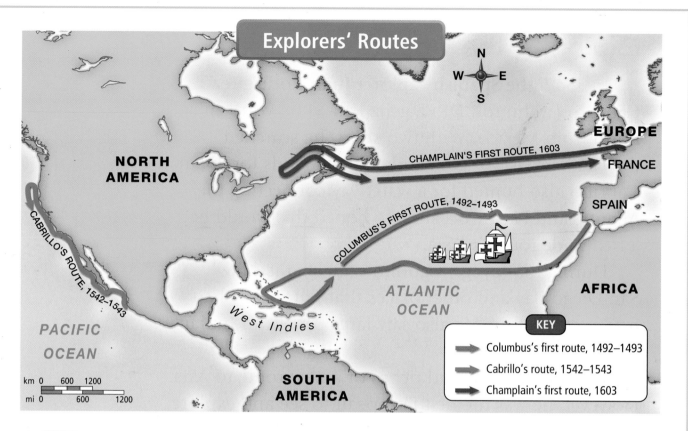

Explorers' Routes

NORTH AMERICA

CHAMPLAIN'S FIRST ROUTE, 1603

COLUMBUS'S FIRST ROUTE, 1492–1493

CABRILLO'S ROUTE, 1542–1543

EUROPE

FRANCE

SPAIN

AFRICA

ATLANTIC OCEAN

West Indies

PACIFIC OCEAN

SOUTH AMERICA

km 0 600 1200
mi 0 600 1200

KEY
- Columbus's first route, 1492–1493
- Cabrillo's route, 1542–1543
- Champlain's first route, 1603

Skill **Reading Maps** Which ocean did Columbus and Champlain cross to reach North America?

Looking for Asia

A sailor named **Christopher Columbus** wanted to find a better route to Asia. In those days, Europeans who went to Asia headed east. Columbus had a different idea. He and his crew tried sailing west from Spain in 1492. When they reached land, they thought they were in Asia, but they had landed in North America. At that time, American Indians were the only people living there.

main idea

When he returned to Spain, Columbus told others all that he had seen. Soon, explorers from Spain, France, and Portugal sailed to the Americas. An **explorer** is someone who travels to learn about new places. These explorers also hoped to find gold and the best trade route to Asia.

Review Why did Columbus want to sail to Asia?

Exploring the Coasts

In 1542, the Spanish explorer **Juan Rodríguez Cabrillo** (wahn roh DREE gehz kah BREE yoh) sailed north from Mexico. With two ships, he searched the Pacific coast for gold and claimed lands for Spain. Cabrillo also hunted for a waterway connecting the Atlantic and Pacific oceans. He hoped this would be a rich trade route to Asia.

During his voyage, Cabrillo saw what is now San Diego Bay and other places that Europeans had never seen before. He also saw large American Indian villages.

Cabrillo did not find riches or a new route to Asia. However, he was the first European to see and explore the coast of California.

Cabrillo National Monument
A statue of Juan Rodríguez Cabrillo stands in San Diego, California, near the coast (below).

France Explores the East Coast

Like Spain, France also sent explorers to the Americas. One explorer was **Samuel de Champlain** (shahm PLAYN). Champlain explored the eastern coast of North America. Instead of a route to Asia, he found rich resources such as fish and beaver. These resources helped convince him that settlers from France should live in North America. In 1608, he founded what is today the city of Quebec, in Canada.

Explorers from France, Spain, and other countries sailed to the Americas hoping to find riches and a trade route to Asia. Instead, they met American Indians. They also traveled to places Europeans had never been and sometimes found rich resources.

main idea ★

Review Why did Spain and France send explorers to North America?

Lesson Review

1492
Columbus arrived in North America

1542
Cabrillo explored Pacific coast

1450 — 1500 — 1550 — 1600 — 1650

❶ **VOCABULARY** Use **trade route** and **explorer** in a sentence about Europeans in North America.

❷ 👆 **READING SKILL** Use the information on your chart to list two details that French and Spanish explorers have in common.

❸ **MAIN IDEA: History** What did Columbus do to try to find a trade route to Asia?

❹ **MAIN IDEA: History** What helped convince French settlers to live in North America?

❺ **TIMELINE SKILL** When did Cabrillo explore California?

❻ **CRITICAL THINKING: Draw a Conclusion** What qualities should an explorer have?

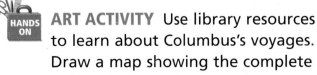
HANDS ON **ART ACTIVITY** Use library resources to learn about Columbus's voyages. Draw a map showing the complete route of one of the voyages.

Champlain's Map

How did explorers keep track of the new places they saw? There was a lot to remember. Maps and notes were helpful to have for later voyages.

In 1607, Samuel de Champlain created a map to show the places he explored along the Atlantic coast of eastern Canada and the eastern United States. He drew the shapes of the waterways and coastlines.

Champlain's Map of 1607

Cape Cod

The Same Area Today

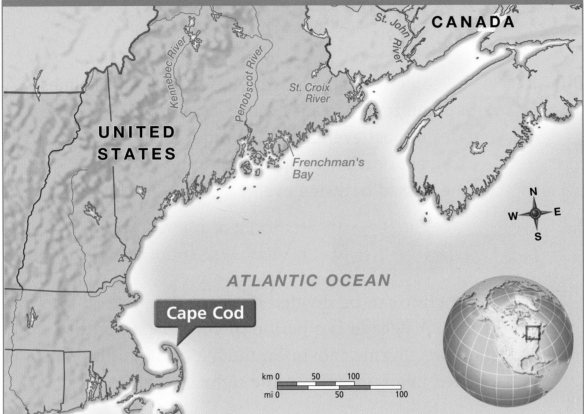

CANADA

St. John River

Kennebec River

Penobscot River

St. Croix River

UNITED STATES

Frenchman's Bay

ATLANTIC OCEAN

Cape Cod

N
W — E
S

km 0   50   100
mi 0   50   100

Look Closely

Compare the shapes of the land on Champlain's map to the map of the same area today. How are they different? What looks the same?

Activities

1. **TALK ABOUT IT** Why do you think old maps are so different from today's maps?

2. **MAKE YOUR OWN** From memory, draw and label a map of your school and the surrounding neighborhood. Which things are hard to remember and draw? Which ones are easier?

 Technology To explore more primary sources for this unit, visit Education Place. www.eduplace.com/kids/hmss05/

Skillbuilder

Read and Interpret a Timeline

► **VOCABULARY**

timeline

decade

century

People who study history often look at timelines to organize important events. A timeline shows the dates of past events and the order in which they occurred. Timelines also help you see how much time passed between events.

Learn the Skill

A timeline can be divided by years, decades, or even centuries. A **decade** is a period of 10 years. A **century** is 100 years. Events shown on the left end of a timeline happened before events on the right.

Step 1: Look at where the timeline begins and ends. Find the points where each time period starts.

Step 2: Find important events on the timeline. Look at the year each event took place.

Step 3: Look at the order in which the events occurred. Think about how one event might affect another.

Use the timeline to answer questions about American history.

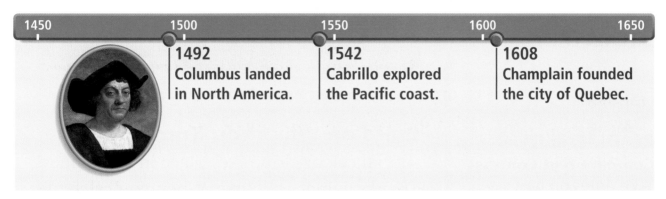

1450   1500   1550   1600   1650

1492
Columbus landed
in North America.

1542
Cabrillo explored
the Pacific coast.

1608
Champlain founded
the city of Quebec.

1 What time period does this timeline cover?

2 What is the earliest event shown on this timeline?

3 What event took place between 1492 and 1608?

4 How many centuries are shown on the timeline?

Apply the Skill

Create a timeline of your own life. Divide it into years. Choose important events or dates in your life, such as your birth or the year you started school.

Colonies in America

800   1200   1600   2000

1620–1780

VOCABULARY

colony

mission

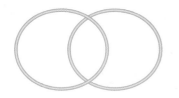 **READING SKILL**

Compare and Contrast
Take notes on how
English and Spanish
colonies were alike and
different.

Build on What You Know What
special celebration takes place in November?
Thanksgiving, of course. When you celebrate
Thanksgiving, you are doing what settlers did
nearly 400 years ago.

The Pilgrims

In 1620, a group of settlers landed at
Plymouth, Massachusetts. We call them the
Pilgrims. They had sailed from England on
a ship called the *Mayflower*.

The Pilgrims were Christians who hoped
to build a colony where they could live and
worship freely. A **colony** is a community
belonging to a distant country.

The Pilgrims' first winter was hard. They
did not have enough food. Half of them died
during the winter. However, during their first
spring the Pilgrims received help from
American Indians who lived nearby.

Plymouth Pilgrim colonists built a small farming town on land that had belonged to the Wampanoag.

The Wampanoag Help

With help from the Wampanoag (wahm puh NOH uhg) Indians, the Pilgrims learned to adapt to their new home. The Wampanoag taught the Pilgrims to fish and hunt deer and turkey. They also showed the Pilgrims how to plant beans, corn, and pumpkins, That fall, the Pilgrims and the Wampanoag held a thanksgiving feast.

Soon, more English families came to New England. They started other settlements. Like the Pilgrims, they wanted to worship freely, but everyone did not agree about how to worship. When **Roger Williams** had a different view, colony leaders forced him to leave. The same thing happened to **Anne Hutchinson**. Over time, laws in New England changed. People came to believe that people should worship as they wanted.

Anne Hutchinson

Review In what ways did the Pilgrims adapt to life in Plymouth?

The Spanish in the West

England's colonies grew quickly. This worried the king of Spain. He feared that England might try to claim Spain's land in the West. So, in the 1700s, Spain sent soldiers and priests to California and other places. They would build forts, convert Indians, and defend the land. To convert means to change from one belief to another.

Spanish Missions

The Spanish priests were Roman Catholics. The priests started missions. A **mission** is a community built around a church. The priests used the missions to teach their religion to American Indians.

Thousands of Indians came to missions in California and other places. Soldiers forced some Indians to leave their homes and join mission life. Others joined willingly. Mission work was hard. For many Indians, though, it became a way to learn new skills and ideas.

Mission San Gabriel Arcángel This mission was home to Gabrielino Indians. **Skill** **Reading Visuals** How are the buildings you see in the painting different?

Mission church

Gabrielino house

A Blend of Cultures

In time, the culture of California became a mix of Spanish and Indian cultures. Priests and soldiers at Spanish missions not only taught Indians, they also learned from them. Some church buildings used both Spanish art and Indian designs. Today, California's culture shows both influences.

Both the Pilgrims and the Spanish came to build settlements. Each group met American Indians and had to adapt to life in a new place. Today, Indian, English, and Spanish culture are part of our American culture.

Review In what ways is California's culture a mix of Spanish and Indian cultures?

California Missions

CALIFORNIA

San Gabriel Arcángel

KEY

• Spanish mission

Lesson Review

1620
Pilgrims landed in Plymouth

1769
Spanish built first mission in California

1600   1650   1700   1750   1800

❶ **VOCABULARY** Choose the best word to complete the sentence.

> **mission**   **colony**

The Pilgrims started a _____ in Plymouth.

❷ 📖 **READING SKILL** Use your chart to **compare** and **contrast** life in an English colony and at a Spanish mission.

❸ **MAIN IDEA: Geography** In what ways did the Wampanoag help the Pilgrims adapt to Plymouth?

❹ **MAIN IDEA: Culture** Why did the Spanish build missions in North America?

❺ **TIMELINE SKILL** Which came first, the arrival of the Pilgrims, or the building of Spanish missions?

❻ **CRITICAL THINKING: Fact and Opinion** Colony leaders forced Anne Hutchinson to leave because of her views. Give your opinion about this fact.

✏️➤ **WRITING ACTIVITY** Write a short story in which a Pilgrim thanks a Wampanoag for his or her help.

Thanksgiving

What was the first Thanksgiving like? In 1621, the Pilgrims invited their Wampanoag neighbors to the feast. Together they celebrated the year's harvest.

At least 90 Wampanoag and their leader, Massasoit (mas uh SOIT), came to the celebration. There were about 50 Pilgrims. The Pilgrims prepared a meal of stews, geese, fish, and lobster.

On Thanksgiving today, friends and families gather to eat and give thanks for the good things in their lives.

1 Pilgrims' Clothing

Look at the Pilgrims' clothing. How is it different from what people wear today?

2 American Indians

The artist painted the wrong clothes on the Wampanoag. The clothing they are wearing is what Indians in the Great Plains region would have worn.

Artist Jennie Augusta Brownscombe painted this in 1914. What words might she have used to describe her painting?

Activities

1. TALK ABOUT IT What Thanksgiving traditions do you know about?

2. WRITE ABOUT IT Write a paragraph explaining how the feast in 1621 is alike and different from Thanksgiving today.

Becoming a Country

VOCABULARY

independence
democracy

READING SKILL
Sequence Chart important events and dates in the order in which they happened.

1	
2	
3	
4	

800   1200   1600   2000

1775–Today

Build on What You Know Your birthday marks the day you were born. Countries have birthdays, too. The birthday of the United States was July 4, 1776.

Fighting for Freedom

Great Britain ruled its colonies in America for more than 150 years. Colonists obeyed British laws and gave money to the government. However, the British sometimes treated the colonies unfairly. Some Americans grew angry. They began to talk of independence. **Independence** means freedom. These colonists wanted freedom from British rule.

In 1775, war broke out. Leaders from the colonies met in Philadelphia, Pennsylvania. At Independence Hall, they named **George Washington** to lead American troops. They also wrote one of the most famous statements in history.

The Liberty Bell

Independence Declared In New York, colonists tear down a statue of the king of England.

The Declaration of Independence

The statement they wrote was called the Declaration of Independence. Its main author, **Thomas Jefferson**, explained why Americans should be free from British rule. He wrote:

" all men are created equal . . ."

At that time, American leaders did not think that women, African Americans, or Indians should be full citizens. **Abigail Adams** thought women should be citizens. She wrote about this to her husband, **John Adams**, who helped write the Declaration.

The leaders agreed to declare independence on July 4, 1776. Later, people rang the Liberty Bell to celebrate. In 1783, Great Britain agreed to peace with the United States. The United States had become a new country.

main idea

Review Why did the colonies fight against Britain?

A New Constitution

After the war, the new country needed new laws. In 1787, leaders met again in Philadelphia. They wrote a constitution, which is a plan for the government.

Throughout the summer, **Benjamin Franklin** and other leaders of the new country discussed their plan. Who would make the laws, and how? How much power should each part of the government have? They decided that the United States would be a democracy. A **democracy** is a government in which the people govern themselves. In a democracy, citizens choose their leaders.

main idea

The U.S. Constitution The Constitution tells the basic ideas and laws of our country.

Skill **Primary Source** Find the words "We the People." What do you think they mean?

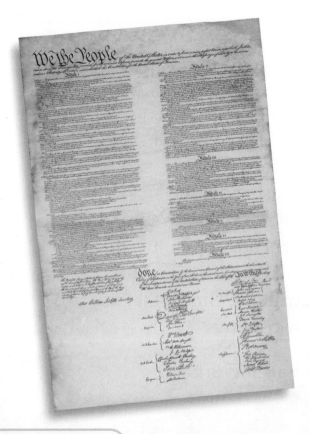

George Washington On April 30, 1789, he became the country's first President.

The Constitution

In September of 1787, the Constitution of the United States was finished. In April 1789, George Washington became the country's first President, or official leader. Americans thought that his bravery and honesty made him the best choice.

Today, the U.S. Constitution is more than 200 years old. Americans still follow its laws. New parts have been added to guarantee the full freedom of women and African Americans. Our Constitution and our nation's laws protect the freedom of all Americans.

Review What is the purpose of the Constitution of the United States?

Lesson Review

1775
War began

1783
Britain agreed to peace

1787
Constitution completed

1770 — 1775 — 1780 — 1785 — 1790

① **VOCABULARY** Use **independence** and **democracy** in a paragraph about the war with Britain.

② **READING SKILL** What is the **sequence** of events between the beginning of the war and the writing of the Constitution?

③ **MAIN IDEA: History** What is the Declaration of Independence and what did it do?

④ **MAIN IDEA: Government** What is the Constitution of the United States and what does it do?

⑤ **TIMELINE SKILL** Was the Constitution written before or after the war with Britain ended?

⑥ **CRITICAL THINKING: Summarize** Why are rules and laws important for a nation?

▶ **WRITING ACTIVITY**
Benjamin Franklin helped to write the Constitution. List three questions a reporter might have asked Franklin about his work.

Freedom's Heroes

What does freedom mean to you? To Benjamin Franklin, Thomas Jefferson, and Abigail Adams, **independence** from Britain was an important goal. They spent much of their lives helping the new United States become a free nation.

Benjamin Franklin 1706–1790

As a boy in Boston, Benjamin Franklin loved to read and write. Later, he moved to Philadelphia and became a printer. He experimented with electricity and made many inventions.

Franklin believed that the colonies should become one free nation. For that reason, he signed the Declaration of Independence. After the colonists won the war against Britain, he helped write the Constitution of the United States.

Thomas Jefferson 1743–1826

Thomas Jefferson was a very talented man. Throughout his life, Jefferson designed buildings, invented things, and started a university.

Thomas Jefferson is perhaps best known for writing the Declaration of Independence. His words showed that freedom and fairness were important to him. In 1801, Jefferson became the third President of the United States.

Abigail Adams 1744–1818

Abigail Adams played a key role in the lives of two United States presidents. She was the wife of John Adams, the second President, and the mother of John Quincy Adams, the sixth President.

While her husband was away during the war against Britain, Abigail Adams cared for their four children and ran the family farm. She was interested in women's independence and the education of girls.

Activities

1. **MAKE IT** Make biography cards of Franklin, Jefferson, and Adams. Tell how they showed **patriotism**, or love of country.

2. **WRITE ABOUT IT** Write a letter to Franklin, Jefferson, or Adams. Say what you think about that person's work for freedom.

Technology Read more biographies at Education Place. www.eduplace.com/kids/hmss05/

129

Skillbuilder

Make a Decision

A **decision** is the act of making up one's mind about what to do. People make decisions every day.

▶ **VOCABULARY**

decision

> Lisa and her brother, Joe, are talking about which way to walk to school. They can take a shortcut, but there are busy streets to cross. They can also take a much longer, safer route, through a park and past a police station. Which route should they choose?

Learn the Skill

Step 1: Identify the decision to be made. What is the goal?

Step 2: Think about possible choices and the different actions that would reach the goal.

Step 3: Gather information that will help you make a good decision. For example, talk with other people.

Step 4: Use the information to list the good sides, or pros, and the bad sides, or cons, of each choice. Predict what might happen if one choice is made instead of another.

Step 5: Review each choice, then make a decision about the best choice.

Practice the Skill

Use the steps and what you know about Lisa and Joe's decision to answer these questions.

1 What decision did Lisa and Joe have to make?

2 Where might Lisa and Joe have found information to help them make their choice?

3 What should they keep in mind as they make their decision?

4 What are the pros and cons of each choice?

Apply the Skill

Suppose that you are a town official who needs to make a decision for your community. Some young people in town want a park for in-line skating. Should you use an area that is now used for dog walkers? Use the steps you have learned to think about your choices. Then write a paragraph explaining your decision.

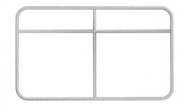

READING SKILL

Compare and Contrast
As you read, take notes on how Canada and the United States are alike and different.

WORLD CONNECTION

Canada

800	1200	1600	2000

1603–Today

Build on What You Know Think about the things you share with your neighbors. You may go to the same school or use the same library. People in the United States and Canada also share many things.

Our Neighbor, Canada

Canada and the United States are neighbors. They have much in common. Both are countries in North America. Both stretch from the Atlantic to the Pacific Ocean. Many of the same natural resources, such as forests and rich soil, can be found in both countries. In both countries, the first people were American Indians. Later, European nations sent explorers to both places and started colonies in each.

Vast areas of farmland are one of Canada's natural resources.

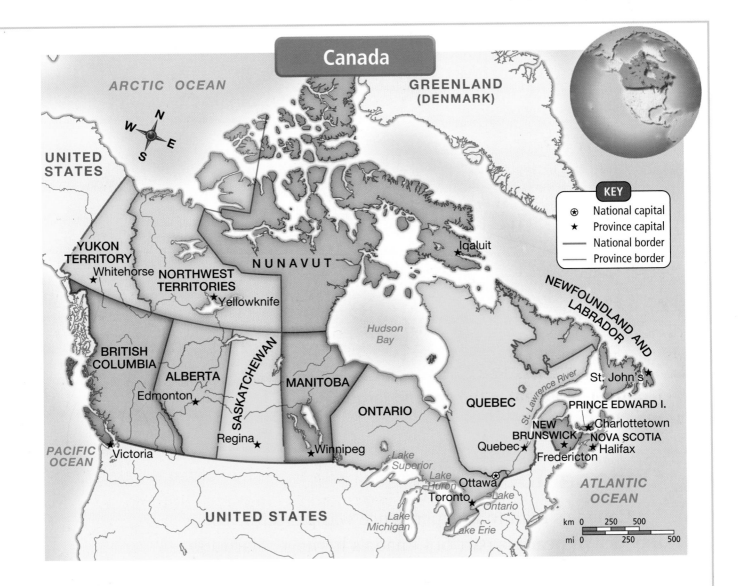

Canada

ARCTIC OCEAN

GREENLAND (DENMARK)

UNITED STATES

YUKON TERRITORY
Whitehorse

NORTHWEST TERRITORIES
Yellowknife

NUNAVUT

Iqaluit

BRITISH COLUMBIA

ALBERTA
Edmonton

SASKATCHEWAN

Regina

MANITOBA

Winnipeg

Hudson Bay

NEWFOUNDLAND AND LABRADOR

St. John's

Victoria

PACIFIC OCEAN

ONTARIO

Lake Superior

Lake Huron

Toronto

Lake Michigan

Lake Ontario

Ottawa

Lake Erie

QUEBEC

St. Lawrence River

Quebec

NEW BRUNSWICK

Fredericton

PRINCE EDWARD I.

Charlottetown

NOVA SCOTIA

Halifax

ATLANTIC OCEAN

UNITED STATES

KEY
⊛ National capital
★ Province capital
— National border
— Province border

km 0   250   500
mi 0   250   500

Canada's Independence

Canada and the United States gained their independence in very different ways. Great Britain and France both had colonies in Canada. For many years, these countries fought each other over the colonies. The British finally won in 1763, but many French colonists remained in Canada. Today, French is an official language of the country.

Unlike the United States, Canadians did not fight a war for independence from Great Britain. They gained their freedom over time. Step by step, Canadians made their own laws and gained full independence in 1867.

main ★ idea

Review How did Canadians gain independence?

Montreal Montreal is the second largest city in Canada.

Canada Today

Canada's road to independence was peaceful. Today, the idea of peace is part of Canada's heritage. **Heritage** is the history, ideas, and beliefs that people receive from the past. Canada's heritage includes languages and traditions.

Today, a number of languages are used in Canada. For example, many road signs are written in both English and French, the country's two official languages. The name Canada comes from a Haudenosaunee word that means "village." British, French, and Indian heritage are part of life in Canada today.

main idea (★)

Canada's Government

You can find clues to Canada's past in its government. It is similar to the British government. Both countries have a constitution. Both also have a government leader called a Prime Minister, and a royal leader, Queen Elizabeth II.

Canada's Symbols

Queen Elizabeth II does not actually rule Canada. She is a symbol of Canada's ties with Great Britain. A **symbol** is something that stands for something else. Symbols of Canada appear on its stamps and coins. One important Canadian symbol is the maple leaf. It reminds Canadians of the maple trees that grow in many parts of their country.

To summarize, Canada shares many things in common with the United States. It was once a British colony. However, Canada gained its independence peacefully. Today, Canada's heritage is a blend of the many different groups who live there.

Canadian nickel, front and back

Review Where can you find everyday reminders of Canada's heritage?

Lesson Review

| 1763 Great Britain won war with France | 1867 Canada gained independence |

1750   1800   1850   1900

1. **VOCABULARY** Use **heritage** and **symbol** in a sentence about Canada.

2. **READING SKILL** Do the United States and Canada have more differences or things in common?

3. **MAIN IDEA: History** How did Canada gain its independence?

4. **MAIN IDEA: Culture** What do Canada's languages tell about the people who have lived there?

5. **TIMELINE SKILL** For about how many years has Canada been independent?

6. **CRITICAL THINKING: Infer** Where would you look for clues about the heritage of the United States?

HANDS ON **ART ACTIVITY** The symbol on the Canadian flag is a maple leaf. Create a flag for your classroom. Include a symbol that stands for something special about your class.

Canada's Resources

Our neighbor to the north, Canada, is a country rich in resources. Water is one of Canada's precious natural resources. Wood from forests, iron ore, oil, and fish are others. Canada shares many of its resources, such as the electric power it creates with water, with the United States. Some of Canada's most important resources are shown on this map. Study the bar graph to learn more about one of these resources.

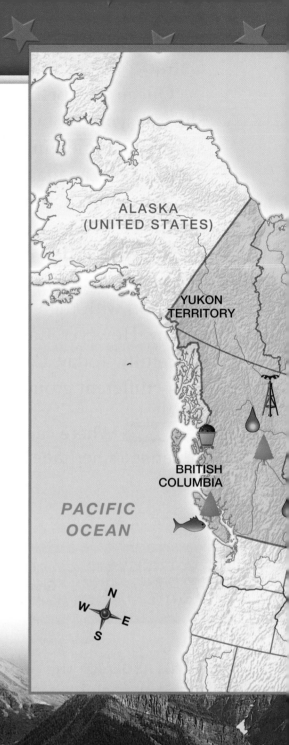

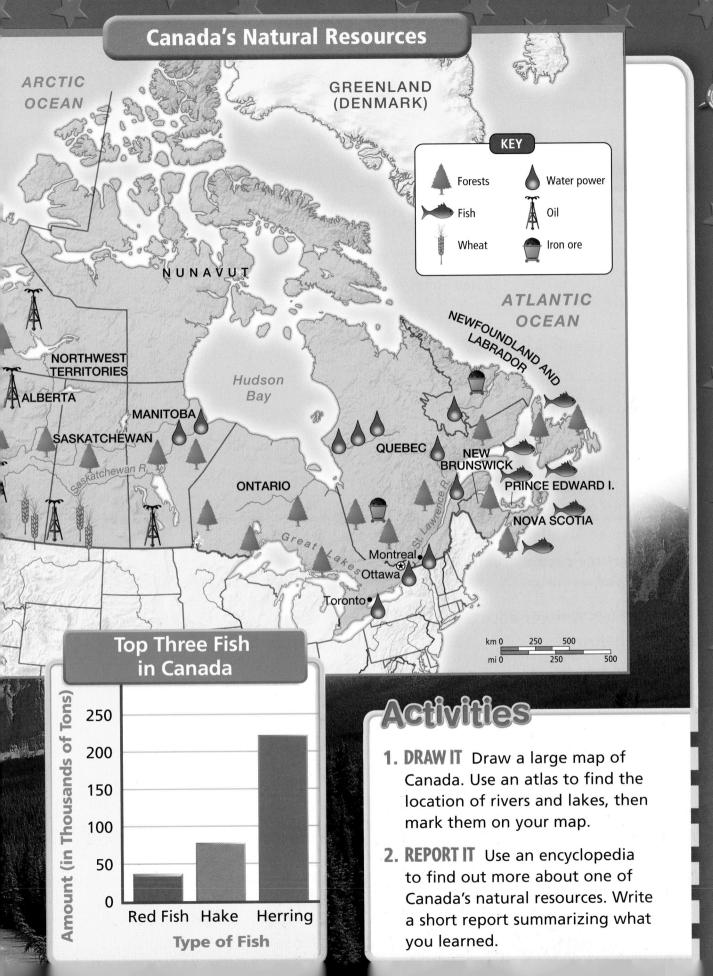

Canada's Natural Resources

ARCTIC OCEAN

GREENLAND (DENMARK)

KEY

- Forests
- Fish
- Wheat
- Water power
- Oil
- Iron ore

ATLANTIC OCEAN

NUNAVUT

Hudson Bay

NORTHWEST TERRITORIES

ALBERTA

MANITOBA

SASKATCHEWAN

Saskatchewan R.

ONTARIO

NEWFOUNDLAND AND LABRADOR

QUEBEC

NEW BRUNSWICK

PRINCE EDWARD I.

NOVA SCOTIA

St. Lawrence R.

Great Lakes

Montreal

Ottawa

Toronto

km 0   250   500
mi 0   250   500

Top Three Fish in Canada

Amount (in Thousands of Tons)

250

200

150

100

50

0

Red Fish   Hake   Herring

Type of Fish

Activities

1. DRAW IT Draw a large map of Canada. Use an atlas to find the location of rivers and lakes, then mark them on your map.

2. REPORT IT Use an encyclopedia to find out more about one of Canada's natural resources. Write a short report summarizing what you learned.

Visual Summary

1–3. ✏️ Write a description of each item or event named below.

United States History, 1542–1776	
🚢 **Cabrillo in California**	
🏠 **Pilgrims in Plymouth**	
📜 **Declaration of Independence**	

Facts and Main Ideas

✔️ **TEST PREP** Answer each question below.

4. **History** Why were European explorers looking for better routes to Asia?

5. **Geography** From which country did the Pilgrims originally come?

6. **Citizenship** Who was the first President of the United States?

7. **Government** In what ways is Canada's government like Britain's government?

Vocabulary

✔️ **TEST PREP** Choose the correct word from the list below to complete each sentence.

colony, p. 118
democracy, p. 126
heritage, p. 134

8. A country's _____ includes its traditions and languages.

9. Before California became part of the United States, it was a Spanish _____.

10. The writers of the United States Constitution decided that their government should be a _____.

980	1492	1620	1867
Vikings in North America	Columbus in North America	Pilgrims in Plymouth	Canada independent

| 800 | 1000 | 1200 | 1400 | 1600 | 1800 | 2000 |

Apply Skills

✓ **TEST PREP** **Read and Interpret a Timeline** Use the Chapter Summary Timeline above to answer each question.

11. What is the earliest event listed on the timeline?

A. Columbus in North America

B. Canada independent

C. Vikings in North America

D. Pilgrims in Plymouth

12. Into what periods of time is this timeline divided?

A. days

B. weeks

C. decades

D. centuries

13. Which event took place between 1800 and 2000?

A. Columbus in North America

B. Canada independent

C. Vikings in North America

D. Pilgrims in Plymouth

Critical Thinking

✓ **TEST PREP** Write a short paragraph to answer each question.

14. **Cause and Effect** What effect did missions have on California's culture?

15. **Summarize** What steps did the thirteen American colonies take to become the United States?

Timeline

Use the Chapter Summary Timeline above to answer the question.

16. In what year did the Pilgrims arrive in Plymouth?

Activities

Speaking Activity Prepare a speech that tells what you think about Thanksgiving.

Writing Activity Suppose the writers of the Declaration of Independence wanted you to sign it. Write a persuasive essay telling why you would or would not sign.

Technology

Writing Process Tips
Get help with your essay at
www.eduplace.com/kids/hmss05/

History Where You Live

Think of the people who lived in your community long before you did. Who were they? Why did they start your town? What traditions did they bring? You can look around your community to find clues to its past.

My Community's History

First people → **First explorers** → **First settlers**

Sod house

Team of horses

Find Out!

This family of settlers lived on the Great Plains in the late 1800s.

Explore the history of your community.

✓ **Start with your library.**
Some libraries have sections for local history. Old maps might show the first streets and buildings.

✓ **Look for memorials.**
They have information about the people who lived in your town.

✓ **Talk with older citizens.**
Older people may recall what your town was like many years ago.

✓ **Visit the historical society.**
This group studies community history. Ask one of the members to speak to your class.

Use your community handbook to keep track of information you find.

Review and Test Prep

Vocabulary and Main Ideas

✓ TEST PREP Write a sentence to answer each question.

1. What did the Yurok **trade** with other Indian nations?

2. What are some of the rules of the **constitution** of the Haudenosaunee?

3. What made colonists begin to think about **independence** from Great Britain?

4. What groups are part of Canada's **heritage?**

Critical Thinking

✓ TEST PREP Write a short answer for each question. Use details to support your answer.

5. **Cause and Effect** What did cold winters cause the Haudenosaunee to do?

6. **Compare and Contrast** In what ways were the explorers from Spain and France alike and different?

Apply Skills

✓ TEST PREP Use the information below and what you know about choosing sources to answer each question.

Todd is writing a report about Plymouth, Massachusetts. He needs to decide which sources to use to find specific information.

7. Which source would Todd probably use to get general information on the Pilgrims?

A. a magazine

B. a newspaper

C. a dictionary

D. an encyclopedia

8. What kind of source would Todd probably use to find out the temperature in Plymouth today?

Unit Activity

The Big Idea

Make a Fact Foldout

- Choose an American Indian nation from the unit.
- Research the people, listing information in a fact file.
- Fold a sheet of paper in half. On one side, list the facts you found.
- On the other side, draw the Indian community. Label your picture.

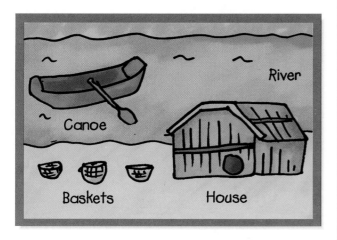

River

Canoe

Baskets

House

At the Library

You may find this book at your school or public library.

Pearl

by Debby Atwell

Pearl tells the story of events she saw in American history.

Connect to Today

Make a timeline of events.

- Find articles about important events from the past year.
- Draw a small picture or map to illustrate two events. Label the date of each event.
- Post your pictures on a classroom timeline.

Technology

Weekly Reader online offers social studies articles. Go to:
www.eduplace.com/kids/hmss/

Read About It

Look in your classroom for these Social Studies Independent Books.

PUEBLO
by Marie Richards

Anne Bradstreet
by Phoebe Beshkin

ON THE BEAMS
by Arlene Krueschek

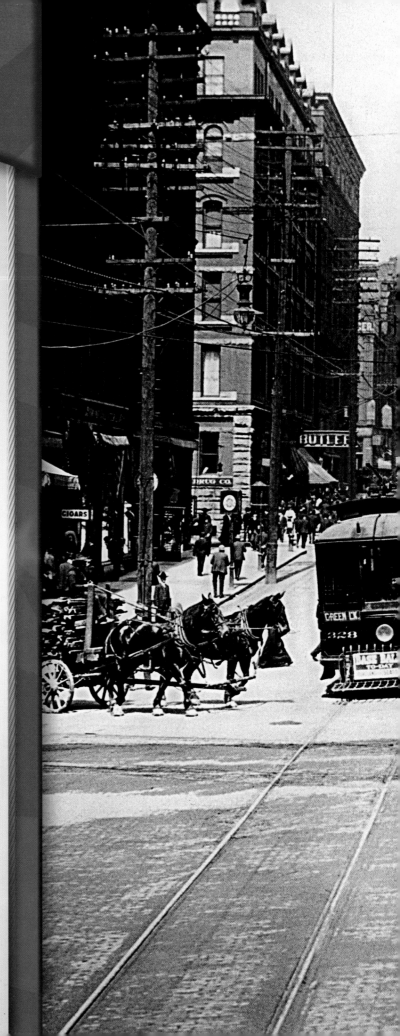

UNIT 3

People Move from Place to Place

The Big Idea

Why do communities change over time?

" . . . [N]othing is fixed, forever and forever and forever, it is not fixed; the earth is always shifting, the light is always changing, . . . "

—James Baldwin, writer, 1964

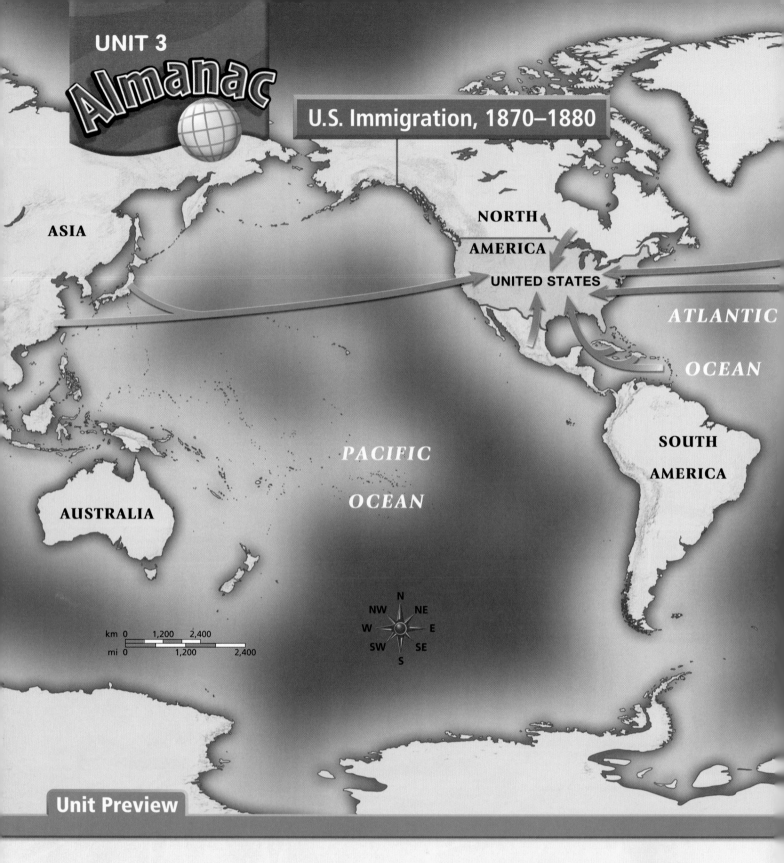

U.S. Immigration, 1870–1880

ASIA

NORTH
AMERICA

UNITED STATES

ATLANTIC

OCEAN

SOUTH
AMERICA

PACIFIC

OCEAN

AUSTRALIA

km 0   1,200   2,400

mi 0   1,200   2,400

N
NW   NE
W   E
SW   SE
S

Unit Preview

St. Louis
A city grows
**Chapter 5,
page 150**

**Trains and
Telegraphs**
People and ideas
move faster
**Chapter 5,
page 160**

**Immigrants
Arrive**
Newcomers
reach
America
**Chapter 6,
page 172**

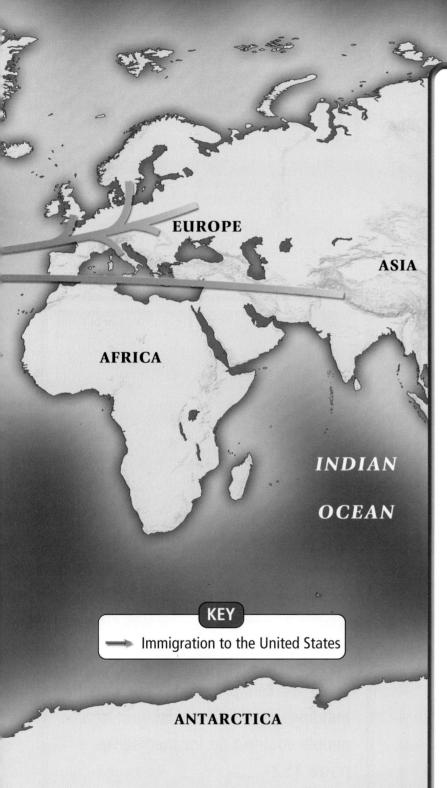

EUROPE

ASIA

AFRICA

INDIAN

OCEAN

KEY

→ Immigration to the United States

ANTARCTICA

Settling in Brazil
Immigrants make new homes
Chapter 6, page 185

Connect to Today

San Francisco, 1870

Newcomers

People born in the United States

In 1870, did San Francisco have more newcomers or more people born in the United States?

San Francisco, 2000

Newcomers

People born in the United States

Compare the circle graphs. In 2000, were newcomers a larger or smaller part of the population in San Francisco than in 1870?

CURRENT EVENTS

WEEKLY (WR) READER

Current events on the web!

Read social studies articles at:

www.eduplace.com/kids/hmss/

Vocabulary Preview

Technology

e • **glossary**
e • **word games**
www.eduplace.com/kids/hmss05/

goods

In the 1800s, boats filled with **goods** went up and down broad rivers. The boats carried many items for people to buy and sell. **page 151**

service

Some workers provided a **service** by building wagons. They did work that people couldn't do for themselves. **page 152**

Chapter Timeline

1764	1844	1869
St. Louis settled	First telegraph line built	Railroads linked coasts

1750   1800   1850

Reading Strategy

Question As you read, ask yourself questions about the important ideas.

Quick Tip List questions you have. After reading, go back to find the answers.

transportation

Many kinds of **transportation** helped people cross the country. They traveled by boat, on horseback, and in wagons. **page 160**

telegraph

With the invention of the **telegraph** people could send messages quickly across the country. **page 162**

1965
St. Louis arch completed

1900　　　　　　　　1950　　　　　　　　2000

Settlers in St. Louis

| 1750 | 1800 | 1850 | 1900 | 1950 | 2000 |

1764–Today

VOCABULARY

goods

service

entrepreneur

profit

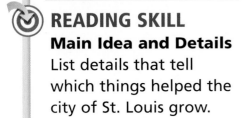

READING SKILL

Main Idea and Details
List details that tell which things helped the city of St. Louis grow.

Main Idea

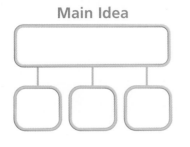

Build on What You Know Has a new person ever joined your class or community? Often, newcomers bring new ideas to a place. Some of the newcomers in St. Louis, Missouri, had new ideas for making money.

St. Louis's First Years

During the 1800s, the United States grew. Thousands of people began to move west. One place they settled was St. Louis.

St. Louis began, in 1764, as a trading post on the banks of the Mississippi River. Not far away, another large river, the Missouri, joins the Mississippi. St. Louis's location where two large rivers meet helped it to grow.

main idea

River Boat
A steamboat travels the Mississippi River during the 1830s.

St. Louis, Missouri

KEY
● City

Cities and Rivers Settlers traveled to St. Louis, and beyond, along rivers. **Skill** **Reading Maps** Which rivers meet north of St. Louis?

Newcomers Arrive

In the 1800s, people used rivers to travel long distances. Boats moved people and goods up and down rivers and all the way to the sea. **Goods** are things people buy or sell.

As more people used rivers for travel and trade, St. Louis became a busy place. The town served as a starting point for settlers moving farther west. Pioneers bought goods there. They wanted saddles, plows, wagons, and other supplies. Newcomers also came from countries such as Germany and Ireland. They found work, farmed, or set up new businesses.

By the 1860s, steamboats filled the docks, and trains connected St. Louis to the East. Thousands of people had built new stores and houses.

Review In what ways did the rivers help St. Louis grow?

Business Boosts St. Louis

As more people came to St. Louis, its economy grew. The people who arrived wanted services. A **service** is work that one person does for another. For example, the boat captains who started businesses provided a service. These entrepreneurs (ahn truh pruh NURS) carried people and goods along the Mississippi River. An **entrepreneur** is a person who takes a risk, or a chance, and starts a business.

In St. Louis, some entrepreneurs started newspapers. Some set up mills. Others raised mules to sell to people heading west. Entrepreneurs who ran their businesses well made a profit. **Profit** is the money a business earns after paying all its costs. Entrepreneurs and other people earned profits by selling private property, such as land. Private property is something that belongs to a person and not to the government.

Profit and Costs A wagon builder in 1847 sold wagons for about $100 each. It cost about $90 to build one. His profit was $10.

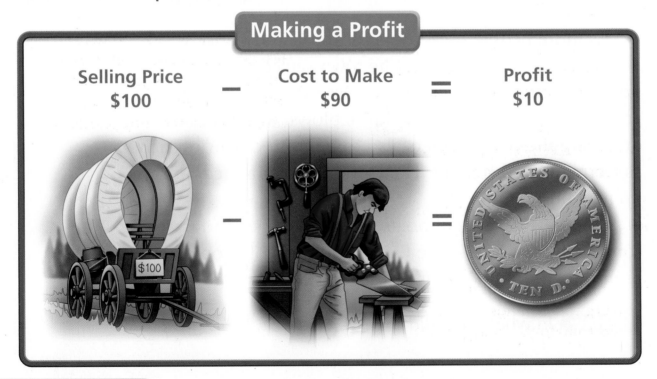

Making a Profit

| Selling Price $100 | − | Cost to Make $90 | = | Profit $10 |

St. Louis Today

St. Louis has changed over the years. The first settlers lived in cabins. Many families now live in tall buildings. Today, people make trucks with motors instead of wagons. Ships, however, still haul goods. More than 300,000 people live in St. Louis today. It is now the second-largest city in Missouri.

Review What made the economy of St. Louis grow?

The St. Louis Arch celebrates the city's past as the "gateway to the west."

Lesson Review

1764 St. Louis settled	1860 Many new stores and homes in St. Louis

1750   1800   1850   1900   1950   2000

1 VOCABULARY Choose the best word to complete the sentence.

> **goods service profit**
> Some businesses in St. Louis made a _____ after paying their costs.

2 READING SKILL Which **details** describe why the number of people in St. Louis grew?

3 MAIN IDEA: Geography In what ways did St. Louis's location help it to grow?

4 MAIN IDEA: Economics What were some things entrepreneurs did to help St. Louis grow?

5 TIMELINE SKILL In what year was St. Louis settled?

6 CRITICAL THINKING: Predict Outcomes Shipping traffic on the Mississippi River began to decline in the late 1800s. In what ways would that affect entrepreneurs in St. Louis?

HANDS ON

MAP ACTIVITY The Mississippi River flows through 10 states. Use a map to find out which states they are. Where does the river begin and end?

Readers' Theater

Hello, St. Louis!

Not every settler journeyed to the far west. In the 1850s, St. Louis, Missouri, was a bustling frontier town. Pioneers often stopped there to pick up supplies and to board boats up the Mississippi River for their journey west. As you will see, though, some families chose to stay in St. Louis.

Characters

Narrator

Joseph Boone: settler, husband of Anna

Anna Boone: settler, wife of Joseph

Conrad Fitzgerald: wagon builder, husband of Elsie

Elsie Fitzgerald: storekeeper, wife of Conrad

Benjamin Boone: son of the Boones, age eight

Rebecca Boone: daughter of the Boones, age nine

Sarah Stanwood: friend of the Fitzgeralds

Narrator: The Boone family, from Virginia, is on its way to California. The Boones have stopped in St. Louis to buy supplies and a wagon. They've gone to a wagon builder's shop to place their order.

Joseph Boone: I guess it's settled then. We'll pick up our wagon in two weeks.

Conrad Fitzgerald: We could have it ready sooner, Mr. Boone, if we weren't so busy. Seems like everybody passing through St. Louis wants wagons.

Elsie Fitzgerald: We're glad for the business. It's too bad more people don't stay and see what St. Louis has to offer.

Anna Boone: Your city is a lively place. There are so many lectures and concerts. I like what I see here.

Benjamin Boone: Me, too. I like watching the boats on the river.

Rebecca Boone: In the newspaper, it said a school for girls is opening. I think that would be wonderful.

Joseph: Hey, now, you all aren't changing your minds about going to California, are you? Rebecca and Benjamin, you were excited about moving there.

Benjamin

Anna

155

Anna: California would be a fine place to live, Joseph. But so would St. Louis.

Rebecca: St. Louis has so much, Pa! It's got a theater, for one thing.

Sarah Stanwood: You're right, Rebecca. We even have a university.

Benjamin: That's where I'd like to go.

Sarah: That's a good goal, Benjamin. We need educated people to help run St. Louis. It's growing very fast.

Joseph: Now you've got me thinking.

Anna: I knew it!

Joseph: A growing town means people need things. We could start a business. Anna and I know a little about horses and mules. We could raise them. What do you think, Anna?

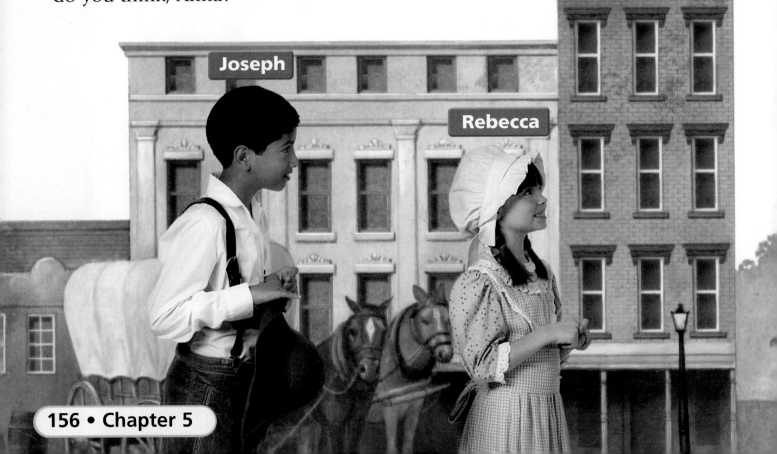

Anna: Mr. Fitzgerald just said everyone's asking him for wagons. They'll need mules to go with them. We would do well, and I'd be happy to stay.

Joseph: Rebecca? Benjamin? Would that suit you, too?

Rebecca and Benjamin: Yes!

Anna: It looks like we all agree, Joseph.

Elsie: You won't need the wagon then, but you will need customers. We'll send our customers to you for mules once they've bought their wagons.

Conrad: We'll help you find a home, too. I know of a house near us that's for rent.

Anna: Customers and a house! I feel settled already.

Joseph: Thank you both. I can't imagine a better welcome to St. Louis.

Sarah

Activities

1. **TALK ABOUT IT** If you were one of the Boones, would you rather stay in St. Louis or travel to California? Why?

2. **ACT IT OUT** Write the next scene in which the Boones start their new business.

Skillbuilder

Read a Line Graph

▶ **VOCABULARY**

line graph

Cities such as St. Louis change over time. You can learn about change by studying a line graph. A **line graph** is a kind of graph that uses lines and dots to show how something changes over time. The steps below will help you to read a line graph.

Learn the Skill

Step 1: Read the title of the line graph. The title tells what kind of information is on the graph.

Step 2: Read the words and numbers along the side and bottom of the graph. The numbers along the side tell you the amount, or what is measured. The numbers along the bottom show the time period.

Step 3: Look at where the dots fall on the graph. The dots show an amount at a specific point in time.

Step 4: Trace the line with your finger. The line shows the change in amount from one time to another.

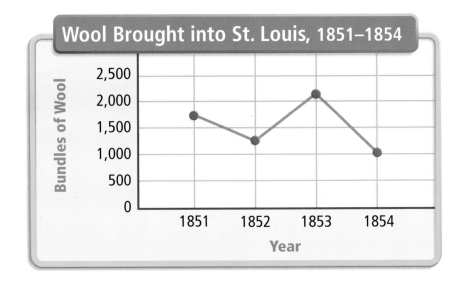

Wool Brought into St. Louis, 1851–1854

Bundles of Wool

2,500
2,000
1,500
1,000
500
0

1851   1852   1853   1854

Year

Practice the Skill

Use the line graph to answer these questions.

1 What time period does the line graph cover?

2 In what year was the largest amount of wool brought into St. Louis? The smallest amount of wool?

3 About how many bundles of wool were brought into St. Louis in 1854?

Apply the Skill

Find the line graph on page 199. Read its title. What does the graph show about the number of women in Congress over time? Write a paragraph describing any changes.

Moving West

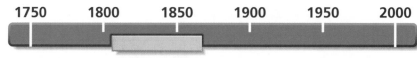

| 1750 | 1800 | 1850 | 1900 | 1950 | 2000 |

1807–1869

Build on What You Know A car can travel over 60 miles an hour. Long ago, there were no cars and few roads. People on foot might need a whole day to travel just 15 miles.

VOCABULARY

transportation
steam engine
railroad
telegraph

READING SKILL

Categorize As you read, organize the information into two categories, transportation and communication.

Transportation in the 1800s

In the 1800s, thousands of people moving west hoped to make new lives in California and Oregon. These settlers used many kinds of transportation on their trips. **Transportation** is the way people and things are carried from one place to another.

In the early 1800s, people usually arrived in St. Louis by horse or boat. From there, they could follow rough trails across the country. Some walked. Others drove large wagons covered in heavy cloth. These settlers made difficult journeys across rivers, mountains, and plains.

Wagons and trains carried people west in the 1860s.

How a Steam Engine Works
1 Burning fuel makes heat.
2 The heat turns water to steam.
3 The steam forces the wheels to turn.

Steamboats and Railroads

Over time, moving west became easier. The steam engine made transportation faster. A **steam engine** is a machine that turns steam into power. **Robert Fulton** built the first useful steamboat in 1807. It used a steam engine for power. Steamboats traveled on rivers and oceans. Travelers to the West could take steamboats to St. Louis. They might travel by wagon for the rest of their journey.

Railroads also changed how people traveled. A **railroad** is a track with two steel rails on which trains move. By the 1830s, railroads had been built in the East. Within a few years, steam engines powered the trains.

Review In what ways did steam engines change transportation?

Communication in the 1800s

Another invention, the telegraph, let people get information more quickly. A **telegraph** is a machine that sends signals by electricity. The signals speed along a wire stretched between telegraph stations. **Samuel Morse** helped invent the telegraph. In 1844, telegraph lines could send messages between cities in minutes.

Trains and telegraphs made life easier in the East. However, transportation and communication were slower in the West. Communication is the way people pass information to each other. People depended on ships and stagecoaches for news. Then came the Pony Express. This group of young horseback riders carried the mail. They could gallop from Missouri to California in about 10 days.

The Telegraph Samuel Morse helped invent the telegraph. People sent messages by typing the Morse Code into the device below, called a telegraph key.

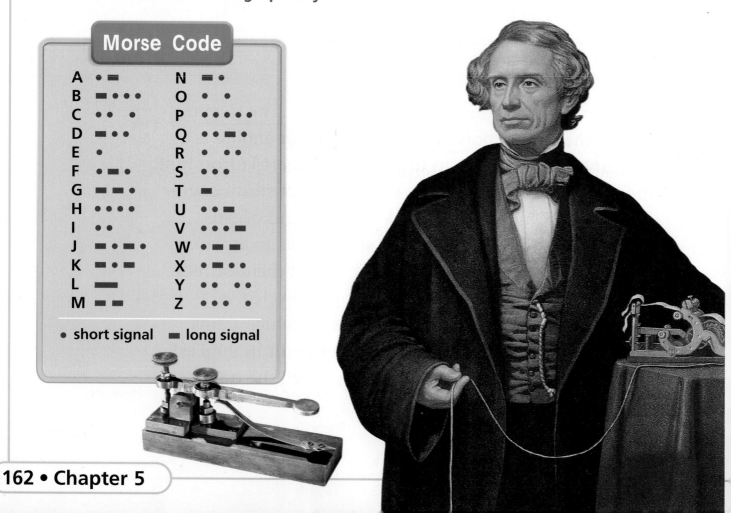

Morse Code

A	•　■		N	■　•
B	■　•　•　•		O	•　•　•
C	•　•　•　•		P	•　•　•　•　•
D	■　•　•		Q	•　•　■　•
E	•		R	•　•　•
F	•　■　•　•		S	•　•　•
G	■　■　•		T	■
H	•　•　•　•		U	•　•　■
I	•　•		V	•　•　•　■
J	■　•　■　•		W	•　■　■
K	■　•　■		X	•　■　•　•
L	■		Y	•　•　•　•
M	■　■		Z	•　•　•　•

• short signal   ■ long signal

Linking East and West

As fast as they went, the riders could not keep up with the telegraph. After the first telegraph line crossed the country in 1861, the Pony Express ended. Then in 1869, a railroad linked the East and West coasts for the first time. <u>The telegraph and the railroad united the country.</u>

A Pony Express rider

main ★ idea

In the mid-1800s, the railroad, the steamboat, and the telegraph changed travel and communication in the United States. They made it possible for Americans to cross the country and send news more quickly than ever before.

Review In what ways did the telegraph affect the United States?

Lesson Review

1807	1844	1869
First useful steamboat	**First telegraph line**	**Railroads linked coasts**

1800   1820   1840   1860   1880

❶ **VOCABULARY** Use **telegraph** in a sentence about Samuel Morse.

❷ **READING SKILL** Did you **categorize** the Pony Express under communication or transportation? Tell why.

❸ **MAIN IDEA: History** What kinds of transportation did settlers use before the steam engine?

❹ **MAIN IDEA: History** Why did the Pony Express end?

❺ **TIMELINE SKILL** What year did the railroad first connect the East and West coasts?

❻ **CRITICAL THINKING: Analyze** In what ways did railroads and steamboats make life easier for people in the 1800s?

✏️ **WRITING ACTIVITY** The first train has just arrived in a western town. Write two headlines about the event for the town's newspaper.

Transportation Then and Now

People have always traveled, but they haven't always moved very fast. Not so long ago, people traveled only as fast as they could walk or as fast as the wind could push their sailboats. Some people traveled by horseback or in wagons pulled by animals. When the **steam engine** came along, **transportation** picked up speed.

Steam engines powered trains and boats. By the late 1800s, cars, buses, and trucks started to roll. Gasoline, not steam, fueled many of their engines. A few years later, small airplanes began to fly. Today, big jets speed through the sky. Cars zip along wide, smooth highways. Long trips don't take as long as they did in the 1800s.

Wagon

- In the 1860s, wagons heading west traveled on bumpy trails.

- The trip from the Missouri River to California was about 2,000 miles.

- Loaded with goods and people, the wagons could go 10 to 15 miles a day.

1–2 miles per hour

Railroad

- The western link for the first cross-country railroad stretched from the Missouri River to California.

- The trip was 1,776 miles long.

- One train company promised the trip could be made in fewer than four days.

 **25–35 miles per hour**

Jet

- Jets today can carry more than 350 people.

- A 2,000-mile trip can take about three and a half hours.

- Jets can cruise at about 600 miles per hour.

 **600 miles per hour**

Activities

1. **DRAW IT** Suppose your job is to sell tickets for the first cross-country train ride. Make a poster to persuade people to make the trip.

2. **FIGURE IT OUT** How much faster is a jet today than a train from the 1800s?

Skillbuilder

Read a Map Scale

In the 1800s, people traveled long distances to move west. What can you do to find out how far they traveled? You can use a map scale. A **map scale** helps you to measure distance.

Learn the Skill

Step 1: Look at the map scale. It shows that 1 inch on the map stands for 300 miles in the real world.

Step 2: Use a ruler to find the distance between Ogden and Sherman Summit on the map. The ruler measures 1 inch, so the distance between these two places is about 300 miles.

Step 3: For longer distances, multiply the number of inches by 300 miles. For example, suppose you measure 2 inches between the places on the map. When you multiply 2 times 300, you get 600 miles.

Practice the Skill

Use a ruler and the map scale to answer the questions.

1 In northern Nevada, about how many miles is it between the east and west borders?

2 About how many miles is it from Elko to Promontory Point?

3 About how many miles is it from San Francisco to Ogden?

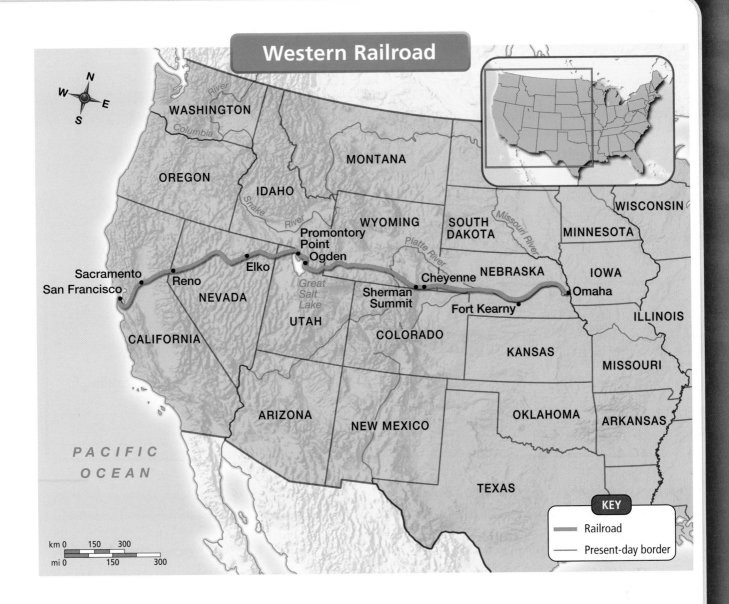

Western Railroad

WASHINGTON

OREGON

IDAHO

MONTANA

WYOMING

SOUTH DAKOTA

WISCONSIN

MINNESOTA

Promontory Point

Ogden

Elko

Sacramento

San Francisco

Reno

NEVADA

Great Salt Lake

CALIFORNIA

UTAH

Sherman Summit

Cheyenne

NEBRASKA

IOWA

Omaha

ILLINOIS

Fort Kearny

COLORADO

KANSAS

MISSOURI

ARIZONA

NEW MEXICO

OKLAHOMA

ARKANSAS

PACIFIC OCEAN

TEXAS

Columbia River

Snake River

Platte River

Missouri River

KEY

━━ Railroad

── Present-day border

km 0   150   300

mi 0   150   300

Apply the Skill

Turn to the political map of the United States in the atlas. Using the scale, find the distance between the following cities on the map:

- **Columbus, Ohio, and Tampa, Florida**

- **Phoenix, Arizona, and San Diego, California**

167

Visual Summary

1–3. Write a description of each item named below.

Changes over Time

St. Louis

_____

_____

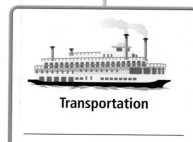

Transportation

_____

_____

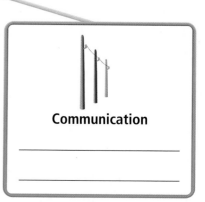

Communication

_____

_____

Facts and Main Ideas

TEST PREP Answer each question below.

4. **Geography** In what ways did the location of St. Louis help it to grow?

5. **Economics** What is private property?

6. **History** Name at least three ways that people traveled west in the early 1800s.

7. **History** In what ways did the steam engine change life in the 1800s?

Vocabulary

TEST PREP Choose the correct word from the list below to complete each sentence.

entrepreneur, p. 152

profit, p. 152

railroad, p. 161

8. Business owners in St. Louis sold goods to make a _____.

9. When the _____ linked the East and West coasts, travel across the country became easier.

10. The _____ took a risk, or a chance, and started a new business.

1764	1807	1844	1869
St. Louis was settled	First useful steamboat built	First telegraph line built	Railroad linked the coasts

1760   1780   1800   1820   1840   1860   1880

Apply Skills

☑ **TEST PREP** **Read a Line Graph**
Study the line graph below. Then use your line graph skills to answer each question.

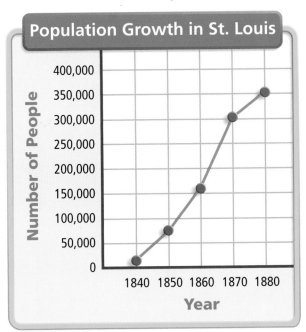

Population Growth in St. Louis

11. About how many people lived in St. Louis in 1850?
    A. 20,000
    B. 80,000
    C. 160,000
    D. 310,000

12. In what year did about 310,000 people live in St. Louis?
    A. 1840
    B. 1850
    C. 1860
    D. 1870

Critical Thinking

☑ **TEST PREP** Write a short paragraph to answer each question below.

13. **Draw Conclusions** Why did entrepreneurs move to St. Louis in the 1800s?

14. **Cause and Effect** In what ways might faster transportation help a community to grow?

Timeline

Use the Chapter Summary Timeline above to answer the question.

15. In what year did Americans first send telegraph messages across the country?

Activities

 Research Activity What did children do on the long wagon trips west? Use library and Internet resources to find out. Prepare a short talk telling about a typical day.

 Writing Activity Write instructions for a way to earn a profit. Number your instructions.

 Technology
Writing Process Tips
Get help with your instructions at
www.eduplace.com/kids/hmss05/

Vocabulary Preview

Technology

e • **glossary**
e • **word games**
www.eduplace.com/kids/hmss05/

diversity

Because people from many different countries live in the United States, the nation has great **diversity.**
page 172

immigrant

People from other countries moved to both the East and West coasts. These **immigrants** left their own countries to work and live in the United States. **page 174**

Reading Strategy

Predict and Infer Use this strategy before you begin reading.

Quick Tip Look at titles and pictures. What can you tell about the people you will read about?

ancestor

Most people living in the United States have older relatives, or **ancestors,** who came from another country.
page 186

generation

Ancestors pass traditions to the next **generation.** People who were born around the same time belong to the same generation.
page 186

Core Lesson 1

VOCABULARY

diversity

slavery

immigrant

READING SKILL

Draw Conclusions
List details that will help you explain why immigrants to the United States settled on the West Coast.

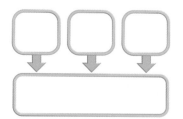

Coming to America

Build on What You Know When you flip through a phone book, you see many different names. Where do these names come from? Many belong to people who came to the United States from other countries.

People From Many Places

The United States is a mix of many people. This mix of people makes our country a place of great diversity. **Diversity** means variety. The people in the United States come from diverse backgrounds. They may be of different ages and abilities, but many of their traditions have blended, creating our American culture.

main ★ idea

Skill **Reading Graphs** During which years did the most newcomers arrive?

Newcomers to the United States

Newcomers (in Millions)

Year	
1851–1900	
1901–1950	
1951–2000	

Freedom Frederick Douglass (right) escaped from slavery and worked for freedom. By 1900, thousands of free black children attended schools.

Africans in the Americas

Some settlers chose to leave their homes to come to the United States, but not everyone who arrived wanted to come. For over 300 years, millions of Africans were captured, brought to the Americas, and forced into slavery. **Slavery** is a system under which people have no freedom. They are forced to work for no pay. People who resisted slavery might be beaten or killed. Many slaves did resist. Some even escaped, or found ways to buy their freedom.

During the 1700s and 1800s, free Africans sometimes settled in their own communities. Some lived in large cities, while some farmed in rural areas. Others started businesses, or worked as ministers, teachers, and lawyers. Still, African Americans were sometimes treated unfairly. Many formed groups to help each other succeed. In the 1860s, the U.S. government finally outlawed slavery.

Review What types of jobs did free Africans in the United States have?

Moving to the West

In 1542, Europeans arrived in California, on the West Coast of what is now the United States. At first, California belonged to Spain. From 1822 to 1848 it was part of Mexico. Spanish and Mexican settlers brought their language and traditions to their new home. Then, in 1848, California became part of the United States. That same year, gold was found there. People from around the country and the world rushed to California.

Many people moving to the United States settled on the West Coast. Among the immigrants were people from China. An **immigrant** is someone who leaves one country and moves to another. Many Chinese came to California to earn money for their families back in China.

main idea (★)

California and the West Coast
Immigrants from China, Ireland, Japan, Mexico and many other countries came to work and to find a better life.

Gold Rush, 1850s

Building the Railroad, 1860s

More Immigrants Follow

Later, other immigrants came to the West Coast. Farmers arrived from Japan, Korea, and the Philippines. From 1910 until 1940, the first stop for most Asian immigrants traveling to the West Coast was Angel Island, in San Francisco Bay. Immigrants had to wait at Angel Island until the government of the United States decided whether they could come into the country.

People also came to California from Spanish-speaking places, including Mexico and Central America. Today, more than one-fourth of the people of California are from a Latino background.

Review Why did many immigrants leave their home countries to move to a new country?

Angel Island, 1910s

California Today

Moving to the East

During the late 1800s and early 1900s, millions of European immigrants continued to come to the East Coast of the United States. Many of them arrived by boat at Ellis Island, in New York Harbor. Like Angel Island, Ellis Island was a government center for immigrants. One of the first sights to greet immigrants in New York Harbor was the Statue of Liberty. It was a sign of welcome.

Making a New Life

For immigrants on the East and West coasts, settling in a new country was hard. Some Americans worried that immigrants would take their jobs. Chinese immigrants sometimes had to wait for weeks or even months for permission to leave Angel Island. Many Irish immigrants to the East Coast found it hard to find jobs.

Immigrants to New York saw the Statue of Liberty, a gift to the United States from the people of France.

Making Contributions

The newcomers didn't give up, though. They worked hard and made contributions to the United States. Chinese workers helped build railroads that crossed the country. A Russian American named **Vladimir Zworykin** (VLAD uh mihr ZWAWR ih kihn) helped invent television. Many immigrants have worked hard and done well in their new country. Immigrants continue to come here today and add to our country's diversity.

Vladimir Zworykin

Review In what ways have immigrants contributed to our country?

Lesson Review

1 VOCABULARY Use **immigrant** in a short paragraph describing what it was like to come to the West Coast.

2 READING SKILL Why did different groups of immigrants settle on the West Coast of the United States?

3 MAIN IDEA: History In what ways did free African Americans succeed in the United States?

4 MAIN IDEA: History Why was life hard for some new immigrants?

5 PLACES TO KNOW Where is Ellis Island?

6 CRITICAL THINKING: Compare In what ways were the experiences of immigrants to the East and West coasts alike?

WRITING ACTIVITY Different countries have different kinds of food. Find the restaurant section in your phone book. List three countries shown and write a sentence for each telling what you know about the people there or their foods.

Hannah's Journal

by Marissa Moss

Hannah and her cousin Esther leave their small village in Lithuania to go to America. As **immigrants,** they hope to find freedom and jobs. Before boarding the ship to America, they meet Samuel, an orphan from Russia.

November 6, 1901

A most magnificent day! We're here at last, in America! Our first sight was of the statue everyone talks about—a giant green goddess raising high the torch of Liberty, promising freedom to all who reach her shores. And her other arm holds a book— is it a sign I will get the education I've dreamed of?

Everyone crowded on deck to see her. Men cheered. Women waved their kerchiefs. Children clapped excitedly. Even Esther, for the first time since the storm, came out to see the famous statue. She looked so thin and pale in the buttery autumn light, I felt terrible for her. I'd said I'd take care of her, but really I hadn't. I'd avoided steerage as best I could, leaving her to her misery. I promised myself that in America, I'd do better. I'd make sure she was happy and well.

As we stood at the rails, a ferry approached our ship. I wished I knew English and could understand what was going on.

All I could tell was that men boarded the steamship, names were called, people rushed around, and when the hubbub was over, all the first- and second-class passengers were gone, ferried over to America.

Samuel said we must wait for our own ferry, but we wouldn't be taken to America, not yet. First we had to go to an immigration station on Ellis Island.

Ellis Island? I'd never heard of it, but Samuel said it's called the Island of Tears because so many people fail the inspection and get sent back.

Another inspection? After coming so far, we could be sent back?! I had no idea that was possible! Esther heard the word inspection, and all her fears flooded back. I told her not to worry, I would take care of everything. But in my heart I wondered, what will we do? How can I be sure they let us in?

We had to answer questions even to get off the ship. The inspector asked me if I could read and write. I was terrified! Would I have to show him this journal? Then I thought of Papashka's prayer book, and I showed how I could read the first page. See, Papashka, it wasn't a waste to teach me. In America, it matters what you know!

Walking a plank from the large steamship to the small ferry made me nervous, but Samuel joked and tried to turn the crossing into a game. He even got a smile out of Esther, tired and fretful though she was.

The ship had been crowded, but that was nothing compared to the numbers on Ellis Island. And now I hear even <u>more</u> languages—Greek, Irish, Italian, Turkish, too many to guess at. Long lines snaked everywhere we looked. We stood and stood, and barely moved forward. We weren't even in the building yet!

INSPECTION CARD
(Immigrants and Steerage Passengers.)
Port of Departure *Hamburg*
Name of Ship *Atlanta*
Name of Immigrant *Rivka*
Solomon
Last Residence *Berdichev*
Inspected and passed
Passed at quarantine, prt of
Ship's list or manifest

Immigrants had to wear tags or cards that gave information such as their names.

Activities

1. **TALK ABOUT IT** Describe three things Hannah sees when she arrives in America.

2. **WRITE ABOUT IT** Hannah says, "In America, it matters what you know!" Do you agree? Do you disagree? Write a statement telling what you think.

Skillbuilder

Identify Primary and Secondary Sources

Many immigrants have written about their lives. These accounts, or stories, are primary sources. A **primary source** is information recorded by a person who was there. Primary sources are different from secondary sources. A **secondary source** is information recorded by a person who was not there.

Read the two descriptions below. One is a primary source and the other is a secondary source.

> At a quarter to ten we steamed for Ellis Island. . . . We could not move an inch from the places where we were awkwardly standing. . . . All were thinking—"Shall I get through?" "Have I enough money?" "Shall I pass the doctor?" . . .
>
> Stephen Graham, 1914

> The government began using Ellis Island as an immigration station in 1892. About 35 buildings were constructed on the island. Newcomers were taken to the main building. . . . The immigrants were questioned by government officials and examined by doctors.

Step 1: Read the sources carefully. What are they about?

Step 2: As you read, look for clues that show that the writer was part of the event. The writer of a primary source may use words such as *I*, *me*, or *we*.

Step 3: Look for clues that show the writer was not part of the event. If the account is based on what the writer heard or read about the event, it is a secondary source.

Practice the Skill

Answer these questions about the two accounts.

1 What makes these two stories different?

2 Which is the primary source? Explain your answer.

3 Which is the secondary source? Explain your answer.

Apply the Skill

Look through Lesson 1 again. List three facts or statements you might find in a secondary source about Angel Island.

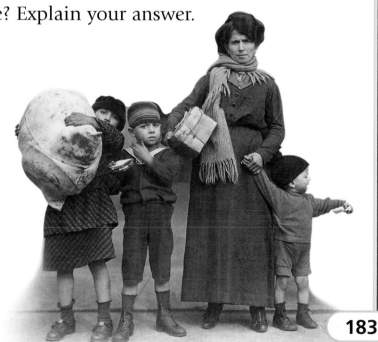

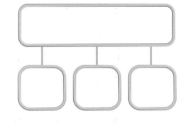

READING SKILL
Main Idea and Details
List details that tell where immigrants to Brazil came from and why they came.

WORLD CONNECTION
Brazil

Build on What You Know People have come from most parts of the world to live in the United States. Many other countries have citizens from around the world, too.

Land of the Amazon

Brazil is the largest country in South America. In land size, it is a little smaller than the United States. Find Brazil on the map.

Brazil is a land of many natural resources. The second longest river in the world, the Amazon, winds through a vast region of rain forest in the north. Sandy beaches hug Brazil's coast. Brazil also has good soil for farming and grasslands for grazing.

The Amazon River is about 4,000 miles long.

Coming to Brazil

Immigrants from around the world have made Brazil their home. American Indians lived in Brazil long before the first European settlers arrived in the 1500s. The European newcomers were from Portugal and spoke Portuguese. Today, most people in Brazil speak Portuguese.

Not everyone who went to Brazil did so freely. Millions of enslaved people were taken there from Africa. Many were forced to work on huge sugar cane farms. Brazil finally ended slavery in 1888.

Over the years, more people from other countries moved to Brazil. Many hoped to find work. Immigrants from Germany settled in southern Brazil. The climate there reminded them of their European homes. Workers from Japan and Italy also went to work on large coffee farms. Some bought small farms of their own.

Review Why did some European settlers go to Brazil?

Brazil

Amazon River

BRAZIL

São Paulo

PACIFIC OCEAN

ATLANTIC OCEAN

Brazil is home to people whose families came from around the world.

New Lives, Old Ways

Many immigrants in a new country keep some of their own ways of doing things, but learn new ways, too. They often live in neighborhoods with people from their home countries. The largest city in Brazil, São Paulo (sown POW loh), has a big Italian community. There is also a large Japanese neighborhood. Some stores there have signs in Japanese. People print newspapers in Japanese and make Japanese crafts.

The people of Brazil have ancestors from many parts of the world, including Africa, Europe, and Asia. An **ancestor** is a relative who was born long ago. Ancestors help pass their traditions on to the next generation. A **generation** is a group of people born and living at about the same time. Your grandmother is one of your ancestors. You and your friends are in the same generation.

Many Japanese immigrants in Brazil pass on their traditions to their families. These traditions include dancing and wearing kimonos.

New Ways

Today, Brazilians use new ways to stay connected with the world. Millions of Brazilians use cell phones and the Internet to communicate. They use email, or electronic mail, to send messages that travel between computers in seconds. Like people all over the world, Brazilians depend on satellites to communicate. A satellite is a machine that travels in space, getting and sending information such as television or telephone signals.

Review In what ways might immigrants pass their traditions to new generations?

Brazilians of all ages use cell phones and other new ways to stay in touch.

Lesson Review

1 **VOCABULARY** Choose the best word to complete the sentence.

ancestor   generation

People in my _____ use many types of new technology.

2 **READING SKILL** What **details** in your chart tell why immigrants came to Brazil?

3 **MAIN IDEA: Culture** What did some German immigrants like about Brazil?

4 **MAIN IDEA: Technology** In what ways do email and the Internet help people to keep in touch?

5 **PLACES TO KNOW** Where is the Amazon River?

6 **CRITICAL THINKING: Analyze** If you were moving to a new country, what traditions would you want to keep?

WRITING ACTIVITY Write a list of three or four questions about the ways people use satellites to communicate.

Hi-Tech Brazil

Space is not so hard to reach after all—not if you launch a satellite from Brazil.

In the Amazon River basin, Brazil has built a launching center for satellites. Called Alcantara, the center is in an ideal location near the equator.

The earth spins faster at the equator. The spin helps move the rockets and satellites into space more easily, and this saves fuel.

People in Brazil, and everywhere, depend on satellites. Satellites can send all kinds of information around the world. They help send TV signals, Internet messages, and details about the weather.

Communication

Communication satellites send messages from one part of the world to another. They help students use the Internet.

Navigation

Satellites help scientists track and study jaguars. Some jaguars wear radio collars that allow scientists to follow their daily activities.

Weather

Weather satellites send pictures of the earth to weather forecasters. These pictures help predict the weather.

Activities

1. **TALK ABOUT IT** What things do you do that depend on information from satellites?

2. **WRITE ABOUT IT** If you could design a satellite to help you with tasks on Earth, what would your satellite do? Write a paragraph telling about it.

Visual Summary

1–3. Write a summary of each item shown below.

Immigrants

Angel Island

_____

_____

Ellis Island

_____

_____

Japanese in Brazil

_____

_____

Facts and Main Ideas

✔ **TEST PREP** Answer each question below.

4. **History** When did the United States government outlaw slavery?

5. **History** Why did people come to California from all over the world after 1848?

6. **Culture** What traditions might immigrants keep in their new country?

7. **Citizenship** What are two ways in which immigrants can contribute to a new country?

Vocabulary

✔ **TEST PREP** Choose the correct word from the list below to complete each sentence.

diversity, p. 172
slavery, p. 173
ancestor, p. 186

8. People have no freedom under the system of _____.

9. The many languages spoken in a large city are a sign of the city's _____.

10. Someone in your family from long ago is your _____.

Apply Skills

TEST PREP **Identify Primary and Secondary Sources** Read each source below. Use what you have learned to answer each question.

1

> *January 12th.* When our ship arrived at the port, I was amazed. So many people were on the dock shouting in a language I didn't know. So this was California.

2

> More than 80,000 people arrived in 1849 alone, and by 1852 California's population had soared to over 250,000.

11. What clue word tells you that the writer of one of the quotes was part of the event?

   A. the word "I"

   B. people

   C. population

   D. soared

12. Which quote is probably from a secondary source?

   A. quote 1

   B. quote 2

   C. both

   D. neither

Critical Thinking

TEST PREP Write a short paragraph to answer each question below. Use details in your response.

13. **Compare** In what ways are the lives of immigrants in the United States and Brazil alike?

14. **Summarize** In what ways do people use computers to communicate?

15. **Decision Making** What might be the pros and cons of moving to a different country?

Activities

Interview Activity Prepare five questions you would like to ask someone who has immigrated to the United States.

Writing Activity Write a description of American culture to help an immigrant learn more about it. Include details about routines, clothing, and activities.

Technology
Writing Process Tips
Get help with your description at
www.eduplace.com/kids/hmss/

Changes Where You Live

All communities change over time. Settlers and immigrants helped some communities to grow. Transportation and communication have changed communities, too. In what ways has your community changed over time?

My Community's Changes

| Immigrants and settlers come. | Businesses grow. | Communication improves. | Transportation speeds up. |

Trolley

Horse and carriage

Find Out!

In 1903, some people in Chicago, Illinois, still used horses for transportation.

Explore how your community has changed over time.

✓ **Start with primary sources.**
A local museum or library may have old diaries, letters, and photographs.

✓ **Check out the names of streets, parks, and schools.**
These are often named for people who have made important contributions.

✓ **Read the ads in old newspapers filed in your library.**
The ads tell what kinds of stores and businesses your community once had.

✓ **Ask the Chamber of Commerce about local transportation.**
Highways and airports have affected local businesses.

Use your community handbook to keep track of information you find.

Review and Test Prep

Vocabulary and Main Ideas

☑ **TEST PREP** Write a sentence to answer each question.

1. Who are **entrepreneurs?**

2. In what ways did the **telegraph** improve communication?

3. Why did many **immigrants** come to the United States in the 1800s and 1900s?

4. In what ways do immigrants pass some of their traditions to the next **generation?**

Critical Thinking

☑ **TEST PREP** Write a short answer for each question. Use details to support your answer.

5. **Predict** In what ways might transportation change in the next 200 years?

6. **Draw Conclusions** Describe the ways in which immigrants contribute to a country.

Apply Skills

☑ **TEST PREP** Use the map of Atlanta, Georgia, to answer each question.

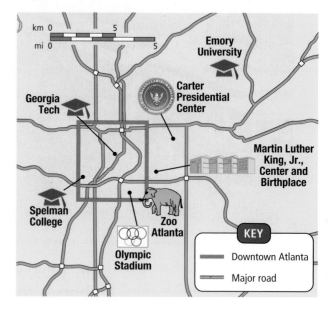

7. About how many miles does one inch equal on the map scale?

8. What is the distance from Spelman College to Emory University?

   A. about 2 miles

   B. about 5 miles

   C. about 9 miles

   D. about 15 miles

Unit Activity

The Big Idea

Make a Pair of "Then and Now" Pictures

- Choose a city that has changed over time. Research new buildings, population growth, and other changes.

- Pick two years that show a great contrast in how the city looked.

- Draw two scenes of the city, one in the early year and one in the later year. Add labels.

At the Library

You may find this book at your school or public library.

We Rode the Orphan Trains by Andrea Warren

Warren tells the stories of eight children who traveled across the country to find new families.

CURRENT EVENTS
WEEKLY (WR) READER

Connect to Today

Present a plan for moving to a new place.

- Find out about a place you would like to move to.

- Find the location of the place on a map.

- Write a plan telling how you would get there and what you would do there.

Technology

Weekly Reader online offers social studies articles. Go to: **www.eduplace.com/kids/hmss/**

Read About It

Look in your classroom for these Social Studies Independent Books.

UNIT 4

Community Government

The Big Idea

What makes someone a good citizen of the United States?

"*The noblest question in the world is: What good can I do in it?*"

—Benjamin Franklin, inventor and statesman, 1737

Levels of Government

ARCTIC OCEAN

km 0 300

mi 0 300

PACIFIC OCEAN

PACIFIC OCEAN

km 0 50 100

mi 0 50 100

PACIFIC OCEAN

Colorado Springs **CITY**

COUNTY

EL PASO COUNTY

STATE

Colorado Springs

COLORADO

N
NW NE
W E
SW SE
S

MEXICO

Common Good
Citizens work together
Chapter 7, page 203

The U.S. Constitution
Protecting citizens' rights
Chapter 7, page 212

Local Leaders
Sheriffs work for safety
Chapter 8, page 228

SHERIFF
8

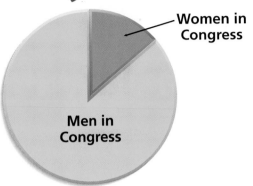

CANADA

L. Superior

L. Michigan

L. Huron

L. Ontario

L. Erie

⊛ Washington, D.C.

ATLANTIC

OCEAN

Gulf of
Mexico

km 0   150   300
mi 0   150   300

KEY

⊛ National capital

— National border

— State border

▢ County area

● City

U.S. Congress

Women in
Congress

Men in
Congress

In 2003, there were 74 women
in Congress.

Women in Congress

Number of Women
in Congress

60

40

20

0

1935 1955 1975 1995

Year

How many women are in your
state government?
Your county government?
Your local government?

CURRENT   EVENTS

WEEKLY (WR) READER

Current events on the web!

Read social studies articles at:

www.eduplace.com/kids/hmss/

**The American
Flag**
A symbol of
our nation
**Chapter 8,
page 242**

Chapter 7

Being an Active Citizen

Vocabulary Preview

Technology

e • **glossary**
e • **word games**
www.eduplace.com/kids/hmss05/

common good

People who work together to help others in their community work for the **common good.**
page 203

volunteer

Anyone can be a **volunteer.** Many people help others in their school or community.
page 203

Reading Strategy

Summarize Use this strategy to help you understand important information in this chapter.

Quick Tip Use main ideas to help you summarize.

right

The U.S. Constitution protects the freedom of all citizens. All have the **right** to say their opinions.
page 212

responsibility

Citizens have a **responsibility** to respect others. Obeying laws is also part of being a responsible citizen.
page 214

Citizens Make a Difference

 READING SKILL
Main Idea and Details List details that show ways in which citizens help communities.

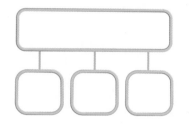

Build on What You Know Who helped you today? Perhaps someone in your family made your lunch. Perhaps your teacher taught you something new. When people help one another, they are practicing good citizenship.

Citizens Can Help

Every day, people in your community help one another. Helping the community is part of being a good citizen. You can practice good citizenship, too. You can speak up to make things more fair. You can obey laws, or help change them to make them better. By being a good citizen, you make your community a better place to live.

 main idea

Community Helper
This crossing guard helps to keep people safe.

The Common Good Volunteering to work at an animal shelter or to help people are two ways to work for the common good.

Working Together

Citizens can help even more by working together. Suppose you want to pick up trash at a nearby park. If your classmates helped, the cleanup would go faster. If community groups and local leaders joined in, it might take just a few hours.

When people work together to benefit their community, they work for the common good. The **common good** is whatever helps the most people in a community. It can mean keeping parks clean, working to change unfair laws, and solving community problems.

Some people take part in their school or community by working as volunteers. A **volunteer** is a person who works freely, without pay. Volunteers care about other people, not just themselves.

Review In what ways can students practice good citizenship?

Paradise Valley, Arizona These Arizona students helped build a new house in their town.

Students Help Others

In Paradise Valley, Arizona, a group of students wanted to help people in their community. The students talked with community leaders. After sharing their ideas, they decided to build 10 houses in 10 years. To reach this goal, the students worked with Habitat for Humanity (HFH). HFH is a volunteer group that helps families all over the world build houses. Working with HFH, the students came up with a plan to build their first house for a family in their town.

Raising Money

The students raised money for supplies and materials. Their school district organized a carnival. The students sold T-shirts, washed cars, and held a dance. They also asked community leaders for help. Teachers, principals, and parents volunteered. Many business owners gave money. Some gave supplies, such as paint and wood.

Building a New Home

Then, the students and other volunteers started building. They had lots of help. Habitat for Humanity workers showed them how to plan and build. Carpenters showed older students how to cut wood. Painters taught younger students to paint walls. The family that would own the house also worked with the volunteers.

At last, the house was finished. Everyone celebrated. The students felt proud. By helping to build a house, the students and volunteers had worked for the common good.

Young volunteers paint.

main idea

Review What steps did students take before starting to build the house?

Lesson Review

1 VOCABULARY Choose the best word to complete the sentence.

common good   **volunteer**

A _____ chooses to help a community without getting paid.

2 READING SKILL Name two **details** that support the **main idea** that good citizens help in their communities.

3 MAIN IDEA: Citizenship Why is it important for people to be good citizens?

4 MAIN IDEA: Citizenship In what ways did students in Arizona help their community?

5 CRITICAL THINKING: Analyze Why did the students start their project by raising money?

WRITING ACTIVITY Think about your own community and what you would like to improve. Write a letter to the editor of a newspaper, explaining your idea.

SAVING SOCCER

How can students work to change a plan? When members of a soccer team learn that a new building might replace their field, they talk about what they can do.

Ana

Characters

Ana: student

Sean: student

Tam: student

Jennifer: student

Coach Wilson: soccer coach

Coach Sánchez: assistant coach

Ana: Hey, did you hear the news?

Sean: Yes! They're going to build a movie theater in town!

Tam: All right! Now we won't have to travel ten miles.

Jennifer: There's one small problem, though. They want to build it where our soccer field is.

Sean: What? Coach Wilson, is that true?

Coach Wilson: I'm afraid so, Sean. According to the paper, our field is one of the places where they're thinking about building the theater.

Coach Wilson

Sean

Ana: That's not fair!

Jennifer: They can't make us give up our field.

Coach Sánchez: Well, they haven't made a decision yet.

Tam: I think a movie theater is better than a soccer field.

Jennifer: Tam! How can you say that?

Tam: I just really like movies, that's all.

Sean: Tam has a right to his opinion, Jennifer.

Jennifer: You're right. I know, but this is our field we're talking about!

Ana: Isn't there anything we can do?

Coach Sánchez: Sure there is. You can let people know how you feel about the building plan.

Sean: We could write a letter to the editor of the newspaper.

Coach Sánchez

Tam: Yes. We could say that we want a movie theater, but just not in our field.

Jennifer: Now you're talking.

Ana: Let's write a petition that says that and ask people to sign it.

Coach Sánchez: Those are both great ideas.

Coach Wilson: I understand there's a town meeting next week. They're planning to talk about the movie theater.

Jennifer

Sean: We can give them our petition.

Jennifer: Will you go, Coach Wilson?

Coach Wilson: Absolutely. Your family members can come, too. Maybe we can fill a school bus.

Ana, Sean, Tam, and Jennifer: Great!

Tam: Will we have to say anything?

Coach Wilson: It's up to you. If you want your voice to be heard, I think you should tell people how you feel.

Ana: You bet we will!

Coach Sánchez: I like this plan.

Tam

Sean: In the meantime, why don't we start working on our letter and petition?

Tam: Wait a minute. We're forgetting something.

Jennifer: What?

Tam: Soccer practice!

Activities

1. **TALK ABOUT IT** As the soccer team talked, how did they show **respect** for each other?

2. **RESEARCH IT** What does freedom of expression mean? Find out what the U.S. Constitution says about it. Does it apply to young people as well? Share what you learn with your classmates.

Resolve Conflicts

VOCABULARY

conflict

compromise

Citizens who work well together can help communities. Sometimes, though, people have very different ideas. When they do not agree on something, they face a conflict. A **conflict** is a disagreement. Knowing how to listen to others and trying to solve conflicts is an important part of working together.

Learn the Skill

Step 1: Identify a conflict. For example, students may have different ideas on how to use a free period.

Step 2: Ask people or groups to share their ideas. For example, some students may want the free period for more computer time. Others might want to spend the period playing outdoors. Listen carefully to all the ideas.

Step 3: Brainstorm different solutions. The class might split the time between the soccer field and the computer room. Or, students could take turns doing different activities on different days.

Step 4: As a group, agree to one of the solutions. Each side may have to make a compromise. A **compromise** is a plan that everyone agrees on. When people make a compromise, each person usually has to give something up. Work on the plan until everyone agrees with at least some part of the solution.

Practice the Skill

Use the steps in Learn the Skill to answer these questions about solving conflicts.

1 Why should people share their ideas?

2 Why is listening important in solving conflicts?

3 How can you find out if everyone agrees to the solution?

Apply the Skill

Suppose that people in your community want to improve the local park. Different groups have different ideas about what to do. One group wants to plant a flower garden. Another group wants to build a stage for concerts. Write a paragraph about how these two groups could work together to solve the conflict. Remember that they will probably have to reach a compromise.

Rights and Responsibilities

 READING SKILL

Compare and Contrast As you read, list ways in which rights and responsibilities are alike and different.

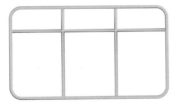

Build on What You Know In some countries, many children cannot go to school. In the United States, however, children are free to go to public school. The freedom to learn brings with it the duty to learn.

Knowing About Rights

Most newspapers print letters from their readers. In their letters, people tell what they think about articles in the paper. People in the United States share their opinions freely. They have the right to say what they think. A **right** is a freedom.

United States citizens have many rights. Some are stated in the Bill of Rights, which is part of the Constitution of the United States. The Constitution explains the nation's government. It says that one job of the government is to protect the rights of its citizens.

main idea

A student shares her opinion in a letter to the editor.

> Dear Editor,
> I read in your newspaper what the leader of our town said about the traffic on Palm Drive. I ride my bike to school along that street. Ms. Lee was right when she

What Are the Rights of Citizens?

One right that U.S. citizens have is called freedom of religion. Citizens may practice their religion, or no religion at all. Another right is freedom of assembly. This means citizens can meet together whenever they choose. They can protest unfair laws. Americans have the right to own property. They also have the right to privacy, or to keep secrets. Citizens are free to do these and many other things, as long as they obey the law.

Review What are some rights that citizens have?

Freedom of Religion

Freedom to Own Property

Our Rights

Freedom of Speech

Freedom of the Press

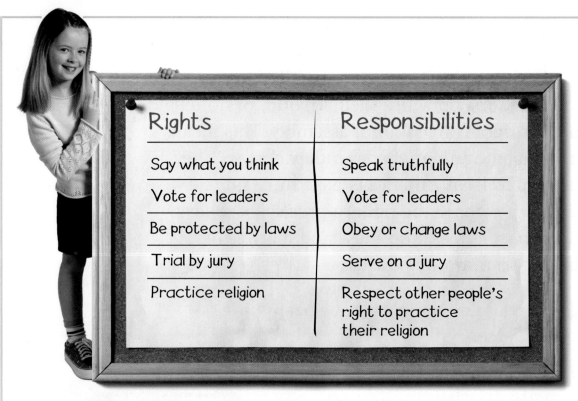

Rights	Responsibilities
Say what you think	Speak truthfully
Vote for leaders	Vote for leaders
Be protected by laws	Obey or change laws
Trial by jury	Serve on a jury
Practice religion	Respect other people's right to practice their religion

Skill **Reading Charts** What right is also a responsibility?

Knowing Our Responsibilities

Citizens have many rights, but rights have limits. For example, you are free to say what you think. However, it is against the law to shout "Fire!" in a public place when there is no fire.

In other words, rights come with responsibilities. A **responsibility** is something you should do for the common good. Every person has responsibilities. One responsibility is to respect other people's property. You may not take another person's coat or bike without their permission. That would interfere with their right to own property. It would also break the law.

Obeying laws is very important. Laws explain our responsibilities. A person who does not obey a law may pay a fine or go to jail. If a law is unfair, however, citizens are responsible for changing it.

Voting Is a Right and a Responsibility

Adult citizens have many responsibilities. For example, they may serve in the military or on a jury. Adults also have the responsibility to vote. To **vote** means to make an official choice.

The Constitution says that every adult citizen has the right to vote. Citizens vote to choose leaders for community, state, and national governments. Sometimes citizens vote about changing the laws.

To vote wisely, citizens first need to learn about issues in their community. Then, on voting day, they need to vote. Unless citizens vote, their opinions may not count.

A student votes on an important class issue.

Review What responsibilities do citizens have?

Lesson Review

① **VOCABULARY** Write a paragraph telling about some of the **rights** and **responsibilities** you have in your community.

② 👆 **READING SKILL** Use your chart to tell about ways in which rights and responsibilities are **different** from one another.

③ **MAIN IDEA: Citizenship** Name two rights that citizens in the United States have.

④ **MAIN IDEA: Citizenship** Why is obeying laws an important responsibility?

⑤ **CRITICAL THINKING: Analyze** In what ways can knowing your responsibilities help you benefit your community?

HANDS ON **ART ACTIVITY** Make a poster that tells people why voting is important and reminds them to vote.

Class President

by Johanna Hurwitz

Whether you are voting for your favorite dessert or for class president, voting is an important **right** and **responsibility.** In this story, students **vote** to elect other students to be their class leaders.

⭐

Arthur stood up. "It doesn't matter where Julio was born," he said. "He'd make a very good class president. He's fair, and he's always doing nice things for people. When I broke my glasses, he was the one who thought of going to Mr. Herbertson so that we could still play soccer at recess. That shows he would make a good president."

"But Julio is not one of the top students like Zoe or Lucas or me," Cricket said.

"He is tops," said Arthur. "He's tops in my book."

Julio felt his ears getting hot with embarrassment. He had never heard Arthur say so much in all the years that he had known him.

"Thank you, Arthur," said Mr. Flores. "That was a very good speech. We still need someone to second the nomination. Do I hear a second?"

Lucas raised his hand.

"I second the nomination of Julio Sanchez," he said.

Mr. Flores turned to write Julio's name on the board. Lucas was still raising his hand.

Mr. Flores turned from the board and called on Lucas again.

"Do you wish to make a campaign speech?" he asked Lucas.

"Yes. I'm going to vote for Julio, and I think everyone else should, too."

"Aren't you even going to vote for yourself?" asked Cricket.

"No," said Lucas. "I want to take my name off the board. Julio is a good leader, like Arthur said. When we went to see Mr. Herbertson, Cricket and I were scared stiff, but Julio just stepped in and did all the talking."

"Are you asking to withdraw your name from nomination, Lucas?" asked Mr. Flores.

"Yes, I am. Everyone who was going to vote for me should vote for Julio."

Julio sat in his seat without moving. He couldn't say a word. He could hardly breathe.

"Are there any other nominations?" asked Mr. Flores.

Zoe raised her hand. "I move that the nominations be closed."

"I second it," said Lucas.

Then Mr. Flores asked the two candidates if they wanted to say anything to the class.

Cricket stood up. "As you all know," she said, "I'm going to run for President of the United States some day. Being class president will be good practice for me. Besides, I know I will do a much, much better job than Julio." Cricket sat down.

Julio stood. "I might vote for Cricket when she runs for President of the United States," he said. "But right now, I hope you will all vote for me. I think our class should make decisions together, like how we should spend the money that we earned at the bake sale. We should spend the money in a way that everyone likes. Not just the teacher." Julio stopped and looked at Mr. Flores. "That's how I feel," he said.

"If I'm president," said Cricket, "I think the money should go to the Humane Society."

"You shouldn't tell us what to do with the money, either," said Julio. "It should be a class decision. We all helped to earn it."

"Julio has made a good point," said Mr. Flores. "I guess we can vote on that in the future."

Mr. Flores passed out the ballots. Julio was sure he knew the results even before the votes were counted. With one boy absent, Cricket would win, twelve to eleven.

Julio was right, and he was wrong. All the boys voted for him, but so did some of the girls. When the votes were counted, there were fourteen for Julio Sanchez and nine for Cricket Kaufman. Julio Sanchez was elected president of his class.

"I think you have made a good choice," said Mr. Flores. "And I know that Cricket will be a very fine vice-president."

Julio beamed. Suddenly he was filled with all sorts of plans for his class.

Activities

1. **THINK ABOUT IT** What are some of the qualities of a good leader? Is Julio a good leader? Would you vote for him? Why or why not?

2. **WRITE ABOUT IT** As Julio, write a short speech thanking your classmates for having elected you class president.

Visual Summary

1–3. Write a description of each item named below.

Citizenship

Good citizen	
Rights	
Responsibilities	

Facts and Main Ideas

✓ **TEST PREP** Answer each question below.

4. **Citizenship** What are two examples of good citizenship?

5. **Government** What document lists the rights of American citizens?

6. **Citizenship** What are two rights of every citizen?

7. **Government** Who has the responsibility of choosing government leaders?

Vocabulary

✓ **TEST PREP** Choose the correct word from the list below to complete each sentence.

common good, p. 203
volunteer, p. 203
vote, p. 215

8. A _____ might help out at the local library.

9. Speaking up about unfair laws is one way to work for the _____.

10. Americans _____ to choose leaders.

Apply Skills

 **TEST PREP Resolve Conflicts**
Apply what you have learned about resolving conflicts. Read the paragraph below and then answer each question.

> A group of students have different ideas about how to present their history project. Some of the students want to give a speech. The other students would rather make a poster. How should they resolve this conflict?

11. What is the FIRST thing the group should do to resolve the conflict?

12. Which of the following is a compromise?

   A. Make a poster.
   B. Give a speech.
   C. Do separate projects.
   D. Give a speech using a poster.

Critical Thinking

✔ **TEST PREP** Write a short paragraph to answer each question below. Use details to support your response.

13. **Analyze** Why is it important for people to respect the rights of others?

14. **Infer** In what ways can newspapers help citizens vote wisely?

Activities

 Citizenship Activity Make a poster encouraging people to be volunteers in your community.

Writing Activity Write a personal narrative about an experience you have had or an event you have seen that showed good citizenship.

 Technology
 Writing Process Tips
Get help with your narrative at **www.eduplace.com/kids/hmss05/**

Vocabulary Preview

Technology

e • **glossary**
e • **word games**
www.eduplace.com/kids/hmss05/

mayor

There are many types of government. People in cities elect a **mayor,** who leads the city's government.
page 228

governor

States have a leader who makes sure the state laws are carried out. This leader is called a **governor.**
page 235

Reading Strategy

Monitor and Clarify As you read, check your understanding of the information in the text.

Quick Tip When you are confused, go back and reread.

legislature

The United States **legislature** is called Congress. Members of Congress make laws.

page 240

ambassador

Most countries have an **ambassador** who works in Washington, D.C., to represent his or her government.

page 248

Local Government

VOCABULARY

election

tax

mayor

council

county

 READING SKILL

Draw Conclusions
List details that tell what citizens do before they vote. Then draw a conclusion about why they do those things.

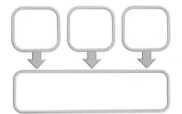

Build on What You Know Think of the last time you went to the school library. Who paid for the books you read or borrowed? Who owns the library building? If you said your local government, you were right.

Citizens Decide

Our country is a democracy. In democracies, citizens decide what the government will do. A citizen may make decisions about local, state, and national government. In this lesson we will look at citizens and local governments.

In some communities, citizens go to a town meeting to make decisions. They take turns speaking. They listen to each other's ideas. Then they vote to decide what to do.

Local governments provide school libraries.

Leadership This citizen wants to win a local election. Beforehand, she meets other citizens to answer questions.

Electing Representatives

In other communities citizens choose people to represent, or speak for, them. Citizens do this by voting in elections. An **election** is the process by which citizens vote for people to represent them.

Before the election, citizens ask questions. How might a leader improve community services? Would a leader spend more money on schools? People try to learn all they can before they vote.

Then the election is held. Citizens vote. The votes are counted. The person with the most votes wins the election. He or she represents the people of that community in local government.

Review What can citizens do to take part in their local government?

What Local Government Does

Local government is part of your daily life. It makes laws and provides services you use every day. These laws and services are for the common good.

Laws can help keep the community safe. In some communities, a law says that bike riders must wear helmets when they are riding their bikes. By obeying such laws, citizens keep themselves safer.

Different laws tell how to run local government. These laws say what jobs leaders will have. Some laws set up special groups, such as the department of public safety and the department of public health. What do you think these groups do?

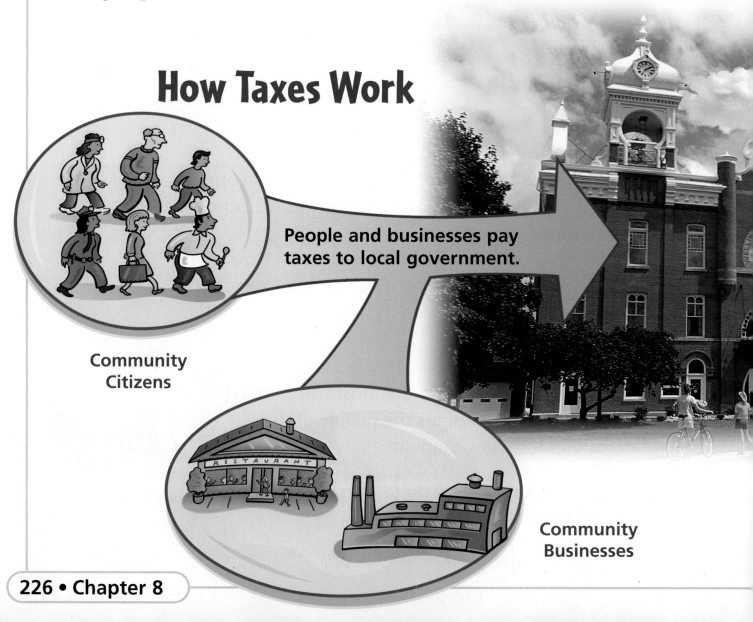

How Taxes Work

People and businesses pay taxes to local government.

Community Citizens

Community Businesses

Paying for Services

To pay for services, the government collects taxes. A **tax** is a fee citizens and others pay to the government. Communities may place a tax on houses, land, or businesses. They may also tax goods that you buy. The money collected goes to pay for such things as buses, subways, trash collection, and running water.

Paying taxes is an important part of being a citizen. So is taking part in making decisions about taxes. Many communities vote to decide when to raise or lower their taxes. They may also vote on how taxes should be used.

Review What are some of the local services paid for by taxes?

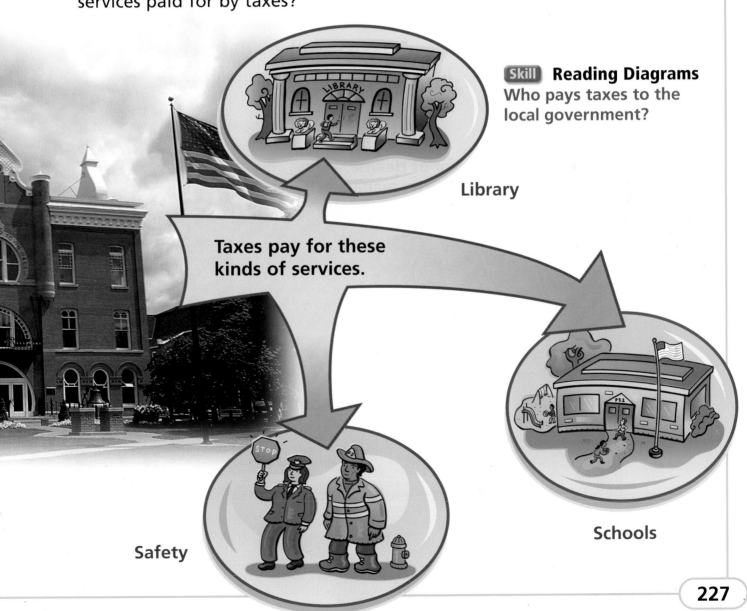

Skill **Reading Diagrams**
Who pays taxes to the local government?

Library

Taxes pay for these kinds of services.

Safety

Schools

Types of Local Government

Different communities have different types of government. In some communities, citizens elect a mayor. A **mayor** is the leader of a city's government. Every day, he or she makes important decisions that help the local government run smoothly.

main idea (★)

City Government

In almost all cities, citizens elect a city council. A **council** is a group of officials who make rules or laws. The council and the mayor have different responsibilities. However, they must work together to get things done.

In some communities, the city council hires a manager to run the city. A city manager is different from a mayor. A manager does not help make laws. He or she obeys the council. Other communities have everything: a mayor, a council, and a city manager.

Working Together The mayor of Hearne, Texas, discusses local issues with the city manager.

BILLY R. McDANIEL
MAYOR–PLACE I

FLOYD T. HAFLEY
CITY MANAGER

County Government

Many counties also have governments. A **county** is an area of the state that includes several communities. County citizens vote for local officials, such as sheriffs and commissioners (kuh MIHSH uh nurs). Commissioners run the county government.

Fulton County, Georgia, has seven commissioners. They make decisions for the communities in the county. They make sure the people of Fulton County get services such as police and fire protection.

Review Why do communities have different types of government?

Sheriffs protect citizens and make sure laws are followed.

Lesson Review

1 VOCABULARY Use **election** in a sentence describing the way citizens choose government leaders.

2 READING SKILL What might happen if citizens did not ask questions before they voted?

3 MAIN IDEA: Citizenship In what ways do citizens help decide what local government should do?

4 MAIN IDEA: Economics What are taxes, and how are they used?

5 CRITICAL THINKING: Compare and Contrast How are city and county governments the same? How are they different?

WRITING ACTIVITY Write a friendly letter to a city council. Thank the members for providing services that children and schools use. Include details to describe those services.

How to Vote

"All in favor, say 'Yes!'" That's one way people vote. In class, you might raise your hand. To vote in local, state, or national **elections,** people follow several steps. Join Charlie and his mother as she follows the steps to vote.

❶ Register to Vote

After moving to a new town, Charlie and his mother go to town hall so she can register to vote. She fills out a form and sends it to the town's election office.

TOWN HALL

VOTER REGISTRATION

② Learn About the Issues

Before voting, Charlie's mother wants to know more about who is running for office and what the important issues are. She and Charlie watch debates on television. She reads newspaper articles and talks to neighbors about the election.

When you elect me for mayor...

DAILY NEWS

RUNNING FOR MAYOR

③ Vote

On voting day, Charlie and his mother go to the right voting location. She marks her choices on her ballot and makes sure she didn't make a mistake. Then she turns in her vote.

Drop Ballot Here

Activities

1. **DRAW IT** Make a poster encouraging people to fulfill their **responsibility** by voting in the next election.

2. **WRITE ABOUT IT** Write an editorial explaining why it is important for students to learn the steps it takes to vote.

Skillbuilder

Point of View

▶ **VOCABULARY**

point of view

Citizens in some communities go to town meetings. There, each citizen can share his or her point of view. A **point of view** is the way a person thinks about an issue. Sharing your point of view is an important part of being a good citizen.

Learn the Skill

Follow the steps below to share your point of view.

Step 1: Read or listen carefully to other people's points of view about a subject. If possible, ask questions about anything you do not understand.

Step 2: Think about what other people have said. Is it similar to what you think? In what ways is it different?

Step 3: Using the information you gathered, write or tell about your point of view.

Town meeting tonight at 7 pm

Practice the Skill

Suppose there is an empty lot in your community. A group of community citizens agree that the space should be used for the good of the whole community. They have different points of view about how to use the space, though. Read the points of view below and then answer the questions.

"This lot would be a good place for sports. We could have a volleyball or basketball court."

"It would be a great place for a stage. We could build rows of benches and have plays and concerts."

"We could plant flowers and vegetables and watch them grow most of the year. We could also build bird feeders."

1. Summarize each opinion in your own words.

2. What is one question that you might ask about each opinion?

3. Which idea do you agree with the most? Explain why.

Apply the Skill

Write a paragraph to share your own point of view about how to use the lot. Make sure to give reasons why you have this point of view.

State Government

VOCABULARY

capitol

governor

READING SKILL

Main Idea and Details As you read, list the details that show the work done by each branch of state government.

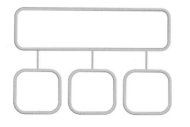

Build on What You Know There are 50 states in the United States. Each one has its own government. What state do you live in? Who leads your state government?

What Is State Government?

Citizens elect people to lead their state government. Many of these leaders work in the state capitol. The **capitol** is the building where leaders meet to make the laws.

Each state has its own constitution, which is the plan for the state's government. Though all state governments are different, they share things in common. Each has three branches, or parts. The branches have different responsibilities. All three branches of state government work together to run the state.

main idea

Members of the Pennsylvania government work in the state capitol in Harrisburg.

Three Branches of State Government

The branch of state government that makes laws is led by lawmakers. Lawmakers represent the people of their communities. They tell other state lawmakers what their communities need. They write new laws that they think will improve the state.

If lawmakers vote for a law, it goes to the governor. The **governor** is the head of the state's second branch. People in each state elect their governor. The governor's main job is to carry out the state laws. He or she signs laws to make them official. Governors may also veto, or stop, new laws, if they don't agree with them.

The courts make up the third branch of government. Judges in a court make sure laws follow the state and national constitutions. They also decide whether state laws have been broken. If someone breaks a law, the court decides the punishment, based on the law.

Review What do state lawmakers do?

State Government

Lawmakers

- Write new state laws
- Rewrite old laws
- Vote on laws

Governor

- Signs laws
- Carries out laws
- Selects state workers to head departments

Judges

- Make sure laws follow state and national constitutions
- Decide punishment when laws are broken

States Offer Services

Like local government, state government provides services to citizens. The government pays for these services with taxes. The governor plans how the state will spend the tax money. He or she may suggest using it for new state roads, schools, or hospitals.

Each state has departments that are in charge of different services. The governor chooses people to run the departments. One department hires state police to patrol highways and make them safe. Another department helps protect state land and water from pollution. There is even a department that decides what you should learn in school each year.

California State Parks Cactus flowers bloom in Anza Borrego Desert State Park. In Oakland (right), a park ranger teaches students about nature.

The States and the Nation

Each state is part of the nation. The government that leads the nation is called the national government. State governments cooperate with the national government. They work together on projects important to the whole country.

For example, the national and state governments have created highways that cross the United States. Workers from different states have planned, built, and fixed the highways. Workers from the national government have made sure the plans for highways are safe. These highways make it easier for people to travel around the country.

Review What are some of the services that state governments provide?

State and interstate highway signs

Lesson Review

1 VOCABULARY Choose the best word to complete the sentence.

capitol   governor

State lawmakers work in the state _____.

2 🕐 **READING SKILL** Use the **details** you listed to explain what the courts do.

3 MAIN IDEA: Citizenship List three responsibilities of a governor.

4 MAIN IDEA: Government What is one way that state governments and the national government work together?

5 CRITICAL THINKING: Analyze Why is it important for people in a community to have lawmakers to represent them?

 RESEARCH ACTIVITY Use library resources to find out about your governor and your community's state lawmakers. List some facts you learned.

State Capitals

What city is the capital of your state? Do you know why it's the capital? Some capitals were chosen because of their location. They might be along a river or main road. Today, some capitals are the largest city in the state.

Sacramento, California

When gold was found in 1848, people rushed to Sacramento. It became the state capital in 1854.

Columbus, Ohio

In 1812, Columbus was named after the famous explorer, Christopher Columbus. Columbus was chosen as Ohio's capital because it was in the center of the state.

NEW HAMPSHIRE
VERMONT
MAINE
★Augusta
Montpelier★
Concord
★
MASSACHUSETTS
Albany★
★Boston
NEW YORK
★Providence
Hartford
RHODE ISLAND
CONNECTICUT
PENNSYLVANIA
★Trenton
Harrisburg★
NEW JERSEY
★Dover
OHIO Washington D.C.
★DELAWARE
★Columbus
⊛★Annapolis
MARYLAND
ILLINOIS INDIANA
Charleston WEST
★Richmond
Springfield★
Indianapolis★
VIRGINIA
Jefferson
VIRGINIA
City★
★Frankfort
★Raleigh
MISSOURI
KENTUCKY
NORTH CAROLINA
★Nashville
Columbia
TENNESSEE
★
SOUTH
OKLAHOMA
CAROLINA
★
★Atlanta
Oklahoma
ARKANSAS
City
★
ALABAMA GEORGIA
Little
Rock
MISSISSIPPI
★Montgomery
Jackson
★
LOUISIANA
★Tallahassee
TEXAS
Baton Rouge
★Austin
FLORIDA

NORTH DAKOTA
★Bismarck
MINNESOTA
MICHIGAN
SOUTH DAKOTA
St. Paul★
WISCONSIN
★Pierre
Madison
★
Lansing
★
IOWA
NEBRASKA
★Des Moines
Lincoln★
Topeka★
KANSAS

Tallahassee, Florida

Tallahassee (tal uh HAS ee) was chosen as the capital because it was between two large cities. It means "old town" in the Creek language.

KEY
⊛ National capital
★ State capital

km 0   200   400
mi 0   200   400

Activities

1. **TELL ABOUT IT** Use an encyclopedia to find and share fun facts about your state capital.

2. **REMEMBER IT** Test your knowledge of states and their capitals. Make flash cards for each state and practice with them.

National Government

VOCABULARY

legislature
executive branch
judicial branch
monument

READING SKILL
Categorize As you read, put the duties of each branch of national government into categories.

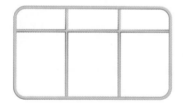

Build on What You Know What is the capital of our nation? National leaders meet and work in Washington, D.C.

The Three Branches

Our nation's government has three parts or branches. The United States Constitution describes the role of each branch. The main role is to protect citizens' rights.

The first branch is the **legislature,** or Congress of the United States. This branch makes the nation's laws. Congress is divided into two parts, the House of Representatives and the Senate. Citizens elect lawmakers to serve in the legislature.

The U.S. Capitol
Congress meets in the Capitol Building in Washington, D.C.

The White House
The President lives and works there.

The Executive and Judicial Branches

The second branch is the executive branch. The **executive branch** carries out the laws. The President heads this branch and approves or rejects laws made by Congress. If laws are approved, the President makes sure they are carried out. American citizens vote to decide who will be President.

The courts are the third, or judicial, branch of government. The **judicial branch** decides what the laws mean and whether they obey the Constitution. The Supreme Court heads this branch.

Citizens and others pay taxes to support the branches of U.S. government. Taxes pay for the armed services that protect the country. They also pay for departments that provide services, such as the National Park Service.

Review In what ways do citizens take part in national government?

The Supreme Court Its nine members form the highest court in the United States.

Symbols and Monuments

When you look at the back of a one dollar bill, you will find a symbol of the United States. It is a bald eagle. The eagle is a symbol of freedom. Freedom is an important value to Americans.

The American flag is another symbol of our country. The 50 stars on the flag stand for the 50 states in the United States. The 13 stripes stand for the first 13 colonies that became the United States.

The bald eagle was chosen as our national bird in 1789.

The Lincoln Memorial

Many national monuments are located in Washington, D.C. A **monument** is a building or statue that helps people remember a person or event. The Lincoln Memorial holds a large stone statue of **Abraham Lincoln**. As our 16th President, Lincoln worked for freedom and equality. He ended slavery in our country.

The Lincoln Memorial The statue of Lincoln is 19 feet tall.

Skill **Reading Visuals** From the statue, can you tell what the sculptor thought about Lincoln? How?

The Washington Monument

The Washington Monument was built to remember **George Washington**. Washington was our first President. The monument stands for his leadership and courage. American symbols and monuments remind us of the ideas and values we share, such as freedom and equality.

The Lincoln Memorial and the Washington Monument are two symbols of great leaders in our history. These symbols help us remember the values those leaders stood for and fought to uphold.

Review What is the purpose of our national symbols and monuments?

The Washington Monument
Completed in 1884, it is just over 550 feet tall.

Lesson Review

1 VOCABULARY Use **executive branch** and **judicial branch** in a sentence about national government.

2 READING SKILL Write a paragraph describing the duties you **categorized** as belonging to Congress.

3 MAIN IDEA: Government Which branch of government makes laws?

4 MAIN IDEA: Citizenship Why are national symbols and monuments important to people in the United States?

5 PEOPLE TO KNOW What did **Abraham Lincoln** work for when he was President?

6 CRITICAL THINKING: Compare What do Congress, the President, and the Supreme Court have in common?

ART ACTIVITY There are many symbols that represent the United States. Choose one, and draw a picture of it. Tell what it symbolizes and why it is important to you.

Primary Sources

Red, White, and Blue

What has 50 stars and 13 stripes? If you said the flag of the United States, you're right. It didn't always have this number of stars and stripes, though. The flag has changed as our nation has changed.

The stars and stripes tell a story about United States history. The stars represent the number of states in the nation. As the United States grew, more stars were added.

Thirteen-star Flag

In 1777, this became the official United States flag. The 13 stars and 13 stripes stand for the 13 colonies. This was the flag during George Washington's first term as President.

Fifteen Stars and Stripes

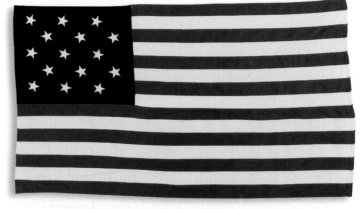

When Kentucky and Vermont joined the country, two more stars and two more stripes were added. This was the official flag from 1795 to 1818.

The 1818 Flag

In 1818, there were 20 states, but there wasn't enough room on the flag for 20 stripes. A new design returned 13 stripes to the flag. There were 20 stars for the 20 states.

Our Flag Today

Today's flag has 50 stars and 13 stripes. The last two stars added to the flag stand for Alaska and Hawaii. They became states in 1959.

Activities

1. **THINK ABOUT IT** Why do you think people added stars to the flag as the nation grew?

2. **MAKE IT** Draw or paint a flag that stands for your classroom. It might include symbols such as stars or circles.

 Technology Learn about other primary sources for this unit at Education Place. www.eduplace.com/kids/hmss05/

Skillbuilder

Use an Inset Map

If you were visiting Washington, D.C., how would you find your way around the city? There are many kinds of maps, and each kind tells you different things. An inset map gives you a close-up view of one part of a map.

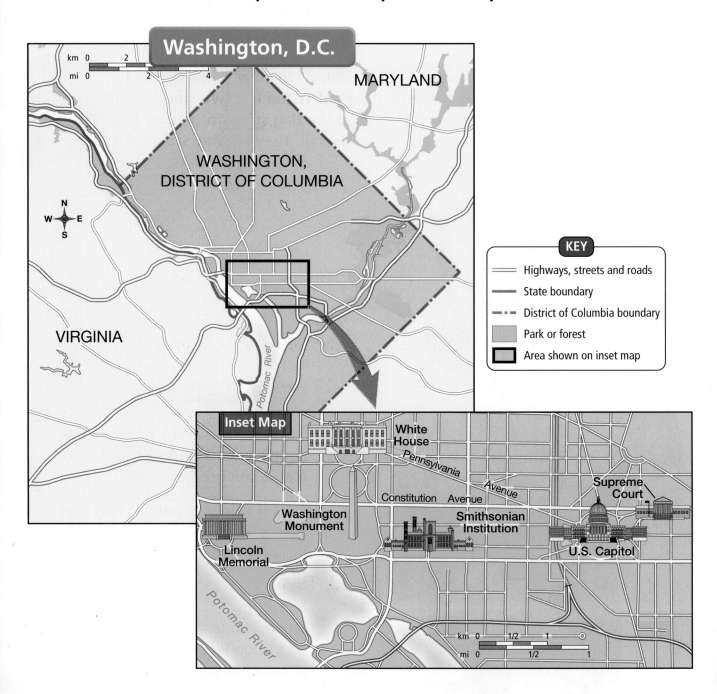

Washington, D.C.

km 0   2
mi 0   2   4

MARYLAND

WASHINGTON, DISTRICT OF COLUMBIA

N
W   E
S

VIRGINIA

Potomac River

KEY
Highways, streets and roads
State boundary
District of Columbia boundary
Park or forest
Area shown on inset map

Inset Map

White House

Pennsylvania

Avenue

Constitution   Avenue

Supreme Court

Washington Monument

Smithsonian Institution

Lincoln Memorial

U.S. Capitol

Potomac River

km 0   1/2   1
mi 0   1/2   1

Step 1: Look at the scales of both maps. What does one inch stand for on each map?

Step 2: Look at the top map. It shows all of Washington, D.C. You can find the states next to the city.

Step 3: Look at the bottom map. This is an inset map. It zooms in on one part of Washington, D.C. You can see more details, such as street names and buildings.

Practice the Skill

Use the information on the two maps of Washington, D.C., to answer the questions below.

1. Which map shows the location of the Lincoln Memorial?

2. Which state is directly west of Washington, D.C.?

3. What street would you take to get from the White House to the U.S. Capitol building?

Apply the Skill

Make a map of your neighborhood. Then make an inset map of your street with your home, street names, and other details.

READING SKILL

Problem and Solution
Keep track of problems
that nations have and
the ways in which they
solve those problems.

Problem   Solution

 **WORLD CONNECTION**

Nations Work Together

Build on What You Know Think of a
time when a friend or family member helped
you do a hard job. Just like friends and family,
countries can help each other.

Governments Team Up

You know that some American leaders
work in Washington, D.C. So do ambassadors
from other countries. An **ambassador** is a
person who represents his or her government
in another country. Ambassadors from India,
South Africa, and many other countries work
in our nation's capital. Ambassadors from the
United States work in the capital cities of these
and other countries.

President George W. Bush
stands with ambassadors
from around the world.

The United Nations Completed in 1953, U.N. headquarters are located in New York City.

Skill **Reading Visuals** What do you think the parts of the U.N. symbol (lower right) stand for?

Reasons to Work Together

Nations work together for many reasons. The United States works with Canada and Mexico to make trade easier in North America. Nations around the world work to keep the oceans safe for travel and trade.

main idea (★)

The United Nations

A group called the United Nations helps countries work together. The United Nations is a team of leaders from most of the world's nations. One of its main jobs is to help countries live in peace. When nations disagree, the United Nations tries to bring them together to solve their disputes. It encourages countries to make a treaty. A **treaty** is an agreement made between nations. Some treaties end wars between countries and lead to peace.

Review Why do countries send ambassadors to other countries?

Freedom in South Africa

Members of the United Nations work in countries across the world. They work to make sure all nations respect human rights. For instance, the United Nations played a part in helping people gain rights in South Africa.

South Africa is a country located at the southern tip of Africa. For many years, black and other non-white South Africans were denied their rights. They were not allowed to vote. They were not free to live or work where they wanted.

Many people in South Africa and across the world helped South Africans gain their rights. **Nelson Mandela** (man DEHL uh) spent much of his life working for equal rights for black South Africans. The United Nations supported Mandela and others who worked for equality. Finally, in 1994, all South Africans won their right to vote.

main (★) *idea*

Freedom Day Each year, South Africans celebrate the first democratic election held in South Africa. It took place on April 27, 1994.

South Africa and the United States

Leaders in South Africa and the United States have created programs to help their nations work together. Scientists from both countries share their research. They study the earth's environment. Doctors seek the best ways to keep people healthy. South African and American teachers have developed programs to help their students learn about life in other parts of the world.

Review What did South Africans do to gain equal rights?

Scientists work to help wildlife, such as penguins.

Lesson Review

1 **VOCABULARY** Match each word with its correct definition.

ambassador   **treaty**

A. An agreement between nations

B. A person who represents his or her government in another country

2 **READING SKILL** What is a way the United Nations tries to help **solve** problems?

3 **MAIN IDEA: Citizenship** Why do countries work together?

4 **MAIN IDEA: Citizenship** What rights did Nelson Mandela and others work to gain?

5 **CRITICAL THINKING: Making Decisions** What might be the pros and cons of a decision to make trade with Mexico and Canada easier?

WRITING ACTIVITY If you were a U.S. ambassador, what would you tell people about your country? Write a speech about it. Revise your speech once.

Biography

Nelson Mandela

Nelson Mandela spent more than 20 years of his life in jail. Why? He spoke out against harsh treatment towards black South Africans. The all-white government put Mandela in jail several times to silence him. Yet he would not stop fighting for his beliefs.

In 1962, Mandela was sent to prison. People all over the world were upset that Mandela was in prison. In the 1980s, many countries would not do business with South Africa. They hoped this would force the South African government to free Mandela and end inequality in South Africa.

Finally, the government released Mandela from prison in 1990. Then, in 1994, South Africans elected him to be their president. As president, Mandela worked to improve life for all South Africans.

"This is one of the most important moments in the life of our country. I stand here before you filled with deep pride and joy. . . . This is a time to heal the old wounds and build a new South Africa."

Activities

1. **TALK ABOUT IT** In what ways did Nelson Mandela show **fairness** throughout his life?

2. **WRITE ABOUT IT** Suppose it is 1989. Write a letter to the South African government, asking for Mandela to be freed.

Technology Visit Education Place for more biographies. www.eduplace.com/kids/hmss05/

253

Visual Summary

1–4. Write a description of each item shown below.

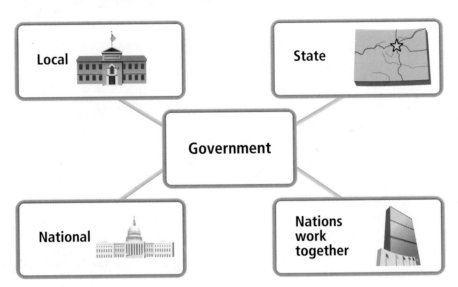

Local

State

Government

National

Nations work together

Facts and Main Ideas

✓ **TEST PREP** Answer each question below.

5. **Citizenship** How do citizens choose government leaders?

6. **Economics** What is one way that local, state, and national governments raise money?

7. **Government** What does the judicial branch do?

8. **History** In what country did Nelson Mandela help people gain equal rights?

Vocabulary

✓ **TEST PREP** Choose the correct word from the list below to complete each sentence.

tax, p. 227
capitol, p. 234
monument, p. 242

9. The Lincoln Memorial is an important _____.

10. Leaders of state government meet inside the _____ to make laws.

11. A _____ is a fee that pays for government services.

✔ **TEST PREP** **Point of View** Read the paragraph below. Then apply what you have learned about point of view to answer each question.

> Students in your school have to wear school uniforms. People have different points of view about the rule.
>
> "I should be able to wear what I want. The school shouldn't decide that for me."
>
> "I think it's a good rule. I won't have to worry about what to wear to school."

12. Which statement summarizes one of the points of view?

   A. Our school knows what is best.

   B. I want to choose what to wear.

   C. Uniforms are okay as long as they are blue.

   D. I don't care either way.

13. What is one step to take to find out someone's point of view?

   A. Listen to other points of view.

   B. Disagree with other points of view.

   C. Tell your point of view.

   D. Do not tell your point of view.

✔ **TEST PREP** Write a short paragraph to answer each question below.

14. **Compare and Contrast** What are the differences between a mayor, a governor, and the President?

15. **Summarize** What is the role of each branch of the national government?

16. **Analyze** In what ways does a democracy benefit from having three branches of government?

Activities

Art Activity You have read what citizens do for government. You have also read what government does for citizens. Draw a diagram or other organizer that shows this.

Writing Activity Use library or Internet resources to find out about a service your city or town provides. Then write a short report about this service and how it helps the community.

Technology
Writing Process Tips
Get help with your report at
www.eduplace.com/kids/hmss05/

Government Where You Live

Think about who governs your community. Who are the local leaders? What goods and services does your community provide? What are some community laws? Knowing how government works is the responsibility of every citizen.

Local Government Highlights

- Mayor, town council, or city manager

- Elections or town meetings

- Services, such as libraries and trash collection

- Taxes to pay for services

TOWN HALL

Learn About Candidates for Mayor

National symbol

Find Out!

Many local officials work in the town hall.

Explore your local government.

☑ **Start with the phone book.**
Look at the pages that list your city or town government. What departments and services do you see?

☑ **Visit local government buildings.**
With an adult you know, find out where government activities take place.

☑ **Look online.**
Find out whether your city or town has a website. If it does, read about what your community does for its citizens.

☑ **Read a local newspaper.**
Newspapers usually have sections that give local news.

Use your community handbook to keep track of information you find.

Review and Test Prep

Vocabulary and Main Ideas

✔ **TEST PREP** Write a sentence to answer each question.

1. Name three ways citizens can work for the **common good.**

2. What are some **rights** that adults have?

3. What responsibilities does a city **council** have?

4. What does a **governor** do?

5. What is one of the duties of the **legislature?**

6. Why might one country make a **treaty** with another country?

Critical Thinking

✔ **TEST PREP** Write a short answer for each question. Use details to support your answer.

7. **Cause and Effect** What is one effect of paying taxes?

8. **Summarize** Why do nations work together?

Apply Skills

✔ **TEST PREP** Use the maps of Washington, D.C., to answer each question.

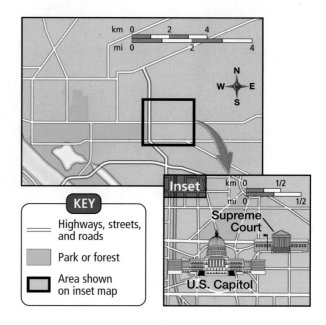

KEY
— Highways, streets, and roads
▨ Park or forest
▢ Area shown on inset map

9. Which map shows the location of the United States Capitol, the top map or the inset map?

10. Which map shows the largest area of Washington, D.C.?

   A. the top map

   B. the inset map

   C. neither map

   D. both maps

Unit Activity

The Big Idea

Create an Election Button

- Think about ways citizens help leaders get elected.

- Make a list of issues you would support in a person running for office.

- Use that list to create an election button and a poster that states what your person stands for.

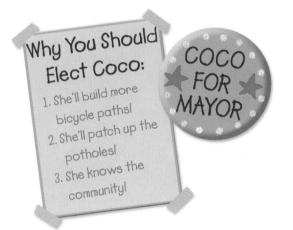

Why You Should Elect Coco:
1. She'll build more bicycle paths!
2. She'll patch up the potholes!
3. She knows the community!

COCO FOR MAYOR

At the Library

You may find this book at your school or public library.

A Castle on Viola Street
by DyAnne DiSalvo

Andy and his family help a community organization fix an abandoned home.

CURRENT EVENTS
WEEKLY (WR) READER

Connect to the Community

Make a poster of volunteers.

- Find information about volunteers who work for their communities.

- Choose four volunteers for your poster. Draw a picture of each.

- Write a short summary for each volunteer and put the summaries under the drawings.

Technology
Weekly Reader online offers social studies articles. Go to:
www.eduplace.com/kids/hmss/

Read About It

Look in your classroom for these Social Studies Independent Books.

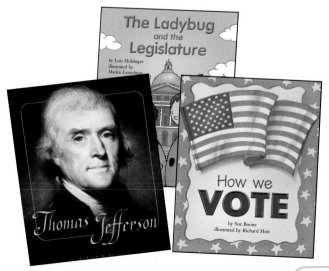

The Ladybug and the Legislature
by Lois Holsinger
illustrated by Martin Lemelman

Thomas Jefferson

How we VOTE
by Sue Boone
illustrated by Richard Hoit

UNIT 5

Making Economic Choices

The Big Idea

Why do you think people work?

"To love what you do and feel that it matters — how could anything be more fun?"

—Katharine Graham,
newspaper publisher, 1974

Almanac

Products of the United States

ARCTIC OCEAN

km 0   300
mi 0   300

ALASKA

PACIFIC OCEAN

WASHINGTON

OREGON

IDAHO

MONTANA

NORTH DAKOTA

MINNESOTA

SOUTH DAKOTA

WYOMING

NEBRASKA

IOWA

CALIFORNIA

NEVADA

UTAH

COLORADO

KANSAS

MISSOURI

NEW MEXICO

ARIZONA

OKLAHOMA

TEXAS

PACIFIC OCEAN

km 0 50 100
mi 0   50 100

HAWAII

PACIFIC OCEAN

N
NW   NE
W   E
SW   SE
S

MEXICO

Unit Preview

Banks
Understanding money
Chapter 9, page 269

Economic Choices
People choose what they buy
Chapter 9, page 274

Bandereen

Free Enterprise
Freedom to make, buy, and sell
Chapter 10, page 288

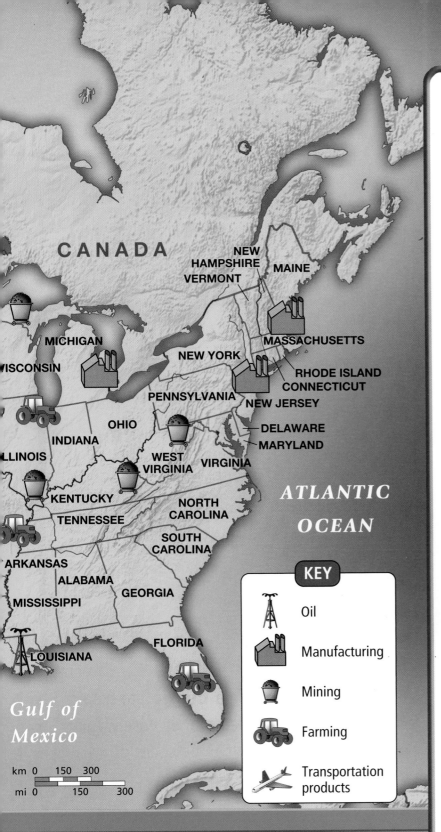

CANADA

MICHIGAN
WISCONSIN
NEW HAMPSHIRE
VERMONT
MAINE
NEW YORK
MASSACHUSETTS
RHODE ISLAND
CONNECTICUT
PENNSYLVANIA
NEW JERSEY
OHIO
INDIANA
DELAWARE
MARYLAND
ILLINOIS
WEST VIRGINIA
VIRGINIA
KENTUCKY
NORTH CAROLINA
TENNESSEE
ARKANSAS
SOUTH CAROLINA
ALABAMA
GEORGIA
MISSISSIPPI
FLORIDA
LOUISIANA

ATLANTIC OCEAN

Gulf of Mexico

km 0   150   300
mi 0   150   300

KEY

Oil

Manufacturing

Mining

Farming

Transportation products

Resources
Three kinds are needed to make products
Chapter 10, page 292

Connect to
The Nation

U.S. Airlines' Airplanes

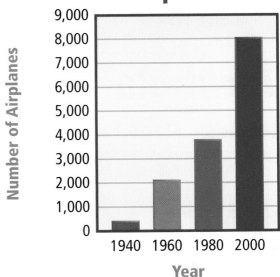

Number of Airplanes

9,000
8,000
7,000
6,000
5,000
4,000
3,000
2,000
1,000
0

1940 1960 1980 2000

Year

In which year were the most airplanes used?

How do you think the increase in airplanes has affected the U.S. economy?

CURRENT EVENTS
WEEKLY WR READER

Current events on the web!

Read social studies articles at:
www.eduplace.com/kids/hmss/

Chapter 9

Economics Every Day

Vocabulary Preview

Technology

e • **glossary**
e • **word games**
www.eduplace.com/kids/hmss05/

income

People who work earn an **income.** The amount of money people earn depends on their job.
page 268

budget

People may use a **budget** to help them spend their money wisely. This plan lists what can be spent or saved. **page 268**

Reading Strategy

Question Ask questions as you read the lessons in this chapter.

Quick Tip Ask yourself about the information. Do you need to reread for the answers?

opportunity cost

Sometimes you may have to give up one thing to buy another. What you give up is the **opportunity cost.**
page 275

competition

One store might charge lower prices than another store for the same items. This **competition** can attract buyers.
page 275

Using Money

VOCABULARY

income
budget
interest

READING SKILL
**Compare and
Contrast** As you read,
compare and contrast
money and barter.

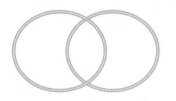

Build on What You Know What would
you do if you had fifty dollars? Thinking
about your choices can help you use your
money wisely.

What Is Money?

What do shells, cows, and whale teeth
have in common? All have been used as
money. Money can be anything that is widely
accepted in exchange for goods and services.
It lets people know easily how much things
are worth. In the United States, people use
dollars and cents as money. People who make
goods and provide services accept U.S. dollars
as payment.

Skill **Reading Charts** Compare the peso and the
rand. What differences do you see?

Money in Three Countries

Japan	yen	
Mexico	peso	
South Africa	rand	

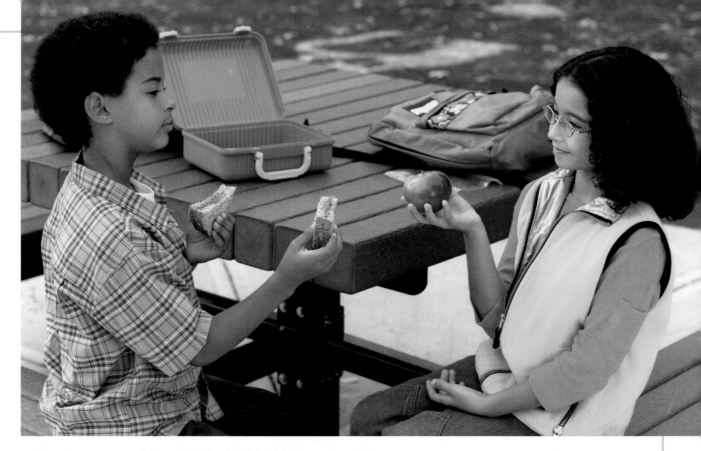

What's for Lunch? These students are bartering, or trading, food.

Money or Barter?

Most people around the world use money to pay for goods and services. Still, many people barter. Barter is the direct trading of goods and services. It allows people to get what they want when they do not have money to spend. When you trade carrot sticks for cookies, you are bartering.

Using money is often easier than bartering. Money tends to be small in size. It is easy to carry. Things used for barter might be any size. People agree on what money is worth. When bartering, people must decide the worth of the goods or services being traded. Barter works only when each person has something the other wants. Money can be used whenever someone is ready to buy or sell.

(★) *main idea*

Review In what ways is money useful?

Earning and Spending

To earn money, people work. They earn different incomes for different jobs. **Income** is the money people earn for work. Workers with special skills usually have higher incomes than others. People who go to college usually earn more than those who do not. Earning money is just one reason to go to college. Some people go to college to learn to do work that they enjoy.

Being Smart About Money

People use the income they earn to pay for goods and services. Families spend money on things they need and want. Some families make budgets. A **budget** is a plan for using money. It shows a person's or family's income. It also shows how much of that income can be spent or saved. People make budgets to decide the best way to use their money.

main idea

Money Planning A budget can help you see how much money you have to spend. **Skill** **Reading Visuals** How much money did this boy save?

My Budget This Week		
What I will earn:	Allowance	$1.00
	Gardening	$3.00
	Total:	$4.00
What I will spend:	Bottle of water	$0.75
	Present for Sam	$3.00
	Total:	$3.75
What I will save:		$0.25

Saving Money

Many people save the money they don't spend right away. They might save for things such as cars, homes, and school. They might collect coins for fun. Saving money is one way to prepare for the future.

To save money, people may put it in a bank. Banks help you save or borrow money. When you save money in a bank, your money earns interest. **Interest** is the money the bank pays you for keeping your money there. The longer you save money at a bank, the more interest your money can earn.

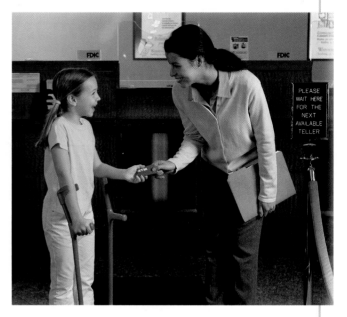

Banks Children might place money in a bank to save for college (above). The United States Mint issues special coins for collecting (below).

Review Why do people work?

Lesson Review

❶ **VOCABULARY** Write a sentence that explains **budget** and **income**.

❷ 📖 **READING SKILL** In what ways are barter and money **alike** and **different**?

❸ **MAIN IDEA: Economics** Why do more people use money than use barter?

❹ **MAIN IDEA: Economics** Name two ways people can earn money.

❺ **CRITICAL THINKING: Cause and Effect** When bartering, what happens if no one wants the item you want to trade?

MATH ACTIVITY Make a sample budget for one week. Plan how you would use ten dollars. Include the amounts that you would spend and save.

MAX MALONE
Makes a Million

by Charlotte Herman

Max Malone wants to earn money. He and his friend Gordy try several ways. Max's sister, Rosalie, laughs at them. Nothing they do seems to make Max rich. To make things worse, Max's friend Austin found a great way to earn a good **income.**

"Pure profit," said Max. "We get the shells for free, and then we sell them."

They were walking their bikes along the shore. And they were barefoot. Gentle waves slapped at their feet and tickled their toes.

"I just wish we would find them already," said Gordy. "All we ever see are pebbles."

"Ouch!" said Max, rubbing his foot. "And some of them are sharp too." Max had been to the beach lots of times. And thinking about it now, he didn't remember ever seeing any seashells. But maybe it was because he hadn't been looking for any.

They walked along the beach, getting splashed by kids who were jumping into the water. They walked around little kids who were digging in the sand. Probably trying to reach China, Max thought. And all that time, Max and Gordy kept their eyes open for seashells. Conchs, like Austin sold. Any kind.

But there were no conchs. There was nothing but pebbles. And tiny pieces of shells that looked like eggshells. Wet and sandy, and with their bike bags empty, Max and Gordy pedaled home.

Rosalie was lying on the grass in front of the house. She was reading *Gone With the Wind*. Max had bought it for her at one of Mrs. Filbert's garage sales.

"You look like drowned rats," she told Max and Gordy when she glanced up from her book.

"We just came from the beach," Max explained. "We were looking for seashells like Austin had. But we couldn't find any."

Rosalie began rolling in the grass and laughing hysterically. "You were looking for conchs in Lake Michigan? I can't believe it." She rolled around some more, and then she sat up. "You can't find those kinds of shells at the lake. You've got to go to the ocean." She started laughing all over again.

That Rosalie. She was always acting like such a know-it-all. When he made his million, he would buy her a house of her own. Then he wouldn't have to live with her.

"Thanks for telling me," said Max. "I'll just go see if I can find an ocean somewhere."

Max and Gordy did not go looking for an ocean. Gordy went home. And later, Max went looking for Austin. He didn't have to look far. He found him sitting on the curb in front of his house, counting money. Real money. Not just nickels, dimes, and quarters. But dollar bills.

"Hey, Austin," said Max. "Where did you get all that money?"

"From the bank," said Austin. "I changed all my coins for dollar bills. The coins were getting too heavy."

"You earned all that money yourself?"

"Sure. Some from the lemonade. And some from the seashells."

"That was a nice shell you sold my mom," Max said. "Did you get it from the ocean?"

"No," said Austin. "From the pet store. That was my source. And I bought in quantity. It's cheaper that way. Thirty shells to a package. I paid two dollars, and I sold each shell for a quarter."

Austin divided his money into two piles. "I'm saving some and spending some," he said, running into his house and back out again. "See you later, Max. I'm going to the pet store."

"For more shells?" Max asked.

"No," said Austin. "I don't need any more. I've already sold to most of the people in the neighborhood. And I'm not allowed to go to strange houses. Now I'm going to buy something I've always wanted. A red-spotted newt."

Max stood at the curb and watched Austin run down the street. It wasn't fair. First Anthony Baker, and now Austin Healy. Everyone, it seemed, was making money. Everyone except Max Malone.

Activities

1. **TALK ABOUT IT** In what ways would you describe Austin?

2. **WRITE ABOUT IT** Think of another job Max could do to earn money. Write a short conversation between Max and Gordy as they talk about whether it would work.

Making Choices

VOCABULARY

opportunity cost
competition
scarcity

READING SKILL

Sequence List the order of steps Marisa follows to make decisions.

1	
2	
3	
4	

Build on What You Know "Should I buy a yo-yo now or save for a new bike?" If you have ever had thoughts like these, you already know something about making economic choices.

Marisa Makes a Choice

Meet Marisa. She recently made a choice about what to buy. One thing she thought about was price. Marisa's favorite music group had made a CD. The price of the CD was ten dollars. Marisa saved twelve dollars. She could buy the CD. Then she remembered that she was saving to buy a maroon jacket. She had to make a choice. People make choices when they decide what to buy.

main idea

Marisa thinks about her choices.

Opportunity Cost

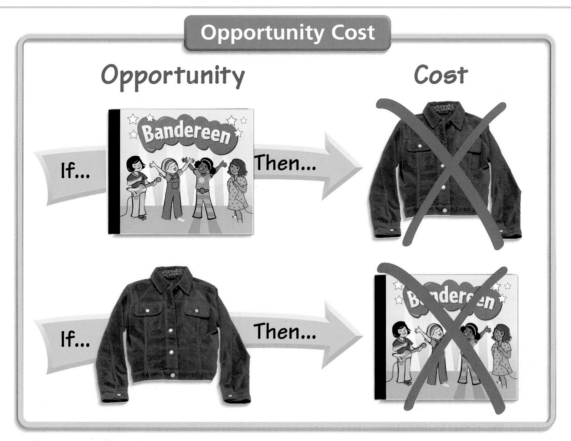

Opportunity   **Cost**

If...   Then...

If...   Then...

Skill   **Reading Diagrams**   What will happen if Marisa buys the CD?

Opportunity Cost

After thinking about it, Marisa chose to keep saving for the maroon jacket. By choosing the jacket, she gave up the CD. The CD was the opportunity cost of the jacket. **Opportunity cost** is the thing that people must give up in order to do what they most want. Marisa's first choice was the jacket. The CD was her second choice.

Competition Between Sellers

When Marisa had enough money, she found two stores that sold maroon jackets. The two stores were in competition with each other. **Competition** is the effort a seller makes to win buyers. When stores compete, they may lower their prices so that more people will shop there. Marisa chose the store with the lowest prices.

Review What is the opportunity cost of the jacket Marisa wants?

Scarcity Limits Choice

Marisa chose to go to the store with low prices, but, once she arrived, she saw only one maroon jacket. The clerk told her that there was a scarcity of maroon jackets. A **scarcity** is a lack of goods or services. Scarcity takes place when people who make goods or provide services cannot provide enough for everyone who wants them.

Scarcity causes people to make tough choices. People must choose because resources are limited. We cannot have everything we want.

Marisa hoped the maroon jacket would fit. When she tried it on, it was too large. A tan jacket fit perfectly. Now what would she do? She could buy the large maroon jacket. She could go to the store with higher prices to see whether it had maroon jackets. Or she could buy the tan jacket that fit.

Scarcity Because there is a scarcity of maroon jackets in her size, Marisa thinks about other choices.

Marisa Decides

Finally, Marisa made her choice. She decided to buy the tan jacket that fit. This was her best choice. She did not want a jacket that was too large or that cost too much. After all, she wanted to start saving for her favorite group's CD!

Marisa made choices before deciding what goods or services to buy. Like many people, she thought about price, opportunity cost, and scarcity before making her choice.

Review What choices did Marisa make?

Marisa decides to buy a tan jacket that fits.

Lesson Review

1 **VOCABULARY** Use **opportunity cost** in a sentence about making choices.

2 👆 **READING SKILL** Complete your **sequence** chart. What was the third decision that Marisa made?

3 **MAIN IDEA: Economics** Why might a store lower its prices?

4 **MAIN IDEA: Economics** Why does scarcity cause some buyers to make tough choices?

5 **CRITICAL THINKING: Summarize** Why did Marisa buy a tan jacket instead of a maroon one?

✏️ **WRITING ACTIVITY** Would you choose to buy a new CD, or save for something more expensive, such as a bike? List the pros and cons of your choice.

Economics

Tricks of the Trade

"Buy the new Zippy Tippy Twister!" says the announcer. "Everyone else is. Why not you? Be cool!"

Have you ever heard advertisements like that? You might see them on television or in magazines and newspapers.

Companies use ads to persuade you to buy goods and services. Ads can give useful information to buyers. Sometimes, however, they use special tricks to play on your feelings. Here are a few.

THIS JUICE IS AWESOME!

EVERYBODY HAS ONE!

Superstar Ads
A movie star or sports hero says that this juice is great. Will you be like them if you buy it?

Bandwagon Ads
A bandwagon ad tells you that everyone else has something. Buy the scooter or feel left out!

THEY'RE GOOD FOR YOU!

Friendly Face Ads
Here is someone friendly. Should you trust him about this cereal?

Before and After Ads
Before you buy the flea collar for your dog, things are bad. After you buy it—wow! Things are great!

Activities

1. **TALK ABOUT IT** Pick one of the ads. What makes it work?

2. **WRITE ABOUT IT** Collect four ads from newspapers or magazines. Explain how each ad works.

279

Skillbuilder

Conduct an Interview

Marisa collected information before making an economic choice. One way to get information is to conduct an interview. An interview is a meeting where one person asks another for facts or ideas.

▶ **VOCABULARY**

interview

Learn the Skill

Step 1: Decide what you want to learn from the interview. You might want to ask an adult how he or she saved enough money to buy something special. You may want to learn about jobs in your community.

Step 2: Choose a person to interview. You might ask an adult at home, at school, or in your community. Let the person know what you want to learn. Set up a time for your meeting.

Step 3: Prepare a list of questions before the interview. Think of questions that begin with *who, what, where, when, why,* and *how*.

Step 4: Interview the person. Listen carefully and write down his or her answers. Say "thank you" when you're done.

Practice the Skill

1 What topic do you want to learn more about?

2 Who should you interview to get that information?

3 Why is it a good idea to set up the meeting ahead of time?

Apply the Skill

Pick a topic. Set up an interview with someone who knows about your topic. Make a list of at least four questions.

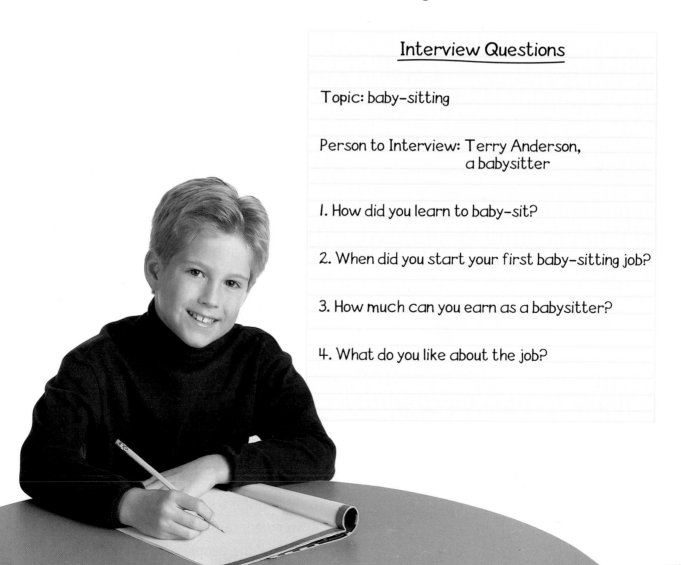

Interview Questions

Topic: baby-sitting

Person to Interview: Terry Anderson,
a babysitter

1. How did you learn to baby-sit?

2. When did you start your first baby-sitting job?

3. How much can you earn as a babysitter?

4. What do you like about the job?

Visual Summary

1–3. ✏️ Write a description of each item named below.

Money

_____

_____

_____

_____

_____

Budget

_____

_____

_____

_____

_____

Bank

_____

_____

_____

_____

_____

Facts and Main Ideas

✓ **TEST PREP** Answer each question below.

4. **Economics** Why might someone barter?

5. **Economics** What is one reason people earn money?

6. **Economics** In what way might competition affect the price of something?

7. **Economics** Why do people have to make choices about the things they want most?

Vocabulary

✓ **TEST PREP** Choose the correct word from the list below to complete each sentence.

budget, p. 268
opportunity cost, p. 275
scarcity, p. 276

8. If you have to choose between buying a tuba and a flute, the _____ of the flute is the tuba.

9. A _____ can help people decide how much money they can save.

10. When there is a _____ of plums, growers cannot provide enough plums for all the people who want them.

Apply Skills

Conduct an Interview
Use the example below and what you have learned about conducting interviews to answer each question.

> You have earned $10.00 walking your neighbor's dogs. Now you want to find out the best way to save that money. You decide to conduct an interview for information on ways to save.

11. Who would be the best person to interview about how to save money?

    A. a salesperson
    B. a police officer
    C. a banker
    D. a reporter

12. Which step would you do LAST?

    A. Write down the answers.
    B. Set up a time to meet.
    C. Ask your questions.
    D. Prepare a list of questions.

Critical Thinking

Write a short paragraph to answer each question below. Use details to support your response.

13. **Draw Conclusions** Why would it be better to save money in a bank than in a wallet?

14. **Cause and Effect** What could happen if people make a budget and don't follow it?

15. **Compare and Contrast** In what ways are needs and wants alike and different? Give two examples of each.

Activities

Math Activity Look in a newspaper or use Internet resources to find out how many Mexican pesos are equal to one United States dollar today.

Writing Activity Write a short story about two children who barter together to get what each wants.

Technology
Writing Process Tips
Get help with your story at
www.eduplace.com/kids/hmss05/

Chapter 10

Communities and Trade

Vocabulary Preview

Technology

e • **glossary**
e • **word games**
www.eduplace.com/kids/hmss05/

producer

Some people are **producers.** They make things or provide services that other people buy or use.
page 286

consumer

People who buy goods and services are called **consumers.** The words "consumer" and "buyer" have the same meaning. **page 287**

Reading Strategy

Predict and Infer What will the lesson be about? Use this strategy as you read.

Quick Tip Look at the pictures and titles to make a prediction.

human resources

People's knowledge, skills, and hard work are **human resources.**
page 293

industry

When people and companies sell similar goods or services, they are part of the same **industry.**
page 303

Who Are Producers?

 READING SKILL

Cause and Effect As you read, list the effects producers can have on consumers.

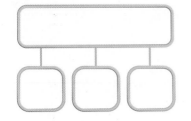

Build on What You Know Think of one thing you would like to buy. Do you know who makes it? Do you know its price? Buying, selling, and deciding on prices are important ideas in economics.

Producers Work

Remember that goods are things that can be bought. A **producer** makes and sells goods. Producers might work together in a large business to make cars or build bridges. Or one single producer can make toys. A farmer who grows crops is a producer, too.

Producers also provide services. A banker and a firefighter are producers. Instead of making things, these producers lend money or put out fires. Producers work to provide goods or services for others to buy or use.

main idea

Making Goods This producer is making snowboards.

Goods

Producers at this outdoor market sell their goods to consumers.

Skill **Reading Visuals**
What is this consumer doing?

Consumer

Producer

Consumers Buy Things

Producers sell their goods and services to consumers. A **consumer** is someone who buys the goods or services sold by a producer. Consumers may buy the services of a barber or vegetables grown by a farmer.

Producers also act as consumers. Toy producers may choose to buy wood or plastic to make toys. They hire workers to make the toys they sell.

Producers Specialize

Many producers specialize. That means that they do one special kind of work. Producers specialize to better meet consumers' wants. For example, an eye doctor learns special skills to help people see better. Some teachers specialize, too. They may study in order to teach a special subject, such as social studies.

Review Why do producers specialize?

287

Free Enterprise

In the United States, producers make or do almost anything they can think of. If the law allows it, producers may run any business they want. Consumers, too, may purchase what they want and can afford.

The right to make such choices is called free enterprise. It means that people can own businesses if they choose to do so. They can create new goods and services to earn money.

What Is Supply?

Producers are free to sell what they want, and consumers are free to buy what they want. What do consumers want? How much will they pay? Producers must think about these things. Then they make a supply. A **supply** is the amount producers will make for a certain price. At high prices, producers make more things. They may also provide more services. At lower prices, producers make less.

main (★) idea

Free Enterprise In Pasadena, California, producers choose to sell many types of goods and services to consumers.

What Is Demand?

Consumers create demand for the goods and services they want. **Demand** is the amount consumers are willing to buy for a certain price. At high prices, consumers buy less. At lower prices, consumers buy more.

Review At higher prices, will consumers want to buy more or less of a good or service?

This girl thought about demand before deciding how many bottles of water to sell.

Lesson Review

1 VOCABULARY Choose the correct word to complete the sentence.

   supply   demand

The _____ for a product is how much consumers are willing to buy.

2 READING SKILL What is the **effect** on consumers when the price of a product they want goes up?

3 MAIN IDEA: Economics What do producers do?

4 MAIN IDEA: Economics When prices are low, will producers usually make more or less of a product? Explain your answer.

5 CRITICAL THINKING: Analyze If you were a producer, what would make you decide to create a large supply of your product?

WRITING ACTIVITY Think about the different producers you have read about. Write a song about one of them, telling what that person does.

The Price of Juice

Sometimes prices go up. Sometimes they go down. Why do prices change? Prices change when **consumers** want to buy more or less of something. Prices also change when **producers** decide to make more or less of something.

Supply

Demand

One day, Jay and Lia decided to sell juice. Jay chose to sell his for a dollar. Lia chose to sell her juice for ten cents. Jay made lots of juice. Lia didn't make nearly as much.

At the price of one dollar, not many consumers were willing to buy juice. Many more consumers wanted ten-cent juice. Lia didn't make enough for everyone who wanted it.

Supply and Demand, Balanced

Juice 50¢

Juice 50¢

Jay wasn't selling juice and he wasn't earning money. Lia sold so much juice that she ran out! But her price was so low that she didn't earn much money. Jay and Lia asked themselves: How much juice would the most consumers buy for the highest price?

Wrap It Up!

To sell juice at a better price, Jay and Lia balanced **supply** and **demand**. They found the highest price at which a larger number of consumers would buy their juice.

Activities

1. **ACT IT OUT** Act out the three scenes about supply and demand.

2. **WRITE ABOUT IT** Write about a product that you would like to sell. At what price would you sell it? Why?

291

Making Goods

VOCABULARY

human resources
capital resources
factory
assembly line

READING SKILL

Sequence As you read, list in order each numbered step needed to make a pair of jeans.

1	
2	
3	
4	

Build on What You Know Do you have a pair of blue jeans? Millions of people around the world love to wear them. It may take many producers, working together, to make blue jeans.

Using Resources

To make products such as blue jeans, people use three kinds of resources. The first, natural resources, are found in nature. Soil, sun, and water are natural resources. Farmers use these to grow cotton, which is used to make blue jeans. Cotton is grown in the southern and western United States, and in other countries.

Other Resources

The second kind of resource producers use is human resources. **Human resources** are the skills, knowledge, and hard work that people bring to their jobs. The third resource people use to make products is called capital resources. **Capital resources** are things made by people that help workers make goods or provide services. Machines, roads, tools, and buildings are all examples of capital resources. The picture below shows how people use the three kinds of resources to pick cotton.

Review What three resources are needed to make blue jeans?

Three Kinds of Resources

Human Resources
The work and skills of people, such as this driver, are human resources.

Natural Resources
These include the water and soil used to grow cotton plants.

Capital Resources
A spindle picker is a machine used to pick cotton.

From Cotton to Blue Jeans

After workers harvest the cotton, they send it to a factory. A **factory** is a building where workers make goods. Workers follow steps to make products such as blue jeans.

step ❶ Cleaning and Spinning

At the factory, workers use machines to clean the cotton. Then, other workers use machines to spin the cotton into yarn.

step ❷ Dyeing and Weaving

Next, workers dye the yarn blue. They use large machines called looms to weave the yarn into cloth. Businesses that make blue jeans buy the dyed cloth. They send the cloth to another factory.

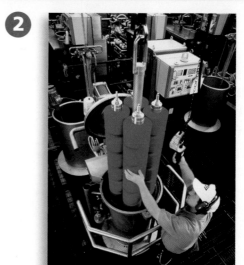

step ❸ Cutting and Sewing

Then, machines cut the cloth into pieces. Next, people on an assembly line sew the pieces together. An **assembly line** is a team of specialized workers. Together, they make a product by following steps. An assembly line can produce goods quickly and at low cost. Each worker completes just one step before passing the product to the next person.

④ Final Steps

After the assembly line, workers pack the jeans and load them onto a plane. The plane delivers the jeans to cities around the world. Then, trucks take them to stores. Finally, the jeans are ready for you to buy.

Review Why do some producers use assembly lines to make goods?

Lesson Review

① **VOCABULARY** Write a sentence using **factory** and **assembly line.** Tell where goods such as jeans are made.

② **READING SKILL** Look at your list. What would happen if you tried to do steps 3 and 4 out of order?

③ **MAIN IDEA: Economics** Name two examples of a capital resource.

④ **MAIN IDEA: Economics** Why do workers follow steps to make products?

⑤ **CRITICAL THINKING: Compare and Contrast** Explain why assembly-line workers can produce goods faster than one person working alone.

HANDS ON **ART ACTIVITY** Identify a product that you would like to produce. Create an illustrated poster showing how the product would be made.

Making Good!

Have you ever thought about how to make a product better? If so, you have something in common with two famous entrepreneurs. Henry Ford and Madame C.J. Walker each started with an idea. They ended up with big businesses and lots of money.

Henry Ford

(1863–1947)

When Henry Ford started the Ford Motor Company, he had a big idea. Ford's idea was to make cars that more people could buy. Few people could afford to buy the first cars that were invented.

Ford used **assembly lines** to make cheaper cars. Without assembly lines, workers needed twelve-and-a-half hours to make a car. Ford's assembly lines could produce a car in an hour and a half. People on assembly lines made his most popular car, the model T.

With workers building more cars each day, the cost of making them went down. Ford lowered the price of his cars.

Madame C.J. Walker

(1867–1919)

Madame C.J. Walker was the first African American woman in the United States to earn a million dollars. How did she do it?

Walker wanted better hair care products. She thought other African American women wanted them, too. So she invented new products, such as "Wonderful Hair Grower" and "Vegetable Shampoo." Then she started her own business to sell them across the country. In 1908, she set up a training center in Pittsburgh, Pennsylvania, to show people how to sell her products. Walker's company grew, and her fame and fortune grew, too.

BIOGRAPHIES

Activities

1. **TALK ABOUT IT** In what ways did Henry Ford and Madame C.J. Walker show **courage** by starting new businesses?

2. **GRAPH IT** Make a line graph that shows the change in cost for cars from 1900 to 1927.

Technology Read more biographies at Education Place. www.eduplace.com/kids/hmss05/

Skillbuilder

Use a Flow Chart

In Lesson 2, you learned how blue jeans are made. You could show that process in a flow chart. A **flow chart** is a diagram that shows how something is done. A flow chart uses words, pictures, and arrows to show each step in the correct order.

Learn the Skill

Step 1: Read the title of the flow chart to find out the subject.

Step 2: Look for numbers and arrows that show the order of the steps.

Step 3: Read the labels and look at the pictures to understand each step.

How a Car Is Made

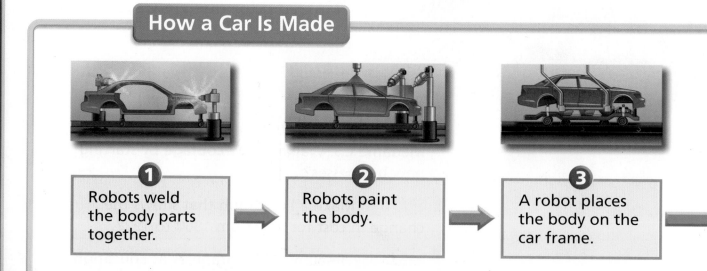

1 Robots weld the body parts together.

2 Robots paint the body.

3 A robot places the body on the car frame.

Practice the Skill

Use the flow chart below to answer these questions.

1 What do the title, labels, and pictures tell you about the subject of the flow chart?

2 How many steps are shown on the flow chart?

3 What step comes after the body of the car is painted?

4 Why is it important to follow the steps in order?

Apply the Skill

Think of a game, hobby, or task, such as bathing a pet or making a sandwich. Create a simple flow chart to show how the activity is done. Draw pictures and write labels and a title. Number the steps and use arrows.

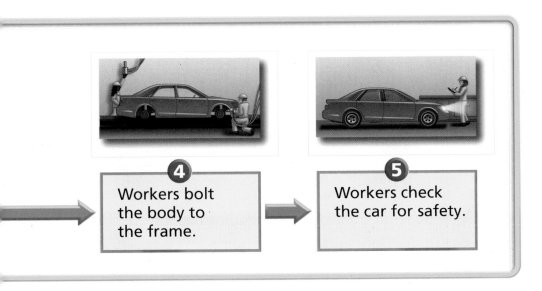

4 Workers bolt the body to the frame.

5 Workers check the car for safety.

Trade Around the World

VOCABULARY

market
import
export
industry

READING SKILL

Problem and Solution As you read, see how countries solve the problem of getting goods they cannot produce themselves.

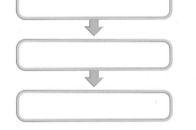

Build on What You Know Do you like bananas? If so, you are not alone. Bananas are a popular fruit. Where do stores in the United States get many of their bananas? They get them from other countries.

International Trade

People in this country eat millions of bananas each year. To meet this demand, some U.S. companies trade with banana producers in Ecuador (EHK wuh dawr). Trading helps both countries. People in different countries often trade with each other to buy and sell goods at lower costs. They look for a market that buys or sells what they want. A **market** is a place where goods may be bought or sold.

main idea (★)

Countries trade for goods that are in demand, such as bananas.

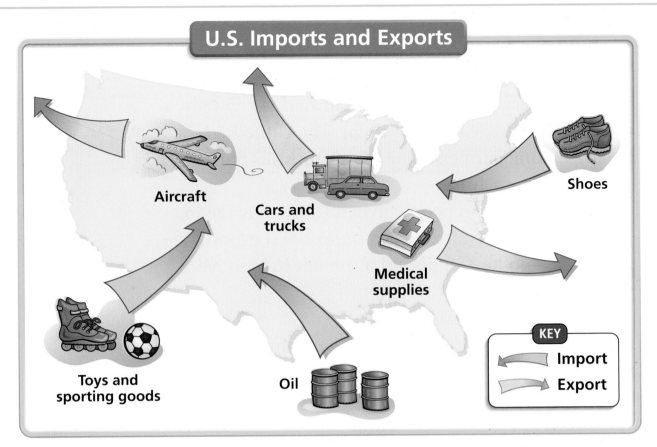

U.S. Imports and Exports

Aircraft

Cars and trucks

Medical supplies

Shoes

Toys and sporting goods

Oil

KEY
Import
Export

Skill **Reading Maps** Name three goods that the United States exports.

Importing Goods

Besides bananas, the United States imports many other types of goods. To **import** means to buy goods or services from sellers in other countries. Importing gives consumers the chance to buy some goods at lower cost. It also gives them more choices of what to buy.

Exporting Goods

Countries also export goods and services. To **export** means to sell goods or services to people in another country. Exporting helps producers sell more goods and services than they could sell in their own country alone. For example, the United States grows a lot of wheat. It uses about half of what it grows and exports the rest.

Review Why do U.S. companies export goods?

Trading Partners

When two or more countries depend on one another for trade, they may become trading partners. Then they work to increase trade between them. The United States has many trading partners. One of our most important trading partners is China.

(★) main idea

More than a billion people live in China. People in both China and the United States import and export goods to one another. Ships and airplanes help move these goods between the two countries.

Trade between China and the United States helps both countries. When American and Chinese companies export goods and services, they earn more money than they could in their own countries alone. When these companies import goods and services, U.S. and Chinese consumers benefit because they have more choices.

China Trades Goods The port of Shanghai (shang HY), China, receives goods from all over the world.

CHINA
Shanghai

Chinese Products

China exports products from many different industries. An **industry** is all of the people and companies that sell similar goods or services. For example, toy makers are part of China's toy industry. The companies that specialize in exporting toys are, too. Some of China's other industries include iron and steel, coal, machinery, clothing, footwear, toys, cars, and electronics.

Review Why is China an important trading partner for the United States?

Chinese workers load goods.

Lesson Review

① **VOCABULARY** Write a short paragraph explaining why countries **import** and **export.**

② **READING SKILL** In what ways is trading a **solution** for countries that want goods from other places?

③ **MAIN IDEA: Economics** Why do countries import and export goods?

④ **MAIN IDEA: Economics** What are two things that China and the United States do as trading partners?

⑤ **CRITICAL THINKING: Predict Outcomes** What would happen if trade with other countries stopped?

MAP ACTIVITY Check the labels on your clothes to see where they were made. Make a list of the countries. On a globe, find each country on your list.

Economics

A Bike from China

Lots of people ride bikes, but did you know that bikes can get rides, too? Bikes from China ride ships thousands of miles across oceans. They ride trucks to stores across the country. Then, when someone buys a bike, it might get a ride home on a car.

Follow a bike's path from Wuxi (WOO SHEE), China, to Boston, Massachusetts.

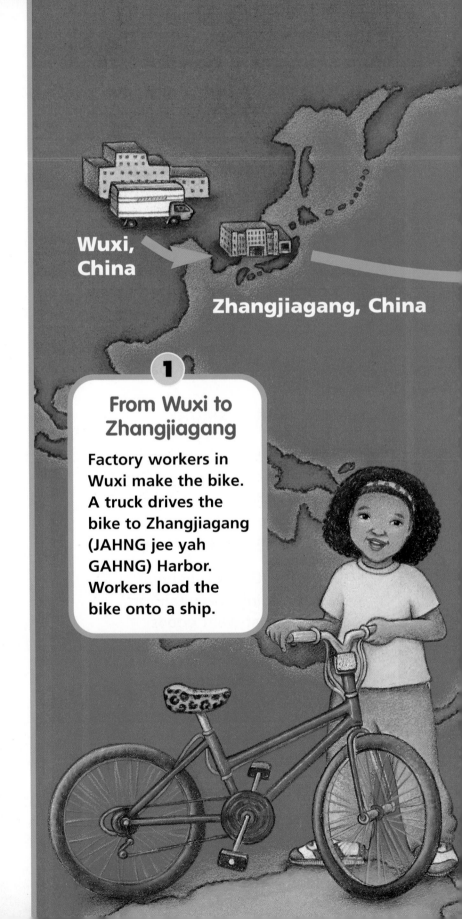

Wuxi, China

Zhangjiagang, China

1

From Wuxi to Zhangjiagang

Factory workers in Wuxi make the bike. A truck drives the bike to Zhangjiagang (JAHNG jee yah GAHNG) Harbor. Workers load the bike onto a ship.

Seattle,
U.S.A.

Boston,
U.S.A.

2 Across the Pacific to Seattle

The ship sails across the Pacific Ocean to the port of Seattle, Washington.

3 Arriving in Seattle

In Seattle, workers take the bike off the ship. Then they load the bike onto a truck.

4 From Seattle to Boston

The truck drives the bike to a store in Boston, Massachusetts. A consumer buys the bike from the store.

PACIFIC OCEAN

Activities

1. **THINK ABOUT IT** If someone in Boston sent his or her bike back to the factory in Wuxi, what route might the bike take?

2. **CHART IT** Make a table that shows three different products and the country in which each is made. Read the label on the product to find out where it is from.

305

Visual Summary

1–3. ✏️ Write a description of each item below.

Goods and Services

Producer

_____

_____

Assembly line

_____

_____

Trading partners

_____

_____

Facts and Main Ideas

🍃 **TEST PREP** Answer each question below.

4. **Economics** Why do producers and consumers depend on each other?

5. **Economics** What is free enterprise?

6. **Economics** Name three kinds of resources that producers use.

7. **Geography** What is the difference between an import and an export?

Vocabulary

✅ **TEST PREP** Choose the correct word from the list below to complete each sentence.

supply, p. 288
demand, p. 289
industry, p. 303

8. Both farmers and cooks work in the food _____.

9. If the price of a good is too high, the _____ may be low.

10. A producer will increase the _____ of goods if prices are high.

Apply Skills

TEST PREP **Use a Flow Chart** Use the flow chart below and what you have learned about flow charts to answer each question.

How to Frost Cupcakes

1. Put the cupcakes on a plate.

2. Find a butter knife.

3. Open a can of frosting.

4. With a knife, spread frosting on the cupcake.

11. Which step comes after putting the cupcakes on a plate?

12. What would happen if you skipped step 4?

  A. You could not open the can of frosting.

  B. You could not frost the cupcakes.

  C. You could not find a butter knife.

  D. You could not put the cupcakes on a plate.

Critical Thinking

TEST PREP Write a short paragraph to answer each question below. Use details to support your response.

13. **Cause and Effect** What can happen when a producer prices a product too high or too low?

14. **Summarize** What are ways that trade between countries helps those countries?

15. **Analyze** In what ways might your work in school help you become a skilled worker in the future?

Activities

Art Activity Make a flow chart that shows how a natural resource is used to make a product. End by showing a consumer using the product.

Writing Activity Write a brief set of numbered instructions to tell someone how to prepare a bowl of popcorn.

Technology

Writing Process Tips
Get help with your instructions at **www.eduplace.com/kids/hmss05/**

The Economy Where You Live

Think about the businesses in your community. What jobs do people do? What kinds of goods and services do producers sell? The answers to these questions tell about the economy where you live.

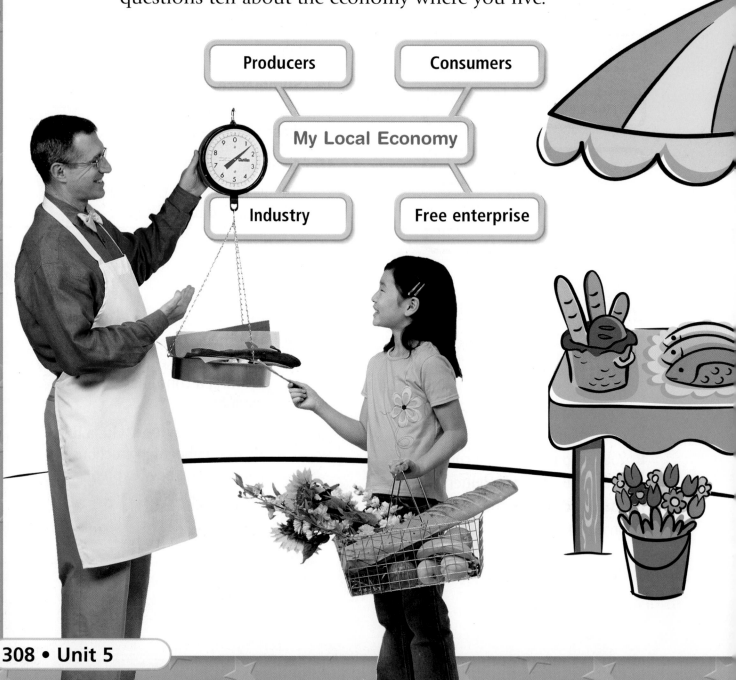

Producers

Consumers

My Local Economy

Industry

Free enterprise

Customer

Bank teller

Banks in local communities are part of the economy.

Explore your local economy.

✔ **Start with your own eyes.**
List some of the jobs and businesses you see or know about.

✔ **Ask the Chamber of Commerce.**
What are the largest industries in your community?

✔ **Interview a worker.**
Ask an adult you know about his or her job. Has it changed over time?

✔ **Interview a person at a local bank.**
Find out about opening a savings account.

Use your community handbook to keep track of information you find.

UNIT 5 Review and Test Prep

Vocabulary and Main Ideas

TEST PREP Write a sentence to answer each question.

1. Why might a person have a **budget?**
2. What is the **opportunity cost** when someone chooses to buy a book instead of a CD?
3. What are some of the **capital resources** that go into making goods?
4. Why would consumers want their country to **import** more goods?

Critical Thinking

TEST PREP Write a short answer for each question. Use details to support your answer.

5. **Make Decisions** Why might someone decide to buy one good instead of another?
6. **Summarize** What steps are needed to make blue jeans?

Apply Skills

TEST PREP Use the flow chart below to answer each question.

How Milk Gets to the Store

1. Farmer milks cow.
2. Milk goes by truck to the factory.
3. Milk is processed and poured into cartons and jugs.
4. Milk goes by truck to the store.

7. What step comes after milk goes by truck to the factory?
8. How does milk get from the factory to the store?

   A. by plane
   B. by boat
   C. by truck
   D. by car

Create a "Needs and Wants" Collage

- Bring in copies of newspapers or magazines.
- Cut out photographs and advertisements of things people need and things people want.
- Tape or glue cutouts on two sheets of paper, one for each category.

Things People Need

At the Library

You may find this book at your school or public library.

A Basket of Bangles
by Ginger Howard

Sufiya and her four friends change their lives by starting their own businesses in Bangladesh.

Connect to Economics

Make a flow chart showing the steps to make a product.

- Find information about how products are made.
- Choose a product and list the major steps it takes to make it.
- Create a flow chart that shows the steps. Illustrate and label it.

 Technology
Weekly Reader online offers social studies articles. Go to:
www.eduplace.com/kids/hmss/

Read About It

Look in your classroom for these Social Studies Independent Books.

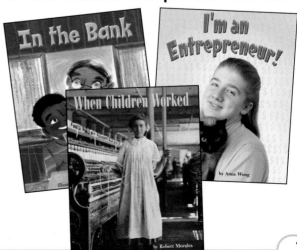

In the Bank

I'm an Entrepreneur!
by Anna Wong

When Children Worked

by Robert Morales

UNIT 6

Celebrating People and Cultures

The **Big** Idea

In what ways are people all the same?

"We all live with the objective of being happy; our lives are all different and yet the same."

—Anne Frank,
writer, 1944

National Monuments

ARCTIC OCEAN

km 0   300
mi 0   300

Aniakchak National Monument

PACIFIC OCEAN

Hanford Reach National Monument

Columbia River

Missouri River

Grand Portage National Monument

Craters of the Moon

Effigy Mounds

PACIFIC OCEAN

Muir Woods

Colorado R.

Arkansas River

Canyons of the Ancients

George Washington Carver National Monument

Navajo National Monument

Cabrillo National Monument

km 0 50 100
mi 0 50 100

PACIFIC OCEAN

Rio Grande

N
NW   NE
W   E
SW   SE
S

MEXICO

Unit Preview

Legends
Johnny Appleseed **Chapter 11, page 319**

School in Russia
Customs students follow **Chapter 11, page 328**

Holiday Customs
Chinese New Year **Chapter 12, page 339**

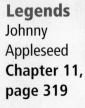

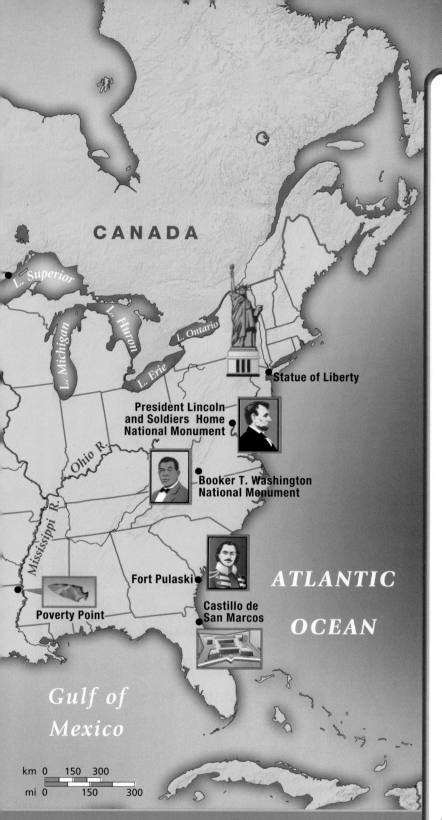

CANADA

L. Superior

L. Michigan

L. Huron

L. Ontario

L. Erie

Ohio R.

Mississippi R.

Statue of Liberty

President Lincoln and Soldiers Home National Monument

Booker T. Washington National Monument

Fort Pulaski

Poverty Point

Castillo de San Marcos

ATLANTIC

OCEAN

Gulf of Mexico

km 0   150   300
mi 0   150   300

Heroes in History
Harriet Tubman
Chapter 12, page 352

Heroes in History
Harriet Tubman
Chapter 12, page 352

U.S. Languages, 2000

More than 231 million people in the United States spoke English as their first language.

Spanish

English

Other

What is the second most commonly spoken language in the United States?

Borrowed Words

Spanish	Arabic	French
patio	admiral	blonde
mosquito	safari	souvenir

American English has borrowed many words from other languages.

CURRENT   EVENTS

WEEKLY WR READER

Current events on the web!

Read social studies articles at:

www.eduplace.com/kids/hmss/

Vocabulary Preview

Technology

e • **glossary**
e • **word games**
www.eduplace.com/kids/hmss05/

legend

People from every land have their own **legends,** or stories that have been told since long ago.
page 319

ethnic group

In the United States, people come from many different cultures and **ethnic groups.**
page 321

custom

Often a **custom,** such as greeting others, is done differently in one country than in another.

page 328

participate

When children **participate,** or take part in, a community activity, they help the common good.

page 329

Culture in a Community

VOCABULARY

legend

ethnic group

READING SKILL

Main Idea and Details
As you read, list the details that show how people learn about their culture.

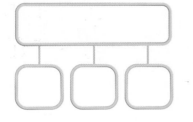

Build on What You Know What do people in your community do for fun? The things people enjoy are part of their culture.

Looking at Culture

Culture is the way of life of people in a community. It includes their ideas, traditions, and languages, their religion, government, and heritage. The clothes people wear and what they learn in school are part of culture. Their work and the tools they use are, too. Every community in the world has a culture.

People don't know the ways of their culture when they are born. They learn them as they grow. <u>Children learn their culture from their families and their community.</u>   (★)

main idea

The music people play or listen to is a part of their culture.

How We Say Hello

In Japan, we bow.

In the United States, we shake hands.

In Thailand, we put our palms together.

Lessons of Culture

Cultures have rules about manners and about how to behave. The rules in your culture may be different from the rules in another culture. Children learn their culture's rules from other children and from adults around them.

Another way children and adults learn about their culture is through stories called legends. A **legend** is a story passed down from an earlier time. Legends tell about a group's important ideas. They also tell about people from the past, though the stories are not always true.

The legend of **Johnny Appleseed** is part of American heritage. He traveled around the country and planted apple seeds. The importance of being unselfish is one of the messages in the Johnny Appleseed legend.

Review In what ways do people learn their culture?

Different Ways of Life

People from all cultures have the same basic needs. The way people meet those needs depends on what they learn from their culture. For example, people need to communicate. In different cultures people use different languages. In Haiti (HAY tee), people speak French or Haitian Creole (HAY shun KREE ohl). In Egypt, many people speak Arabic.

People across the world also need shelter. Because the environments they live in are different, the homes or shelters in which they live are also different. In some parts of Cambodia, people build their homes on stilts. That keeps them out of the water during the rainy season. In dry parts of Sudan, some people make their homes from mud bricks dried in the sun.

main idea

Houses Culture and geography affect the types of houses people build.

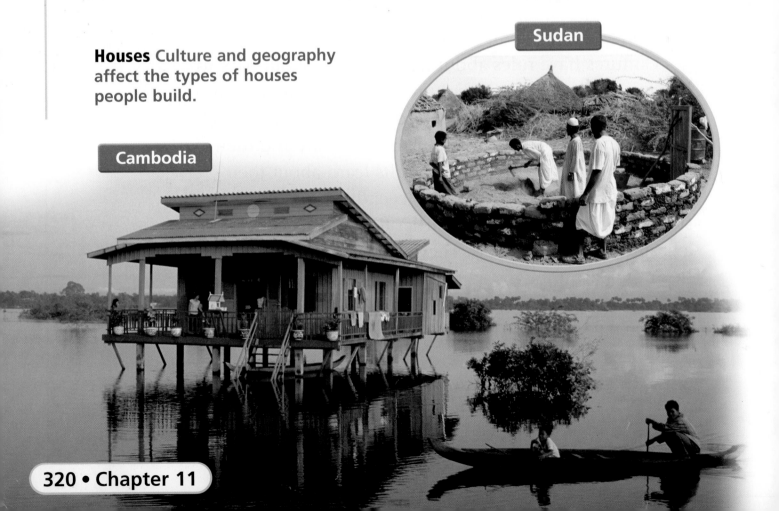

Sudan

Cambodia

A Mix of Cultures

The United States is a mix of people from many world cultures. Many of these people continue to follow some of the traditions of their ethnic groups. An **ethnic group** is a group of people who have their own language and culture. Many ethnic cultures are now part of our American culture. Across the country, Americans dine on pizza from Italy. They play electronic games from Japan. They listen to music from Brazil.

Review In what ways are cultures alike?

Children from many cultures form part of our American culture.

Lesson Review

1 VOCABULARY Use **legend** in a sentence about a culture.

2 READING SKILL Use the **details** you recorded to write a sentence telling how you learned about American culture.

3 MAIN IDEA: Culture What are some ways to learn about ideas that are important in the culture of the United States?

4 MAIN IDEA: Culture What basic needs do people in all cultures have?

5 CRITICAL THINKING: Synthesize Describe two or three features of American culture.

WRITING ACTIVITY Write a list of questions you might ask someone from a different country about their culture.

Johnny Appleseed! Johnny Appleseed!

Retold by Marion Vallat Emrich and George Korson

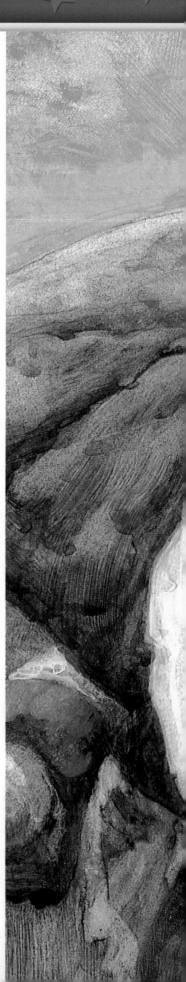

Legends and folktales reveal what's important to a community. In the United States, a well-known folktale tells the story of a man called Johnny Appleseed. The story teaches about generosity and kindness.

✢ ✢ ✢

Of all the tales that Pennsylvanians tell, they may like best the story of a strange fellow who rode into Pittsburgh on the lazyboard of a Conestoga wagon back in 1794. He said his name was Jonathan Chapman, and he built himself a log cabin on Grant's Hill.

There are some people who say he told it around Pittsburgh that he had been born in Boston in the year of the Battle of Bunker Hill and that the first thing his baby eyes ever saw was a branch of apple blossoms outside the window of his home. If that is true, the sight must have influenced the rest of his life, for as soon as he had his house built in Pittsburgh he planted a big apple orchard. There, on the hill now known as Pittsburgh's Hump, the bees in Jonathan Chapman's hives made honey from the apple blossoms, and Jonathan gave it away to his neighbors because, he said, the bees didn't charge him anything for it.

In the twelve years he lived in Pittsburgh an idea kept growing in Jonathan Chapman's brain until it got a powerful hold on him. He would take a load of apple seeds westward to the pioneers on the frontier so that they might have flowering, fruitful orchards like his own.

So, in 1806, Jonathan loaded two canoes with apple seeds and started down the Ohio River. When he got to the Muskingum he followed that to White Woman Creek, and he finally ended up along Licking Creek where his load of seeds ran out. Behind him farmers were rejoicing in their seedlings—soon to be waving orchards—and they talked about the man who had brought them. They called him Johnny Appleseed.

Johnny went back to the Pennsylvania cider mills to get more seeds. They're still talking about him around Shadeland and Blooming Valley and Cool Spring— the odd, blue-eyed man with long hair hanging to his shoulders, barefooted, wearing ragged clothes. When he had disposed of a second load and come back to Pennsylvania for seeds again, his appearance had changed still more. On his head as a cap he wore a tin kettle in which, when he needed it, he cooked his food. His only garment now, winter or summer, was a coffee sack with holes cut in it for his arms and legs.

Strange stories came out of the western frontier.

A trapper had come upon Johnny Appleseed playing with three bear cubs while their mother looked on placidly.

Johnny Appleseed knew direction by instinct and never carried a compass in the trackless woods.

He did not feel the cold and could walk barefoot in below-zero weather without freezing his toes.

Wherever Barefoot Johnny walked, he brought apple seeds.

Soon, hundreds of Ohio acres were abloom with pink blossoms, and Pennsylvania seeds had reached the banks of the Wabash. Everywhere Johnny Appleseed was welcomed by the grateful farmers. When he sat down at table with them he would not eat until he was sure that there was plenty of food for the children. His voice, one good housewife said, was "loud as the roar of wind and waves, then soft and soothing as the balmy airs that quivered the morning-glory leaves about his gray beard."

Farmers who own apple orchards along Johnny Appleseed's path, which stretched over a territory of a hundred thousand square miles, have been blessing him ever since. And all the folks in western Pennsylvania do, too, for they know that when spring comes to the land known now as the Midwest, hundreds of thousands of Ohio and Indiana acres will be pink and white with Pennsylvania apple blossoms.

Activities

1. **LOCATE IT** Where did Johnny Appleseed go? Use a map to find at least three places he traveled.

2. **WRITE ABOUT IT** Write a song about Johnny Appleseed's travels. Include details from the story.

READING SKILL

Compare and Contrast
List ways that schools in Moscow are similar to and different from schools here.

🌐 WORLD CONNECTION
Russia

Build on What You Know What is your school day like? You read and study social studies. You eat lunch with your friends. Maybe you play a sport. What might a school day be like in a different country?

School in Moscow

All over the world, people go to school. In this lesson, you will learn what it is like to be a student in Moscow, Russia. Find Moscow on the map on the next page.

Moscow is the capital of Russia. It is a center for arts, business, and government. The city has about 1,600 schools. Schools in Moscow are like yours in some ways.

Moscow has a mix of old and new buildings.

Skill **Reading Visuals** In what ways is this Russian classroom similar to or different from your classroom?

The School Day

School is important to Russians, just as it is to Americans. School gives people the skills to be good citizens and to get good jobs. With training, students can become scientists. They might become writers or choose to run businesses.

In Moscow, most children between the ages of 6 and 17 go to school. Students in the early grades finish school at 12 or 12:30 P.M. Older students stay in class until 3 P.M.

Many Russian students work hard on math and science. Younger students learn about the Russian language and study stories and poems. They have lessons in history and geography, too. Students who are interested in certain subjects can go to special schools. For example, third graders who want to learn French or English can attend schools that feature those subjects.

Review Why is school important to people in Russia and the United States?

School Customs These Russian children play outside during recess. Some use textbooks (right) to study writing.

Russian Customs

Some customs in Russian schools differ from the customs in our country. A **custom** is something that members of a group usually do. In Moscow, students in early grades often share school buildings with high school students. In the United States, younger students usually have their own schools.

Winters in Moscow are cold, so during the winter, some students don't have recess outside as many students do here. Instead, children in Moscow play in big halls inside their schools.

Some Russian school customs have to do with manners. In many classrooms students stand up when a teacher enters the room. Some students also have a special way of raising their hands in class. They keep their elbows on their desks and lift just the front part of their arms.

Citizenship Projects

Students in Moscow may participate in special projects. To **participate** means to take part in something. The projects make their communities and schools better. For example, students might plant trees and a garden at their school. Taking care of their schools teaches Russian students about being good citizens.

Review What are some Russian school customs?

Red Square, Moscow
These students are taking a trip to learn more about Russian culture.

Lesson Review

1 **VOCABULARY** Use **custom** in a sentence about your family.

2 **READING SKILL** In what way does your school day **contrast,** or differ from, a school day in Moscow?

3 **MAIN IDEA: Culture** Name two customs that are the same in Russian schools and in your school.

4 **MAIN IDEA: Culture** In what ways do Russian students participate in special projects?

5 **CRITICAL THINKING: Analyze** In what way does it help at school when students have good classroom manners?

DRAMA ACTIVITY Prepare a short conversation between you and a Russian student who is visiting your classroom. Remember to include information about your cultures and customs.

Geography

Long Days Short Nights

Imagine playing tag until 9 P.M. when it's still light out. In Moscow you can. There, for more than a month in the summer, the sun lights the sky past 9 o'clock at night.

What causes this? In space, the earth is tilted. During the summer, the northern part of the earth tilts toward the sun. This means the sun shines on the north for more hours. Moscow is not the only northern place that has long summer daylight hours. Parts of Alaska are so far north that the sun never sets during the summer.

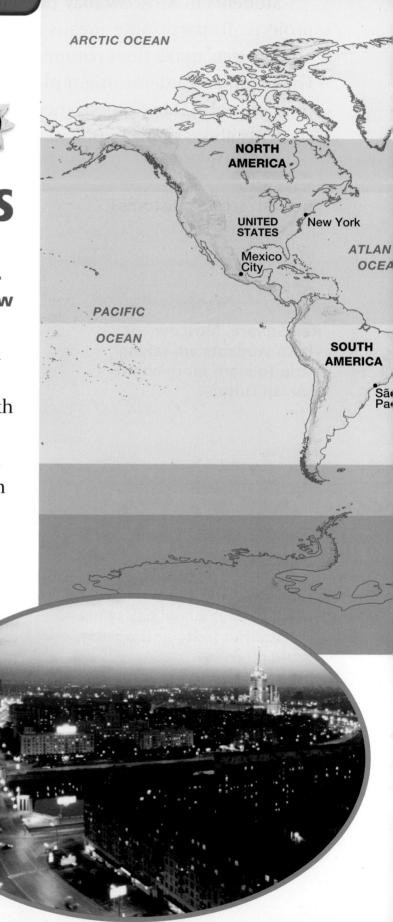

ARCTIC OCEAN

NORTH AMERICA

UNITED STATES   New York

Mexico City

ATLAN OCEA

PACIFIC OCEAN

SOUTH AMERICA

São Pa

Moscow stays light long after sunset in the summer.

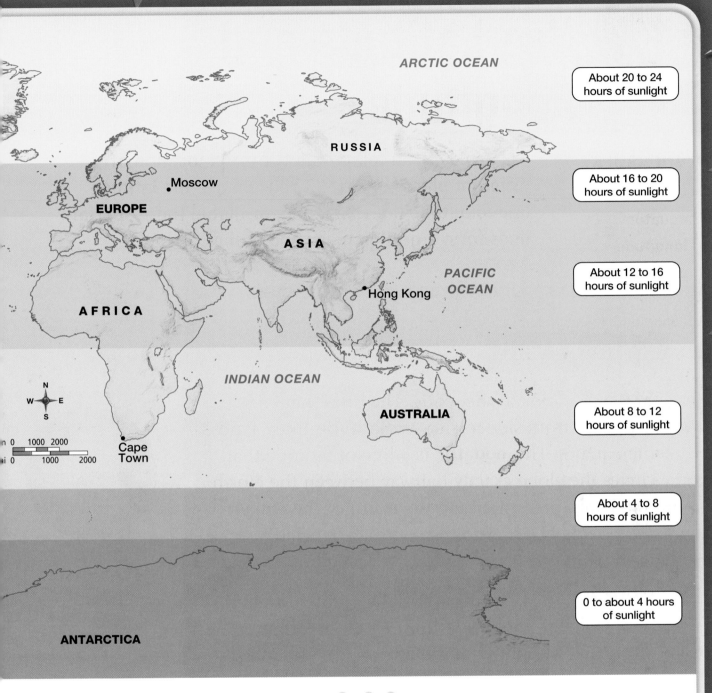

ARCTIC OCEAN

About 20 to 24 hours of sunlight

RUSSIA

About 16 to 20 hours of sunlight

• Moscow

EUROPE

ASIA

PACIFIC OCEAN

About 12 to 16 hours of sunlight

AFRICA

• Hong Kong

INDIAN OCEAN

N
W · E
S

AUSTRALIA

About 8 to 12 hours of sunlight

0   1000 2000
0   1000   2000

Cape Town

About 4 to 8 hours of sunlight

ANTARCTICA

0 to about 4 hours of sunlight

Summer Sun

This map shows the hours of sunlight in different places around the world on June 21.

Activities

1. **FIND IT** Locate Moscow and three other cities on the map. How many hours of daylight do they have compared with Moscow?

2. **DESCRIBE IT** In what ways might your life be different if you lived where the sun never set in the summer? Describe what steps you would take to fall asleep when it's bright out at bedtime.

Skillbuilder

Use Latitude and Longitude

▶ **VOCABULARY**

latitude

equator

longitude

prime meridian

How can you tell others the exact location of different places on Earth? You can use the latitude and longitude lines on a map or globe. These special lines form a grid on maps and globes.

Learn the Skill

Step 1: Look at the globe. The lines that cross the globe from side to side are **latitude** lines. Find the equator. The **equator** is a line of latitude that circles the globe exactly halfway between the North and South poles. Lines to the north of the equator are labeled N. Lines to the south are labeled S.

Step 2: The lines that cross the globe from top to bottom are **longitude** lines. Find the prime meridian. The **prime meridian** is a line that passes through Greenwich, England. Longitude lines to the east of the prime meridian are labeled E. Those to the west are labeled W.

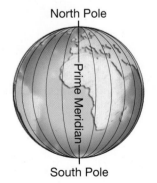

Step 3: Find New Orleans, Louisiana, on the map. Then find the nearest latitude and longitude lines. The location of New Orleans is 30°N, 90°W. The symbol ° means degrees.

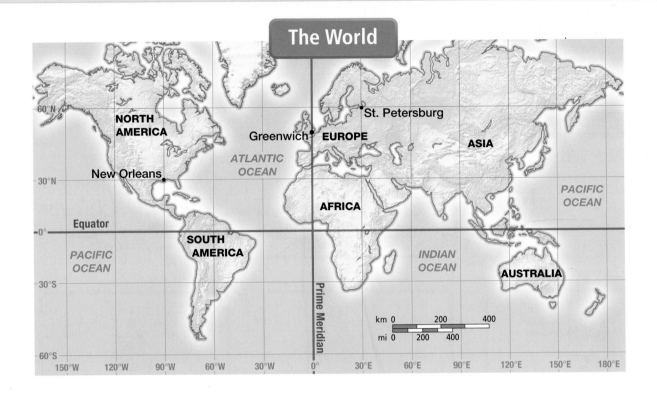

The World

60°N · NORTH AMERICA · Greenwich · EUROPE · St. Petersburg · ASIA · ATLANTIC OCEAN · New Orleans · 30°N · PACIFIC OCEAN · AFRICA · Equator · 0° · SOUTH AMERICA · PACIFIC OCEAN · INDIAN OCEAN · AUSTRALIA · 30°S · Prime Meridian · 60°S · 150°W · 120°W · 90°W · 60°W · 30°W · 0° · 30°E · 60°E · 90°E · 120°E · 150°E · 180°E · km 0 · 200 · 400 · mi 0 · 200 · 400

Practice the Skill

Study the world map above. Use latitude and longitude to answer each question.

1 Which city is located on the prime meridian?

2 What is the latitude and longitude for St. Petersburg, Russia?

3 Through which three continents does latitude 30°S pass?

Apply the Skill

Pick three places on a classroom globe or map. Write down their latitude and longitude numbers. Then ask a classmate to use latitude and longitude to find each place.

Visual Summary

1–3.  Write a description of each item named below.

Culture

Basic needs

_____

_____

Customs

_____

_____

School life in Moscow

_____

_____

Facts and Main Ideas

✓ **TEST PREP** Answer each question below.

4. **Culture** What things are part of a person's culture?

5. **Culture** In what ways do people learn about their own culture?

6. **Culture** Why is school important here and in Moscow?

7. **Culture** What are three subjects that Russian students learn?

Vocabulary

✓ **TEST PREP** Choose the correct word from the list below to complete each sentence.

legend, p. 319
ethnic group, p. 321
custom, p. 328

8. Each _____ has its own culture.

9. A _____ is a kind of story that tells about important ideas.

10. One Russian _____ is that students stand when a teacher enters a room.

TEST PREP **Use Latitude and Longitude** Use the map of Africa below and what you have learned about latitude and longitude to answer each question.

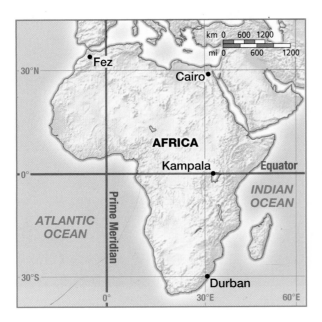

11. Which city is on the equator?

    A. Cairo

    B. Durban

    C. Fez

    D. Kampala

12. What is the latitude and longitude of Cairo?

    A. about 30°N, 30°E

    B. about 30°N, 60°E

    C. about 30°S, 30°W

    D. about 60°S, 30°W

 TEST PREP Write a short paragraph to answer each question below. Use details to support your response.

13. **Analyze** In what ways do legends help children learn more about their culture?

14. **Cause and Effect** In what ways would living in a dry, hot place affect the culture of the people there?

15. **Draw Conclusions** Why are schools in Russia different from schools in the United States?

Activities

 Research Activity Use library or Internet resources to research the clothing of people who live in a culture and climate different from yours.

Writing Activity Write a persuasive essay explaining why your school or community should hold a cultural fair. Give reasons for your point of view.

Technology
Writing Process Tips
Get help with your essay at
www.eduplace.com/kids/hmss05/

335

Chapter 12 Holidays and Heroes

Technology

e • **glossary**
e • **word games**
www.eduplace.com/kids/hmss05/

Vocabulary Preview

holiday

A **holiday** is a time for celebrating. These special days may be patriotic, religious, or cultural.
page 338

liberty

On Independence Day, Americans celebrate the principle of freedom, or **liberty.**
page 346

Reading Strategy

Summarize Use this strategy to focus on important ideas.

 Quick Tip Review the main ideas. Look for details to support them.

patriotism

Flying the American flag is a way to show love for your country. The flag is a symbol of **patriotism.**
page 346

legacy

Heroes have left a **legacy** of freedom in our country.
page 352

Cultural Holidays

VOCABULARY

holiday

principle

READING SKILL

Compare and Contrast Note the ways cultural holidays are alike and different.

Build on What You Know Many cultures have special days. People celebrate them in different ways. What special days do you take part in?

Cultural Holidays

Holidays are one way people share their cultures. A **holiday** is a time to celebrate a special event or person. During holidays, people think about ideas that are important to them. One type of holiday is a cultural holiday. <u>Cultural holidays help people celebrate their history or way of life.</u> *main idea* Kwanzaa (KWAHN zuh) is one example of a cultural holiday.

Kwanzaa Corn, fruit, gifts, and candles are some symbols of this holiday.

Kwanzaa

Many African Americans take part in Kwanzaa to celebrate African heritage. The holiday starts on December 26 and lasts for seven days. Kwanzaa is based on old African celebrations.

Each day of Kwanzaa stands for a principle. A **principle** is a basic truth. Unity and faith are two Kwanzaa truths. People light candles for each of the seven principles. The night before Kwanzaa ends, families and friends gather for a feast.

Chinese New Year

Chinese people around the world celebrate the Chinese New Year. The holiday begins in January or February, depending on the year.

Red is an important color during this holiday. It is supposed to bring good luck. Adults give children money in red envelopes. People light red candles. Fireworks, visits to friends, and a big feast are also part of the fun.

Review What can people learn by celebrating cultural holidays?

Chinese New Year Children wearing a dragon costume celebrate in a holiday parade in Los Angeles, California.

Religious Holidays

Some cultural holidays are religious. A religious holiday is a time for people to think about and practice their beliefs. Often, people attend special services in their places of worship.

main idea

Rosh Hashanah

Rosh Hashanah (rawsh huh SHAW nuh) is an important holiday for Jews. It marks the Jewish New Year and takes place in the fall. During Rosh Hashanah, Jews think about the past year. They look ahead to the new year with hope.

At home, Jewish families and friends share a special meal. They may eat food such as apples dipped in honey. This tradition expresses their hope for a sweet new year.

Rosh Hashanah Jewish children eat apples dipped in honey.

Christmas

Christmas is a religious holiday for Christians. It is celebrated on December 25. Christmas marks the birth of **Jesus,** who lived about 2,000 years ago. Christians follow Jesus' teachings.

In different parts of the world, Christians have different Christmas traditions. Some people give gifts. Others ring church bells the night before. People may also decorate Christmas trees.

Christmas Christian children decorate a Christmas tree.

Ramadan

Ramadan (ram uh DAHN) is a religious holiday for Muslims. Muslims follow a religion called Islam. **Muhammad** (mu HAM ihd) was the founder of Islam. He lived about 1,400 years ago. Ramadan lasts one month. During the holiday, Muslims think about their faith. From sunrise to sunset they fast, or do not eat. At sunset each day, they gather to pray and then share food. A huge feast marks the end of Ramadan.

Ramadan In the evenings, Muslim families and friends share special foods.

Review In what ways do people celebrate religious holidays?

Lesson Review

1 VOCABULARY Choose the correct word to complete the sentence.

> **principle**   **holiday**

We always feast on my favorite _____.

2 READING SKILL What is one difference between Kwanzaa and the Chinese New Year?

3 MAIN IDEA: Culture In what ways do holidays help people celebrate their culture?

4 MAIN IDEA: Culture What are some traditions people practice during religious holidays?

5 CRITICAL THINKING: Analyze Why do you think cultural holidays are important to people?

WRITING ACTIVITY Invent a new tradition for a cultural holiday. Write an entry for the encyclopedia to describe it. Revise your entry.

What We Share

Sometimes a race is more than a chance for fun.
It can raise money for programs in a community.

A race is just one way that Americans come together.
They might celebrate different **holidays** or believe different
things, but they all are part of American culture. In schools
and in offices, on streets and in government centers,
people find ways to have fun and to work together.

Anything Goes Many
thousands of people run,
trot, and walk in the
Bay to Breakers race.
Here, a father and son
run to raise money for
the common good.

Lunch Mates Sharing food and hanging out with friends can make lunch a fun part of the school day.

It's a Deal City and state leaders in New York work together to help New York City's schools.

Activities

1. **DRAW IT** Draw a picture that shows an event in your community.

2. **PLAN IT** What community program would you like to support? Write a plan for an event that would bring people together to help support that program.

343

National Holidays

VOCABULARY

honor
liberty
patriotism

READING SKILL

Cause and Effect
As you read, note the reasons why each national holiday was created.

Cause	Effect

Build on What You Know Whistle! Boom! Crash! When fireworks explode, do you clap your hands over your ears or laugh out loud? Throughout the United States, communities use fireworks to celebrate history.

Holidays in History

National holidays are one way for us to remember our history. They honor important people and events in the United States. To **honor** a group means to show respect for it.

During national holidays, we think about the rights and freedoms Americans have. The holidays help remind us of how we won these rights.

With a salute on Veterans Day, these veterans honor those who have served our country in war.

Memorial Day and Veterans Day

We mark Memorial Day on the last Monday in May. This is a day to honor the men and women who lost their lives during war. On Memorial Day, some people attend religious services. Others march in parades. Many flags fly at half-staff until noon to show respect for those who have died for our country.

On November 11, we celebrate Veterans Day. November 11 was the day World War I ended in 1918. Today, Americans mark that event by remembering all veterans. A veteran is a person who has served in the armed forces. On Veterans Day, people may gather at war monuments in their towns to listen to speeches. In many communities, the day includes parades that honor soldiers.

Review Why is it important to celebrate national holidays?

Memorial Day This holiday parade took place more than 80 years ago.

Skill **Primary Source** In what ways is this picture like the one on page 344?

Independence Day Parades, cookouts, and fireworks are some of the ways people celebrate our nation's birthday.

Independence Day

We celebrate freedom and the Declaration of Independence on Independence Day. American leaders signed the Declaration during the summer of 1776. Today we celebrate Independence Day, or the Fourth of July, as the country's birthday.

Americans still believe in the principles that led them to seek independence. **Liberty,** or freedom, is one of the most important of those principles. Independence Day honors the liberty that Americans have enjoyed for more than 200 years.

Across the United States, people celebrate Independence Day in many ways. It is a time for Americans to show their patriotism. **Patriotism** is love for your country.

Celebrating Together

Many people hang American flags on buildings and flag poles. The flag, with its red, white, and blue colors, is a symbol of patriotism. In some communities, people show their patriotism by reading the Declaration of Independence out loud.

The Fourth of July is also a time for families to gather and have fun. In Washington, D.C., people march through the city in a big parade. Fireworks glow over San Francisco, California, and hundreds of other cities and towns. Chicago, Illinois, celebrates with concerts.

Review What important idea do we celebrate on Independence Day?

Honoring People

Some American holidays honor people who worked for fairness or freedom. **Martin Luther King, Jr.**, spent most of his life working for equal rights. He believed that all people should be treated with respect.

Dr. King lived at a time when African Americans were denied their rights. He worked to change things in a peaceful way. In one speech, Dr. King said,

> 66 **I have a dream that one day this nation will rise up and live out the true meaning of its creed: 'We hold these truths to be self-evident: that all men are created equal.'** 99

We mark Dr. King's birthday on the third Monday of January. People honor him in different ways. Some people participate in marches. Others help children learn to read.

Martin Luther King, Jr. In 1963, Dr. King spoke to a huge crowd. Today, people honor him with parades and other events.

City of Long Beach Parks, Recreation + Marine

Teen Volunteer Program

Presidents' Day

Presidents' Day honors the birthdays of **George Washington** and **Abraham Lincoln**. Washington was born in 1732. He led the country in its fight for freedom from Great Britain. Lincoln was born in 1809. He worked to end slavery and keep the country united. We celebrate Presidents' Day on the third Monday in February.

Review In what ways have some of our leaders worked for fairness?

Mount Rushmore Carved into stone are the faces of four U.S. Presidents: George Washington, Thomas Jefferson, Theodore Roosevelt, and Abraham Lincoln.

Lesson Review

❶ **VOCABULARY** Use **patriotism** and **liberty** in a short paragraph about celebrating Independence Day.

❷ **READING SKILL** Contrast the reasons people celebrate Veterans Day and the Fourth of July.

❸ **MAIN IDEA: History** Name two important events that national holidays help us remember.

❹ **MAIN IDEA: History** What do George Washington, Abraham Lincoln, and Martin Luther King, Jr., have in common?

❺ **CRITICAL THINKING: Analyze** Why do you think Americans honor the birthday of Martin Luther King, Jr.?

HANDS ON **MUSIC ACTIVITY** Choose a patriotic song you know and tell in your own words what it means.

A DAY FOR LEADERS

One gave his life for freedom. The other fought for the rights of farm workers. Both had courage. They are Count Casimir Pulaski (KA sih meer pu LAS kee) and Cesar Chavez (SAY sahr CHAH vehz). Today, special state holidays **honor** these leaders.

Pulaski fought for freedom in Poland. In 1777, he came to America to help in its war against the British.

Chavez grew up picking crops with his family. The pay was poor and the work was hard. As a young man, he decided to speak out for the rights of farm workers. It took many years, but California's leaders took action. They passed laws to help the workers.

Count Casimir Pulaski

In America, Pulaski led and trained United States soldiers. Today, Illinois honors Pulaski with a holiday. It celebrates his birthday on the first Monday in March.

Cesar Chavez Day

California declared a holiday for Cesar Chavez in 2000. Other states also honor him with a holiday each year. The picture above shows people leading a parade to celebrate Chavez. On the banner they carry, the words in quotes mean "march for justice."

Activities

1. **THINK ABOUT IT** Why did it take **courage** for Pulaski and Chavez to act as they did?

2. **PRESENT IT** Research and present a report on a leader who was important in your state.

Our Heroes

Build on What You Know Some storybooks tell about strong people who do bold things. The lives of real people can be as amazing as stories.

VOCABULARY

legacy
justice

READING SKILL
Draw Conclusions
Come to a conclusion about what heroes do. Include details about the traits of heroes.

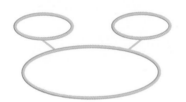

Courageous Heroes

Brave people have done important work for our country. They are American heroes. Some heroes have left us with a legacy of freedom. A **legacy** is something passed on to later generations.

main idea ⭐

Harriet Tubman

Harriet Tubman was a daring hero. Although Tubman was born into slavery in the South, she escaped. Then she worked and raised money to help others flee slavery. She guided slaves on secret escape routes called the Underground Railroad. Over time, Harriet Tubman led about 300 people to freedom.

Harriet Tubman She risked her own freedom many times to help others.

Abraham Lincoln

Abraham Lincoln believed in justice. **Justice** means fairness. When Lincoln became President of the United States, the northern and southern parts of the country could not agree about slavery. The South wanted to leave the nation and continue slavery. Lincoln and the North wanted the country to stay together.

The North and South went to war. As President, Lincoln guided the country through the terrible time. During the war, Lincoln announced that slaves in the South would be freed. His courage helped keep the nation united and end slavery.

Review In what ways did Tubman and Lincoln work for freedom?

Abraham Lincoln In 1863, he issued the Emancipation Proclamation, shown below. This document helped to end slavery.

Americans With New Ideas

Another American hero is **Thomas Edison**. He was an inventor who turned ideas into products. <u>Many Americans, such as Edison, have used their ideas to help our country.</u>

Edison came up with a way to make electric light bulbs glow for hours. Edison also worked on ways to get electricity to people's homes. Before that, people had to use gas lamps or candles for light.

Thomas Edison He invented more than 1,000 products.

Helen Keller

Helen Keller was blind and deaf. She could not see words on a page, nor could she hear if someone read them to her. Yet Keller did something amazing. She learned to read and write. Keller was very determined. She also had a wonderful teacher, **Anne Sullivan**.

Keller believed in education for people who are deaf and blind. She traveled across the country to spread this idea and share her experiences.

Helen Keller Here, Anne Sullivan reads to Helen Keller by using touch.

Maya Lin

Some Americans share their ideas through art. **Maya Lin** makes sculptures. The Vietnam Veterans Memorial in Washington, D.C., is one of Lin's most famous works. The wall of polished black stone honors Americans who died in the Vietnam War or are still missing.

Review In what ways did Edison's ideas help people?

Maya Lin She designed the Vietnam Veterans Memorial when she was in college.

Lesson Review

1. **VOCABULARY** Write a paragraph explaining ways that heroes can pass on a **legacy.**

2. **READING SKILL** Draw a **conclusion** about the traits that heroes share.

3. **MAIN IDEA: History** Why is Abraham Lincoln a hero?

4. **MAIN IDEA: Culture** What are some new ideas that have changed people's lives?

5. **PEOPLE TO KNOW** Who was **Helen Keller** and what did she do?

6. **CRITICAL THINKING: Analyze** What is your definition of a hero? Explain your answer.

WRITING ACTIVITY Prepare for an interview with a person you consider a hero. Write four questions you would ask.

Local and Global Heroes

Superheroes swoop in, save the day, and disappear. At least, that's what happens in the movies. In real life, heroes help people around the world and in their own communities every day.

Roberta Guaspari

When you love something deeply, it's worth fighting for. That's even more true when it helps a whole community. Roberta Guaspari (gwah SPAH ree) loves music. She teaches students to play the violin in New York City schools.

When her school district cut the money for violin lessons, Guaspari took action to save them. She asked parents and famous musicians to help her. Together, the community saved the program. Her love of music and of her students have inspired people to make two films about her.

Nobel Peace Prize

Jimmy Carter

Jimmy Carter (above left) was our 39th President. When he left office, he did what few other presidents have done. He traveled the world helping to improve people's lives.

In Nigeria, Carter worked to help people pick their leaders fairly. He met with General Abdulsalami Abubakar (ab dool sah LAH mee ah boo BA kahr, above right). In 2002, Carter won the Nobel Peace Prize. People who earn this honor have done important work for world peace.

Activities

1. **TALK ABOUT IT** What **civic virtues** do Guaspari and Carter show that make them heroes?

2. **WRITE ABOUT IT** Write a letter to your principal about someone at your school whom you think is a hero.

 Technology Read more biographies at Education Place.
www.eduplace.com/kids/hmss05/

Skillbuilder

Tell Fact from Opinion

Abraham Lincoln was the sixteenth President of the United States. That is a fact. A fact can be proven. Some people believe that Lincoln was the best President. That belief is an opinion. An opinion tells what a person thinks or believes.

► **VOCABULARY**

fact

opinion

Learn the Skill

Step 1: Listen or look for dates, numbers, and events. These are usually facts. They can be checked in sources such as encyclopedias and dictionaries.

Step 2: Listen or look for words that show opinions. Sentences with the words *I think* or *I believe* are usually opinions. Other clue words that show opinions are *perfect, best, worst, always,* and *from my point of view.*

Step 3: Think about how an opinion about a person or event can affect someone's use of facts.

Practice the Skill

Read these two sentences. Then answer the questions about fact and opinion.

> I think the best thing Lincoln ever did was to free slaves.
>
> Lincoln was a soldier, legislator, and lawyer before he became President.

❶ Which statement is a fact?

❷ Which statement is an opinion?

❸ What clue words are used in the opinion?

Apply the Skill

Read this paragraph about Abraham Lincoln. Makea two-column chart. Write the facts in the first column and the opinions in the second column.

> Abraham Lincoln was President from 1861 to 1865. Giving speeches was one of Lincoln's greatest talents. He did a perfect job of explaining things clearly. In 1863, Lincoln gave a speech called the Gettysburg Address. In his speech, he told citizens that "government of the people, by the people, and for the people, shall not perish from the earth."

Visual Summary

1–4.  Write a description of each item named below.

Cultural holidays

_____

_____

_____

_____

Religious holidays

_____

_____

_____

_____

National holidays

_____

_____

_____

_____

National heroes

_____

_____

_____

_____

Facts and Main Ideas

TEST PREP Answer each question below.

5. **Culture** Why do people celebrate holidays?

6. **History** What are two national holidays, and what does each holiday celebrate?

7. **History** Name two people we honor with holidays.

8. **Culture** What are some of the traits that Americans admire in heroes?

Vocabulary

TEST PREP Choose the correct word from the list below to complete each sentence.

principle, p. 339
liberty, p. 346
legacy, p. 352

9. Abraham Lincoln left a _____ of freedom.

10. Each day of Kwanzaa stands for a _____.

11. Independence Day is a holiday that celebrates our country's _____.

Apply Skills

✔ TEST PREP **Tell Fact from Opinion**
Use the text below and what you have learned about telling fact from opinion to answer each question.

- Sandra Day O'Connor was the first woman on the United States Supreme Court.
- When she was young, she read many books.
- O'Connor is the best judge on the Supreme Court.

12. Which sentence is a FACT?

   A. O'Connor is the best judge on the Supreme Court.

   B. O'Connor was the first woman on the Supreme Court.

   C. all of the above

   D. none of the above

13. Which phrase is a clue that a sentence is an OPINION?

   A. read many books

   B. was a judge

   C. the best judge

   D. on the Supreme Court

Critical Thinking

✔ TEST PREP Write a short paragraph to answer each question below. Use details to support your response.

14. **Draw Conclusions** What can you learn about a country and its people from their holidays and heroes?

15. **Summarize** What are some things that people enjoy doing on holidays?

16. **Conclude** Why do people often feel patriotism toward the country in which they live?

Activities

Art Activity Choose a holiday that you enjoy. Design a banner that you could hang in honor of that day.

Writing Activity Write a description of an American hero you admire. Tell what heroic traits that person has or had.

Technology
Writing Process Tips
Get help with your description at
www.eduplace.com/kids/hmss05/

Culture Where You Live

Customs, ideas, and heroes are part of culture. So are cultural and religious traditions. What are some of your community's traditions? Who are some local heroes? Your community's culture affects your life every day.

My Community's Culture

Customs and Traditions

Languages and Religions

Heroes and Holidays

Spanish mission

Adobe house

Find Out!

Many communities have buildings that show the influence of different cultures.

Explore your local culture.

✓ **Talk to adults you know.**
What languages do they speak? What are some customs and traditions that they follow?

✓ **Read the local newspaper.**
Look for the calendar that lists community events.

✓ **Use the phone book.**
Look up restaurants to find out the kinds of food people enjoy.

✓ **Learn about heroes.**
Find out about a hero from your community.

Use your community handbook to keep track of information you find.

Review and Test Prep

Vocabulary and Main Ideas

✔ **TEST PREP** Write a sentence to answer each question.

1. What can a **legend** teach about a culture?

2. In what ways are the **customs** in Russian schools different from customs in American schools?

3. What are some religious **holidays** celebrated by people in the United States?

4. In what ways do American citizens show their **patriotism** on national holidays?

Critical Thinking

✔ **TEST PREP** Write a short answer for each question. Use details to support your answer.

5. **Draw Conclusions** What can you learn about a culture by studying its customs?

6. **Compare and Contrast** Compare and contrast two national heroes.

Apply Skills

✔ **TEST PREP** Use the list below and what you know about fact and opinion to answer each question.

1. Thomas Edison (1847–1931) was the greatest inventor in American history.

2. Edison made advances in many fields, including electric lighting and movie making.

3. I believe Edison's finest achievement was the invention of the first successful light bulb.

7. Which statement is a fact?

8. What clue words are used in the opinions?

   A. greatest

   B. I believe

   C. finest

   D. all of the above

Unit Activity

The Big Idea

Create a Cultural Calendar

- Research holidays celebrated by cultures around the world.
- Add the information you find to a calendar.
- Label the days of the holidays.
- Tape a sheet of blank paper over the picture area of the calendar and include one or more illustrated facts.

Cinco de Mayo celebrates a great victory for Mexico on May 5, 1862

MAY

S	M	T	W	T	F	S
	1	2	3	4	⑤	6

At the Library

You may find this book at your school or public library.

Harvesting Hope
by Kathleen Krull

Cesar Chavez grows from a quiet boy to a civil rights leader.

Connect to Our Nation

Design a poster honoring a national hero.

- Find information about a hero.
- Make a list of that person's accomplishments and draw or find pictures of the hero you chose.
- Include accomplishments and drawings on your poster.

Technology
Weekly Reader online offers social studies articles. Go to:
www.eduplace.com/kids/hmss/

Read About It

Look in your classroom for these Social Studies Independent Books.

HAPPY NEW YEAR!

Hindu Holiday

CESAR CHAVEZ
by Robert Glassman

References

Citizenship Handbook

Resources

Pledge of Allegiance

A pledge is a type of promise. To show allegiance means to be faithful or loyal to a place or a thing. When we pledge allegiance to the flag of the United States, we promise to be loyal citizens of this country.

The Pledge of Allegiance first appeared in a children's magazine in 1892. It was written by Francis Bellamy. That same year, children recited the Pledge for the first time. You continue that tradition today.

I pledge allegiance to the flag
of the United States of America,
and to the Republic for which it stands,
one Nation under God, indivisible,
with liberty and justice for all.

Prometo lealtad a la bandera
de los Estados Unidos de América,
y a la república que representa,
una nación bajo Dios, indivisible,
con libertad y justicia para todos.

Songs of Our Nation

Who wrote the patriotic songs we sing and why did they do it? There are as many reasons as there are songs.

Our national anthem, "The Star-Spangled Banner," was written by Francis Scott Key. In 1814, this American lawyer watched from a ship as the British attacked Fort McHenry near Baltimore, Maryland. The fight lasted all night. As the morning dawned, Key saw the American flag still flying proudly over the fort. The sight inspired him to write these verses.

"The Star-Spangled Banner"

by Francis Scott Key

O say, can you see, by the dawn's early light,
What so proudly we hailed at the twilight's last gleaming,
Whose broad stripes and bright stars, through the perilous
    fight,
O'er the ramparts we watched were so gallantly streaming?
And the rockets' red glare, the bombs bursting in air,
Gave proof through the night that our flag was still there
O say, does that Star-Spangled Banner yet wave
O'er the land of the free and the home of the brave?

On the shore, dimly seen through the mists of the deep.
Where the foe's haughty host in dread silence reposes,
What is that which the breeze, o'er the towering steep,
As it fitfully blows, half conceals, half discloses?
Now it catches the gleam of the morning's first beam,
In full glory reflected now shines on the stream;
'Tis the Star-Spangled Banner, O long may it wave
O'er the land of the free and the home of the brave!

O thus be it ever when free man shall stand
Between their loved homes and the war's desolation!
Blest with victory and peace, may the heaven-rescued land
Praise the Power that hath made and preserved us as a
     nation.
Then conquer we must, for our cause it is just,
And this be our motto: 'In God is our trust.'
And the Star-Spangled Banner in triumph shall wave
O'er the land of the free and the home of the brave.

Fort McHenry

Have you ever heard the tune to the British national anthem? When Samuel F. Smith heard it in 1832, he wrote words so that Americans could sing it. "America," or "My Country, 'Tis of Thee," quickly became a favorite of many people in the United States. It remains a favorite today.

"America"
("My Country, 'Tis of Thee")

by Samuel F. Smith

My country, 'tis of thee,
Sweet land of liberty,
    Of thee I sing;
Land where my fathers died,
Land of the Pilgrims' pride,
From every mountain-side
    Let freedom ring.

My native country, thee,
Land of the noble free,
    Thy name I love;
I love thy rocks and rills,
Thy woods and templed hills;
My heart with rapture thrills
    Like that above.

In 1893, a teacher from the east named Katharine Lee Bates took a trip west. She loved the beauty of the United States, its mountains, plains, and open skies. Bates's poem became the words for the song, "America the Beautiful."

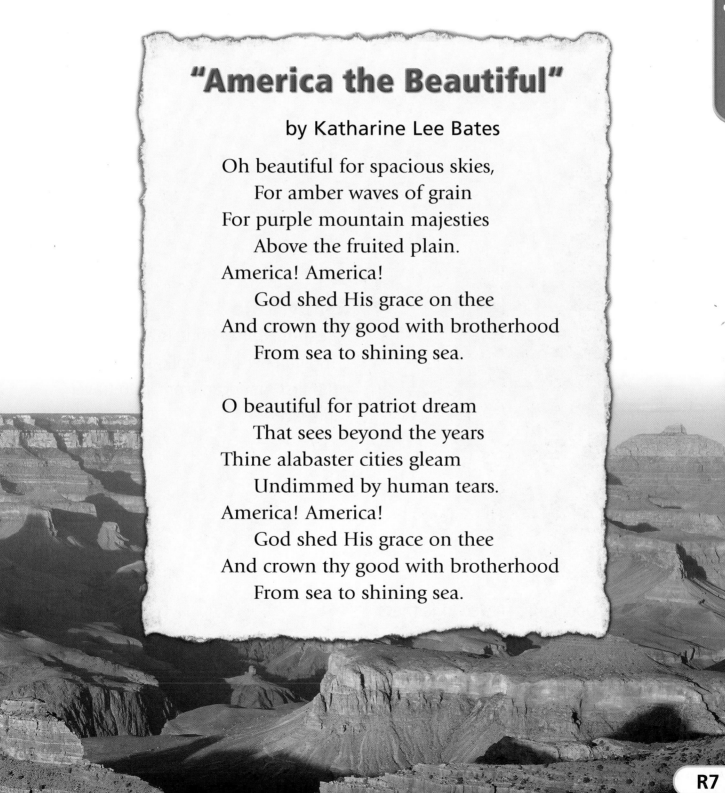

"America the Beautiful"

by Katharine Lee Bates

Oh beautiful for spacious skies,
    For amber waves of grain
For purple mountain majesties
    Above the fruited plain.
America! America!
    God shed His grace on thee
And crown thy good with brotherhood
    From sea to shining sea.

O beautiful for patriot dream
    That sees beyond the years
Thine alabaster cities gleam
    Undimmed by human tears.
America! America!
    God shed His grace on thee
And crown thy good with brotherhood
    From sea to shining sea.

Character Traits

A character trait is something people show by the way they act. A person who acts bravely shows courage, and courage is a character trait.

Character traits are also called "life skills." Life skills can help you do your best, and doing your best leads to reaching your goals.

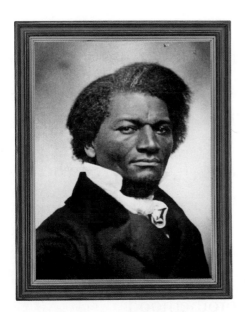

Sally Ride
Responsibility Ride is an astronaut. Through her hard work, she became the first American woman to travel in space.

Frederick Douglass
Fairness Douglass believed in fairness for all people. After escaping from slavery, he spent the rest of his life speaking out against it.

Courage means acting bravely. It takes courage to be honest and tell the truth.

Patriotism is being proud of your country and working for your country's goals.

Responsibility means completing your work. Responsible people are trustworthy. You can count on them.

Respect means paying attention to what other people want and believe. Treating others with respect helps everyone get along.

Fairness means acting to make things fair for everyone.

Civic virtue is good citizenship. It means doing things to help communities live and work well together.

Caring is helping others. Feeling concern is also caring.

Biographical Dictionary

The page number after each entry refers to the place where the person is first mentioned. For more complete references to people, see the Index.

A

Abubakar (ah boo BA kahr), **Abdulsalami** (ab doo sah LAH mee) former leader of Nigeria (p. 357).

Adams, Abigail 1744–1818, wife of John Adams, second President of the United States; noted letter writer (p. 125).

Adams, John 1735–1826, first Vice-President of the United States (1789–1797), second President of the United States (1797–1801) (p. 125).

Adams, John Quincy 1767–1848, son of Abigail and John Adams; sixth President of the United States (1825–1829) (p. 129).

Addams, Jane 1860–1935, worked with the poor of Chicago; won a Nobel Prize in 1931.

Appleseed, Johnny 1775?–1845, American known in legends for planting apple seeds as he traveled; his real name was John Chapman (p. 319).

B

Banneker, Benjamin 1731–1806, American scientist; helped survey Washington, D.C.

Barton, Clara 1821–1912, American who helped injured soldiers during the Civil War; founded the American Red Cross in 1881.

Bates, Katharine Lee 1859–1929, writer, author of "America the Beautiful" (p. R7).

Bethune (buh THOON), **Mary McLeod** 1875–1955, American who worked to improve education for African Americans.

Bloomberg, Michael 1942–, 108th mayor of New York City, took office in 2002 (p. 343).

Brownscombe, Jennie Augusta 1850–1936, American painter and illustrator (p. 123).

Bush, George W. 1946–, 43rd President of the United States (2001–) (p. 248).

C

Cabrillo (kah BREE yoh), **Juan Rodríguez** (wahn roh DREE gehz) died in 1543, explored the coast of California for Spain (p. 112).

Carter, Jimmy 1924–, 39th President of the United States; won the Nobel Peace Prize in 2002 (p. 357).

Champlain (shahm PLAYN), **Samuel de** 1567?–1635, French explorer who sailed to Canada in 1608 (p. 113).

Chavez (CHAH vehz), **Cesar** (SAY sahr) 1927–1993, Mexican American leader who founded the United Farm Workers of America (p. 350).

Columbus, Christopher 1451–1506, explorer who sailed to North America in 1492 (p. 110).

Biographical Dictionary

Douglas, Marjory Stoneman 1890–1998, newspaper reporter from Florida; wrote about the Everglades (p. 43).

Douglass, Frederick 1817–1895, American who escaped from slavery and worked to end it (p. 173).

Edison, Thomas A. 1847–1931, inventor of the electric light bulb and the moving-picture camera (p. 354).

Elizabeth II 1926–, Queen of Great Britain and Canada (p. 134).

Escalante, Jaime 1930–, mathematics teacher who worked with students in East Los Angeles; subject of the 1988 film *Stand and Deliver*.

Flores, Archbishop Patrick 1929–, leader of the Archdiocese of San Antonio, he heads the largest group of Catholic dioceses in the United States.

Ford, Henry 1863–1947, entrepreneur who developed the gasoline-powered automobile (p. 296).

Franklin, Benjamin 1706–1790, author, scientist, and printer; helped write the U.S. Constitution (p. 126).

Fulton, Robert 1765–1815, inventor who built the first useful steamboat in 1807 (p. 161).

Graham, Katharine 1917–2001, publisher of *The Washington Post* newspaper (p. 260).

Guaspari (gwah SPAH ree), **Roberta** music teacher, started the East Harlem Violin Program in New York (p. 356).

Hiawatha (hy uh WAHTH uh) Haudenosaunee leader who helped unite five Haudenosaunee nations (p. 98).

Holmes, Oliver Wendell 1809–1894, Associate justice of the U.S. Supreme Court from 1902–1932.

Hutchinson, Anne 1591–1643, American colonist, sent away from the Massachusetts Bay Colony because of her religious beliefs (p. 119).

Jefferson, Thomas 1743–1826, third President of the United States; wrote the Declaration of Independence (p. 125).

Jesus Christianity was founded on his teachings (p. 340).

Keller, Helen 1880–1968, speaker and writer who was deaf and blind; worked to help people with disabilities (p. 354).

Key, Francis Scott 1779–1843, writer of "The Star-Spangled Banner" (p. R4).

King, Martin Luther, Jr. 1929–1968, American leader who worked for civil rights (p. 348).

Lin, Maya 1959–, sculptor and architect; designed the Vietnam Veterans Memorial in Washington, D.C. (p. 355).

Lincoln, Abraham 1809–1865, 16th President of the United States (p. 242).

Mandela (man DEHL uh), **Nelson** 1918–, South African leader (p. 250).

Mankiller, Wilma 1945–, first female Chief of the Cherokee Nation (p. 91).

Massasoit (mas uh SOIT) 1580?–1661, a Wampanoag leader who helped the settlers at Plymouth (p. 122).

Morse, Samuel 1791–1872, inventor who built the first telegraph line in 1844 (p. 162).

Muhammad (mu HAM ihd), founder of the religion of Islam (p. 341).

Muir (myur), **John** 1838–1914, studied and wrote about land across the United States, including Yosemite Valley in California (p. 42).

O'Connor, Sandra Day 1930–, first female Supreme Court justice (p. 361).

Parks, Rosa 1913–, American civil rights leader.

Pataki, George 1945–, 53rd Governor of New York; took office in 1994 (p. 343).

Peacemaker Haudenosaunee holy man who spread a message of peace to the Haudenosaunee nations (p. 98).

Pulaski (puh LAS kee), **Casimir** (KA sih meer) 1747–1779, Polish general who fought for the colonies in the war against Britain (p. 350).

Ride, Sally 1951–, first American woman in space (p. R9).

Ripken, Calvin Edward, Jr. 1960–, American baseball player known as "Cal", in 1995 he broke the record for consecutive games played.

Robinson, Jack Roosevelt 1919–1972, baseball player known as "Jackie," he was the first African American player in the major leagues.

Roosevelt, Theodore 1858–1919, 26th President of the United States; won the 1906 Nobel Peace Prize (p. 349).

Sacajawea (sak uh juh WEE ah) 1787?–1812, Shoshone guide and interpreter who accompanied the Lewis and Clark Expedition from 1805–1806.

Sequoyah (sih KWOY uh) 1770?–1843, Cherokee leader who invented a system of writing the Cherokee language (p. 92).

Sosa, Samuel 1968–, Dominican-born baseball player known as "Sammy," he broke the record for single-season home runs in 1998.

Sullivan, Anne 1866–1936, teacher of Helen Keller (p. 354).

Tubman, Harriet 1820?–1913, helped many slaves escape to freedom on the Underground Railroad (p. 352).

Walker, Madame C.J. 1876–1919, American entrepreneur; became America's first female independent millionaire (p. 297).

Washington, George 1732–1799, first President of the United States (p. 124).

Williams, Roger 1603?–1683, religious leader, asked to leave Massachusetts because of his beliefs; he later founded Providence, Rhode Island (p. 119).

Woods, Eldrick 1975–, golfer known as "Tiger"; he became the youngest player to win the Masters title in 1997.

Zworykin, Vladimir (VLAD uh mihr ZWAWR ih kihn) 1889–1982, Russian immigrant who helped invent television (p. 177).

Biographical Dictionary

Geographic Terms

bay
an area of a lake or ocean partly surrounded by land

coast
land next to the ocean

coastal plain
an area of low land next to the sea

delta
a triangular area of land formed by deposits of fine soil at the mouth of a river

▲ **desert**
a dry area where few plants grow

gulf
a large area of ocean partly surrounded by land

highland
land that is higher than most of the surrounding land

hill
a raised mass of land, smaller than a mountain

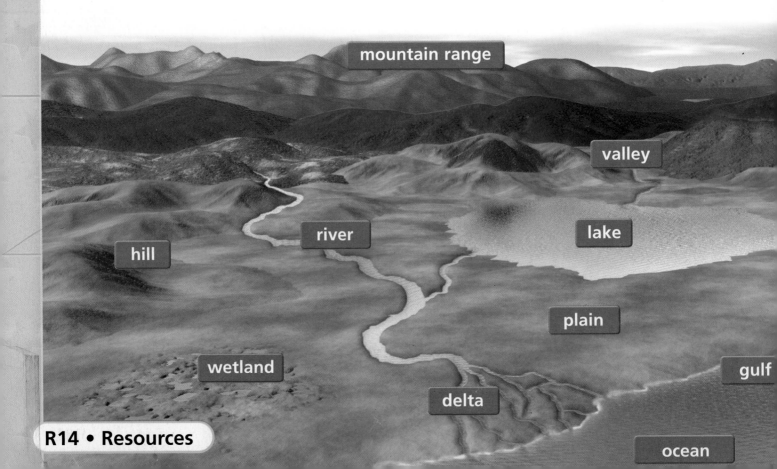

mountain range

valley

river

lake

hill

plain

wetland

delta

gulf

ocean

▲ **island**
a body of land with water all around it

lake
a body of water with land all around it

lowland
land that is lower than most of the surrounding land

mountain
a steeply raised mass of land, much higher than the land around it

mountain range
a row of mountains

ocean or sea
a salty body of water covering a large area of the earth

peninsula
a piece of land nearly surrounded by water

plain
a broad, flat area of land

plateau
a landform that rises above nearby land and may be flat or hilly

river
a large stream of water that runs into a lake, ocean, or another river

sea level
the level of the surface of the ocean

valley
low land between hills or mountains

wetland
a lowland area that is very wet

highland

plateau

lowland

sea level

bay

coastal plain

peninsula

coast

Atlas

The World: Political

ALB.	—Albania
AZER.	—Azerbaijan
BOS. & HERZ.	—Boznia & Herzegovina
CEN. AFR. REP.	—Central African Republic
DEM. REP. OF CONGO	—Democratic Republic of Congo
FR.	—France
IT.	—Italy
LIECH.	—Liechtenstein
LUX.	—Luxembourg
NETH.	—Netherlands
N.Z.	—New Zealand
REP. OF CONGO	—Republic of Congo
SERB. & MONT.	—Serbia & Montenegro
SLOV.	—Slovenia
SWITZ.	—Switzerland
U.A.E.	—United Arab Emirates
U.K.	—United Kingdom
U.S.	—United States

ARCTIC OCEAN

GREENL (Denm

ALASKA (U.S.)

NORTH

CANADA

AMERICA

UNITED STATES

Bermuda (U.K.)

ATLANTI OCEAN

NORTH PACIFIC OCEAN

Midway Islands (U.S.)

Hawaii (U.S.)

MEXICO

Area of index

VENEZUELA COLOMBIA

Galapagos Islands (Ecuador)

ECUADOR

SOUTH

KIRIBATI

Tokelau (N.Z.)

Cook Is. (N.Z.)

SAMOA

American Samoa (U.S.)

French Polynesia (Fr.)

TONGA

Niue (N.Z.)

PERU

AMERICA

BRAZIL

BOLIVIA

PARAGUAY

Pitcairn Islands (Fr.)

SOUTH PACIFIC OCEAN

CHILE

URUGUAY

ARGENTINA

Falkland Islands (U.K.)

South Ge Islands

UNITED STATES

GULF OF MEXICO

BAHAMAS

ATLANTIC OCEAN

MEXICO

CUBA

Turks & Caicos Islands (U.K.)

Virgin Islands (U.S./U.K.)

Cayman Islands (U.K.)

HAITI

DOMINICAN REPUBLIC

St. Martin (Fr./Neth.)

ANTIGUA & BARBUDA

BELIZE

JAMAICA

Puerto Rico (U.S.)

Guadeloupe (Fr.)

DOMINICA

GUATEMALA HONDURAS

CARIBBEAN SEA

Martinique (Fr.)

ST. LUCIA

EL SALVADOR

ST. VINCENT & THE GRENADINES

NICARAGUA

GRENADA

PACIFIC OCEAN

COSTA RICA

PANAMA

TRINIDAD AND TOBAGO

VENEZUELA

km 0 250 500

GUYANA

mi 0 250 500

COLOMBIA

SURINAME

FRENCH GUIANA (Fr.)

ARCTIC OCEAN

RUSSIA

ASIA

ICELAND
(Norway)

Area of Index

EUROPE

KAZAKHSTAN

MONGOLIA

GEORGIA UZBEKISTAN KYRGYZSTAN

ARMENIA TURKMENISTAN

TURKEY AZER. TAJIKISTAN

CHINA

N. KOREA

S. KOREA JAPAN

PACIFIC
OCEAN

TUNISIA CYPRUS SYRIA AFGHANISTAN

LEBANON IRAQ IRAN

ISRAEL JORDAN PAKISTAN

NEPAL BHUTAN

KUWAIT

MOROCCO

ALGERIA LIBYA EGYPT QATAR

WESTERN U.A.E.

SAHARA SAUDI OMAN

(Morocco) ARABIA

MAURITANIA

AFRICA

MALI NIGER

BANGLADESH

INDIA MYANMAR

TAIWAN

Northern
Mariana
Islands
(U.S.)

Guam (U.S.)

MARSHALL
ISLANDS

CHAD ERITREA YEMEN LAOS

SENEGAL BURKINA SUDAN DJIBOUTI THAILAND VIETNAM

GAMBIA FASO NIGERIA CAMBODIA

GUINEA BISSAU GHANA CEN.AFR. ETHIOPIA

GUINEA TOGO REP.

SIERRA IVORY BENIN

LEONE COAST CAMEROON SOMALIA

LIBERIA UGANDA KENYA

EQU. GABON DEM. RWANDA

GUINEA REP. OF REP. BURUNDI

SAO TOME CONGO OF TANZANIA

AND PRINCIPE CONGO

FEDERATED STATES
OF MICRONESIA

PALAU

KIRIBATI

NAURU

SRI LANKA BRUNEI

MALAYSIA

MALDIVES

SINGAPORE

INDONESIA

PAPUA
NEW
GUINEA

EAST
TIMOR

SOLOMON
ISLANDS

TUVALU

ANGOLA MALAWI COMOROS

ZAMBIA

ZIMBABWE MOZAMBIQUE

BOTSWANA MADAGASCAR MAURITIUS

NAMIBIA Reunion
(Fr.)

SWAZILAND

LESOTHO

SOUTH AFRICA

INDIAN
OCEAN

VANUATU

New
Caledonia
(Fr.)

FIJI

AUSTRALIA

km 0   1000   2000

mi 0   1000   2000

ATLANTIC
OCEAN

NEW
ZEALAND

ANTARCTICA

FINLAND

SWEDEN

NORWAY

RUSSIA

ESTONIA

LATVIA

LITHUANIA

RUSSIA

BELARUS

km 0 150 300

mi 0   150 300

NORTH
SEA

DENMARK

UNITED
KINGDOM

IRELAND NETH.

GERMANY POLAND

BELGIUM

LUX. CZECH

REPUBLIC

LIECH. AUSTRIA SLOVAKIA

FRANCE SWITZ. HUNGARY

SLOV.

SAN CROATIA

MARINO BOS. &

HERZ. SERB. &

MONT.

UKRAINE

MOLDOVA

ROMANIA

ATLANTIC
OCEAN

MONACO

Corsica
(Fr.)

PORTUGAL

SPAIN

GIBRALTAR
(U.K.)

Balearic
Islands
(Fr.)

Sardinia
(It.)

ITALY

Sicily (It.)

BULGARIA

MACEDONIA

ALB.

GREECE TURKEY

MEDITERRANEAN SEA

MOROCCO ALGERIA TUNISIA

The World: Physical

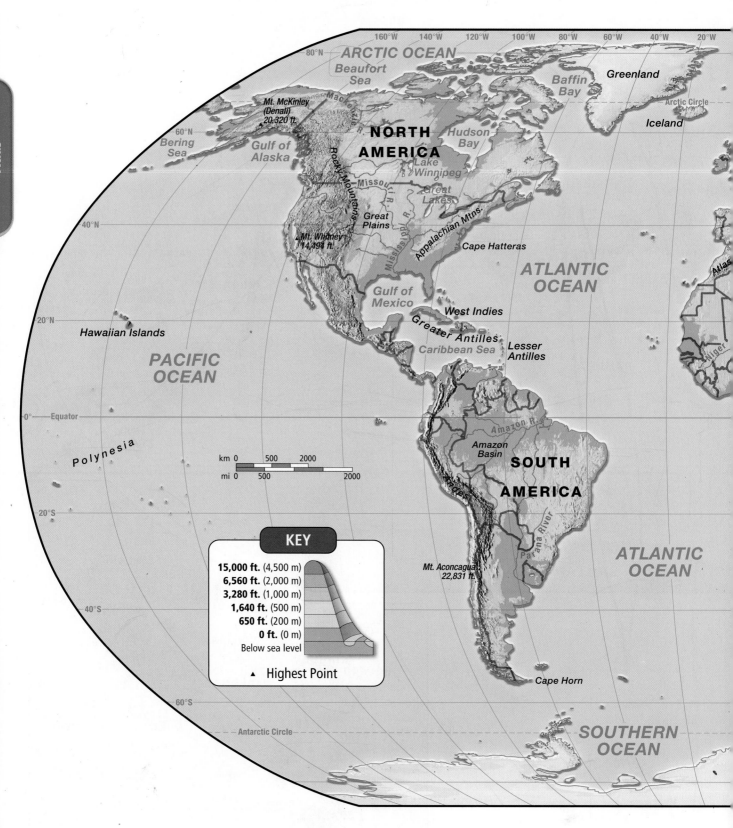

ARCTIC OCEAN

Beaufort Sea

Baffin Bay

Greenland

Arctic Circle

Iceland

Mt. McKinley (Denali) 20,320 ft.

Mackenzie R.

NORTH AMERICA

Hudson Bay

Bering Sea

Gulf of Alaska

Rocky Mountains

Lake Winnipeg

Missouri R.

Great Lakes

Great Plains

Mt. Whitney 14,494 ft.

Mississippi R.

Appalachian Mtns.

Cape Hatteras

ATLANTIC OCEAN

Atlas

Hawaiian Islands

Gulf of Mexico

West Indies

Greater Antilles

Lesser Antilles

Caribbean Sea

Niger

PACIFIC OCEAN

Equator

Amazon R.

Amazon Basin

SOUTH AMERICA

Polynesia

Andes

Parana River

ATLANTIC OCEAN

Mt. Aconcagua 22,831 ft.

KEY

15,000 ft. (4,500 m)
6,560 ft. (2,000 m)
3,280 ft. (1,000 m)
1,640 ft. (500 m)
650 ft. (200 m)
0 ft. (0 m)
Below sea level

▲ Highest Point

km 0   500   2000
mi 0   500   2000

Cape Horn

SOUTHERN OCEAN

Antarctic Circle

Atlas

ARCTIC OCEAN

80°N

20°E 40°E 60°E 80°E 100°E 120°E 140°E 160°E

Barents
Sea

60°N

EUROPE

Northern European Plain

Ural Mountains

Ob River

Yenisey River

ASIA

Lake
Baikal

Sea of
Okhotsk

Amur River

Volga River

Danube

Alps

Caspian Sea

Mt. Elbrus
18,510 ft.

Aral
Sea

40°N

Black Sea

Caucasus
Mountains

Hwang He

Sea
of
Japan

Mtns.

Mediterranean Sea

Himalaya Mountains

Mt. Everest
29,035 ft.

Chang Jiang

East
China
Sea

PACIFIC
OCEAN

SAHARA

Red Sea

Ganges River

20°N

SAHEL

Nile River

Arabian
Sea

Bay of
Bengal

South
China
Sea

Philippine Islands

Micronesia

River

AFRICA

Lake
Victoria

Mt. Kilimanjaro
19,340 ft.

Sumatra

Borneo

Equator 0°

Congo River

Java

New Guinea

Melanesia

INDIAN
OCEAN

Madagascar

Coral
Sea

Great
Sandy
Desert

20°S

Kalahari
Desert

AUSTRALIA

Darling River

Tasman
Sea

Cape of
Good Hope

Mt. Kosciusko
7,310 ft.

North Island

South Island

Prime Meridian

60°S

Antarctic Circle

ANTARCTICA

Atlas

R19

Western Hemisphere: Political

ARCTIC OCEAN

Beaufort Sea

GREENLAND (DENMARK)

Alaska (U.S.)

Hudson Bay

Labrador Sea

CANADA

Great Lakes

Ottawa

Great Salt Lake

UNITED STATES

Washington, D.C.

ATLANTIC OCEAN

Tropic of Cancer

Hawaii (U.S.)

Gulf of Mexico

BAHAMAS

Havana

MEXICO

CUBA

HAITI

Mexico City

BELIZE

Kingston

DOMINICAN REPUBLIC

GUATEMALA

Belmopan

Santo Domingo

U.S. VIRGIN ISLANDS

ST. KITTS AND NEVIS

Guatemala City

JAMAICA

Tegucigalpa

Port-Au-Prince

ST. LUCIA

EL SALVADOR

San Salvador

Managua

BARBADOS

HONDURAS

San José

Panama City

GRENADA

NICARAGUA

COSTA RICA

VENEZUELA

Caracas

Georgetown

Paramaribo

PANAMA

Bogotá

Cayenne

PACIFIC OCEAN

COLOMBIA

GUYANA

SURINAME

FRENCH GUIANA (FRANCE)

Galápagos Is. (Ecuador)

ECUADOR

Quito

Equator

BRAZIL

French Polynesia (France)

Lima

PERU

La Paz

Brasília

BOLIVIA

Sucre

Tropic of Capricorn

PARAGUAY

Asunción

CHILE

N
W   E
S

URUGUAY

Santiago

Buenos Aires

Montevideo

ARGENTINA

Falkland Is. (U.K.)

KEY

⊛ National capital

—— National border

km 0   500   1000

mi 0   500   1000

South Georgia (U.K.)

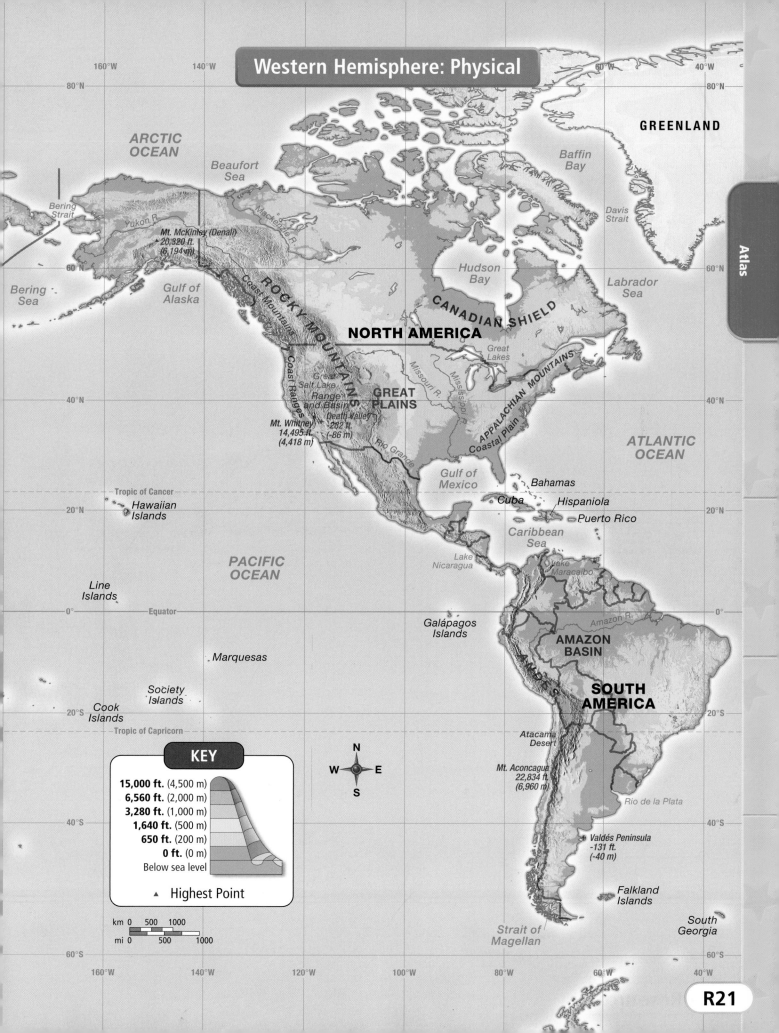

Western Hemisphere: Physical

ARCTIC OCEAN

GREENLAND

Beaufort Sea

Baffin Bay

Davis Strait

Bering Strait

Yukon R.

Mackenzie R.

Mt. McKinley (Denali)
▲ 20,320 ft.
(6,194 m)

Hudson Bay

Labrador Sea

Bering Sea

Gulf of Alaska

Coast Mountains

ROCKY MOUNTAINS

CANADIAN SHIELD

NORTH AMERICA

Great Lakes

Coast Ranges

Great Salt Lake

Range and Basin

Missouri R.

Mississippi R.

APPALACHIAN MOUNTAINS

GREAT PLAINS

Death Valley
282 ft.
(-86 m)

Mt. Whitney
14,495 ft.
(4,418 m)

Rio Grande

Coastal Plain

ATLANTIC OCEAN

Tropic of Cancer

Hawaiian Islands

Gulf of Mexico

Bahamas

Cuba

Hispaniola

Puerto Rico

Caribbean Sea

Lake Nicaragua

PACIFIC OCEAN

Line Islands

Equator

Galápagos Islands

Lake Maracaibo

AMAZON BASIN

Amazon R.

Marquesas

SOUTH AMERICA

Society Islands

Cook Islands

Tropic of Capricorn

Atacama Desert

Mt. Aconcagua
22,834 ft.
(6,960 m)

Rio de la Plata

KEY

15,000 ft. (4,500 m)	
6,560 ft. (2,000 m)	
3,280 ft. (1,000 m)	
1,640 ft. (500 m)	
650 ft. (200 m)	
0 ft. (0 m)	
Below sea level	

▲ Highest Point

Valdés Peninsula
-131 ft.
(-40 m)

Falkland Islands

N
W · E
S

km 0   500   1000
mi 0   500   1000

Strait of Magellan

South Georgia

Atlas

ARCTIC OCEAN

RUSSIA

BROOKS RANGE

ALASKA
(U.S.)

Mt. McKinley
(Denali)

60°N

Bering
Sea

ROCKY MOUNTAINS

CN	—Connecticut
DE	—Delaware
IN	—Indiana
LA	—Louisiana
MA	—Massachusetts
MD	—Maryland
MS	—Mississippi
NH	—New Hampshire
NJ	—New Jersey
PA	—Pennsylvania
RI	—Rhode Island
VT	—Vermont
WV	—West Virginia

WASHINGTON

Mt. Rainier
Mt. St. Helens

IDAH

OREGON

PACIFIC
OCEAN

40°N

CALIFORNIA

NEVADA

COAST RANGES

SIERRA NEVADA

CENTRAL VALLEY

GREAT
BASIN

DEATH
VALLEY

KEY

⊛ National capital

★ State capital

• Major city

▲ Mountain peak

National boundary

State boundary

N
W · E
S

km 0   150   300
mi 0   150   300

Mauna Loa
HAWAII
(U.S.)

20°N

160°W   140°W   120°W

Baffin
Bay

GREENLAND
(U.S.)

Labrador
Sea

60°N

Hudson
Bay

CANADA

Lake
Winnipeg

MONTANA   NORTH DAKOTA   MINNESOTA

Great
Lakes

St. Lawrence River

SOUTH DAKOTA

WISCONSIN

MICHIGAN

Ottawa

MAINE

WYOMING

Mt. Washington

NEW
YORK

VT
NH

Missouri River

NEBRASKA   IOWA

MA
CT   RI

ROCKY MOUNTAINS

ILLINOIS   IN

OHIO

PA

NJ

40°N

UTAH

Pike's Peak

KANSAS

CENTRAL
PLAINS

WV

MD   DE

COLORADO

Arkansas River

Ohio River

Washington, D.C.

GRAND
CANYON

MISSOURI

KENTUCKY

VIRGINIA

ARKANSAS

TENNESSEE

NORTH CAROLINA

ARIZONA

OKLAHOMA

Mississippi River

APPALACHIAN MOUNTAINS

SOUTH
CAROLINA

NEW
MEXICO

MS

ALABAMA

GEORGIA

ATLANTIC
OCEAN

TEXAS

LA

Rio Grande

GULF COASTAL PLAIN

MEXICO

SIERRA MADRE OCCIDENTAL

SIERRA MADRE ORIENTAL

FLORIDA

Gulf of
Mexico

B A H A M A S

C U B A

PUERTO RICO
(U.S.)

20°N

Mexico City

80°W

60°W

R23

United States: Political

ARCTIC OCEAN

RUSSIA

ALASKA

CANADA

Yukon R.

Fairbanks

Anchorage

Juneau

PACIFIC OCEAN

Aleutian Islands

km 0 250 500
mi 0 250 500

N
W E
S

WASHINGTON

Seattle
Olympia ★

Portland
★ Salem

Columbia R.

OREGON

IDAHO

Boise ★

Pocatello

Snake R.

MONTANA

Helena ★

Billings

WYOMING

Casper

Cheyenne ★

NEVADA

Reno
Carson City ★

Sacramento ★

San Francisco

CALIFORNIA

Las Vegas

Los Angeles

San Diego

UTAH

Salt Lake City ★

Provo

Colorado R.

COLORADO

Denver ★

Colorado Springs

Pueblo

ARIZONA

Phoenix ★

Tucson

Santa Fe ★
Albuquerque

NEW MEXICO

El Paso

PACIFIC OCEAN

KEY

⊛ National capital
★ State capital
• Major city
— National boundary
— State boundary

HAWAII

Kauai

Niihau

Oahu Kailua
Honolulu ★ Molokai

Lanai Maui

Kahoolawe

PACIFIC OCEAN

Hilo
Hawaii

km 0 50 100
mi 0 50 100

MEXICO

Gulf of California

Rio Grande

CANADA

NORTH DAKOTA
• Bismarck
Fargo

SOUTH DAKOTA
Pierre
Sioux Falls

MINNESOTA
St. Paul
Minneapolis

L. Superior

WISCONSIN
Madison
Milwaukee

MICHIGAN
Grand Rapids
Lansing

L. Michigan

L. Huron

Detroit

St. Lawrence R.

NEW HAMPSHIRE
VERMONT
Burlington ★ Montpelier

MAINE
Augusta
Portland
Concord
Manchester

NEW YORK
Albany
Rochester
Buffalo

MASSACHUSETTS
Boston
Providence
Hartford
New Haven

RHODE ISLAND
CONNECTICUT

IOWA
Cedar Rapids
Des Moines

NEBRASKA
Omaha
Lincoln

Missouri R.

ILLINOIS
Springfield
Chicago

INDIANA
Indianapolis

OHIO
Columbus
Cincinnati

L. Erie
Cleveland

PENNSYLVANIA
Harrisburg
Pittsburgh

Newark
New York
Trenton
Philadelphia

NEW JERSEY
DELAWARE
Dover

Baltimore
Annapolis
Washington, D.C.
MARYLAND

KANSAS
Kansas City
Topeka

Kansas City
Jefferson City
St. Louis

MISSOURI

Louisville
Frankfort

KENTUCKY

Ohio R.

WEST VIRGINIA
Charleston

Richmond
Norfolk

VIRGINIA

Greensboro
Raleigh

NORTH CAROLINA

OKLAHOMA
Tulsa
Oklahoma City

Fort Smith

ARKANSAS
Little Rock

Mississippi R.

Memphis

Nashville

TENNESSEE

Columbia

SOUTH CAROLINA
Charleston

TEXAS
Dallas
Austin
Houston
San Antonio

LOUISIANA
Baton Rouge
New Orleans

MISSISSIPPI
Jackson

Birmingham
Montgomery

ALABAMA
Mobile

GEORGIA
Atlanta
Savannah

Jacksonville
Tallahassee

FLORIDA
Tampa
Miami

ATLANTIC OCEAN

Gulf of Mexico

BAHAMAS

CUBA

km 0 100 200 300 400 500
mi 0   100   200   300   400   500

United States: Physical

Alaska Inset
ARCTIC OCEAN

RUSSIA

Brooks Range

Yukon R.

CANADA

Bering Strait

Mt. McKinley
(Denali)
20,320 ft.

Alaska Range

Bering
Sea

Gulf of
Alaska

Aleutian
Islands

Kodiak Is.

km 0   250   500
mi 0   250   500

70°N
60°N
170°W   160°W   150°W   140°W

PACIFIC
OCEAN

San Francisco
Bay

Channel Islands

N
W   E
S

35°N
30°N
25°N

LEGEND

15,000 ft. (4,500 m)
6,560 ft. (2,000 m)
3,280 ft. (1,000 m)
1,640 ft. (500 m)
650 ft. (200 m)
0 ft. (0 m)
Below sea level

▲ Highest Point

CASCADE   RANGE

COLUMBIA

PLATEAU

Mt. Rainier
14,410 ft.

Columbia R.

Mt. Hood
11,239 ft.

COAST

Mt. Shasta
14,162 ft.

Sacramento R.

CENTRAL
VALLEY

SIERRA   NEVADA

San Joaquin R.

RANGES

Mt. Whitney
14,494 ft.

Death Valley
282 ft. below sea level

Mojave
Desert

BASIN
AND
RANGE

BITTERROOT RANGE

Snake River

WASATCH RANGE

Green River

Colorado River

Gila River

Sonoran
Desert

Grand
Canyon

Painted
Desert

Colorado
Plateau

CONTINENTAL DIVIDE

Missouri   River

Yellowstone River

ROCKY   MOUNTAINS

BIGHORN MTNS.

GREAT   PLAINS

Black
Hills

Badlands

Pikes Peak
14,110 ft.

SANGRE DE
CRISTO MTNS.

Llano
Estacado

Rio Grande

Pecos River

Edwards
Plateau

110°W
110°W
105°W
115°W

MEXICO

Gulf of California

Tropic of Cancer

Hawaii Inset

160°W   155°W

Kauai
Niihau
Oahu
Molokai
Lanai   Maui
Kahoolawe
Hawaii
Mauna Kea
13,796 ft.
Mauna Loa
13,678 ft.

PACIFIC OCEAN

km 0   50   100
mi 0   50   100

20°N

CANADA

95°W · 90°W · 85°W · 80°W · 75°W · 70°W · 65°W · 50°N

St. Lawrence River

Mesabi Range

Lake Superior

Mt. Washington 6,288 ft.
▲ White Mtns.

Adirondack Mountains

L. Ontario

Lake Michigan

Lake Huron

Connecticut R.

Hudson R.

Catskill Mtns.

ALLEGHENY PLATEAU

Nantucket
Martha's Vineyard

Lake Erie

Sand Hills

Mississippi River

Des Moines River

Missouri River

Platte River

Long Island

Delaware River
Susquehanna River

Delaware Bay

CENTRAL PLAINS

Wabash River

Ohio R.

A P P A L A C H I A N   M O U N T A I N S

Chesapeake Bay

35°N

OZARK PLATEAU

Arkansas River

Mississippi River

Cumberland Plateau

Mt. Mitchell 6,684 ft.

Tennessee R.

BLUE RIDGE MOUNTAINS

FALL LINE

ATLANTIC COASTAL PLAIN

ATLANTIC OCEAN

OUACHITA MOUNTAINS

Red River

Savannah R.

Oconee R.

Sabine River

Tombigbee R.

Pearl River

Alabama R.

Chattahoochee River

Altamaha R.

30°N

Brazos River

Colorado River

G U L F   C O A S T A L   P L A I N

Mobile Bay

Pensacola Bay

Galveston Bay

Gulf of Mexico

Tampa Bay

25°N

Everglades

BAHAMAS

Florida Keys

km 0   100   200   300   400   500
mi 0   100   200   300   400   500

Tropic of Cancer

CUBA

95°W · 90°W · 85°W · 75°W

Gazetteer

Acworth A suburb in Georgia near the city of Atlanta. (34°N, 84°W) page 18

Africa The earth's second-largest continent. (10°N, 22°E) page 185

Alaska A state in the northwestern United States. (64°N, 150°W) page 3

Alps Mountain chain of south central Europe. (46°N, 8°E)

Amazon River The second-longest river in the world. It flows from northern Peru across Brazil. (0°S, 49°W) page 184

Anchorage The largest city in Alaska. It is in the southern part of the state on Cook Inlet. (61°N, 150°W) page 30

Angel Island An island in San Francisco Bay. It once had a government center for immigrants. (38°N, 122°W) page 175

Antarctica A continent on the South Pole. (75°S, 15°E)

Antarctic Circle Line of latitude that encircles Antarctica. (66°S)

Appalachian Mountains A mountain range west of the Atlantic Coastal Plain. (37°N, 82°W) page 40

Arctic Circle Line of latitude just south of the North Pole. (66°N)

Arizona A state in the southwestern United States. Its capital is Phoenix. (34°N, 113°W) page 74

Asia The earth's largest continent. It is separated from Europe by the Ural Mountains. (50°N, 100°E) page 110

Atlanta The capital and largest city in Georgia. (34°N, 84°W) page 17

Atlantic Coastal Plain A plains region along the Atlantic coast. (35°N, 78°W) page 40

Atlantic Ocean The second-largest ocean in the world. (5°S, 25°W) page 41

Australia The earth's smallest continent. (25°S, 133°E)

Basin and Range A region of desert and mountains east of the Sierra Nevada. (32°N, 108°W) page 37

Brazil A country in South America. Its capital is Brasilia. (9°S, 53°W) page 184

California A western state on the Pacific coast. Its capital is Sacramento. (38°N, 121°W) page 46

Cambodia A country of southeast Asia on the Gulf of Siam. Its capital is Phnom Penh. (13°N, 105°E) page 320

Canada The country to the north of the United States. Its capital is Ottawa. (50°N, 100°W) page 101

Central Plains A plains region west of the Appalachian Mountains. (37°N, 78°W) page 38

Central Valley A valley of central California between the Sierra Nevada and the Coast Ranges. (34°N, 119°W) page 36

China A country in eastern Asia. Beijing is its capital. (37°N, 93°E) page 174

Coast Ranges A series of mountain ranges in western North America. They extend from southeast Alaska to lower California. (41°N, 123°W) page 36

Colorado Plateau A plateau region in the southwestern United States. (40°N, 107°W) page 37

Death Valley A desert region in the Basin and Range section of California. It is the hottest place in the United States. (35°N, 115°W) page 37

Egypt A country on the Mediterranean Sea in northeast Africa. Its capital is Cairo. (27°N, 30°E) page 320

Ellis Island An island in New York Harbor where immigrants arrived. (41°N, 74°W) page 176

England A part of the United Kingdom on the island of Great Britain. London is the capital and largest city. (52°N, 2°W) page 118

Europe The sixth-largest continent. It is located between Asia and the Atlantic Ocean. (50°N, 15°W) page 110

Everglades A vast wetland in Florida. (26°N, 80°W) page 41

Feather River A river in northern central California. (40°N, 121°W) page 46

Florida A southeastern state bordered by the Gulf of Mexico and the Atlantic Ocean. Its capital is Tallahassee. (27°N, 82°W) page 41

France A country in Europe. Its capital is Paris. (47°N, 1°E) page 111

Fulton County A county in the state of Georgia. (33°N, 84°W) page 229

Georgia A state in the southeastern United States. Atlanta is its capital and largest city. (32°N, 81°W) page 17

Germany A country in Europe. Its capital is Berlin. (51°N, 10°E) page 151

Grand Canyon A deep canyon in northwest Arizona. (36°N, 112°W) page 37

Great Britain An island off the western coast of Europe. It includes England, Scotland, and Wales. (50°N, 0°W) page 124

Great Lakes A group of five large lakes between the United States and Canada. (45°N, 83°W) page 39

Great Plains A vast region of grasslands east of the Rocky Mountains. (45°N, 104°W) page 38

Gulf Coastal Plain A plain that borders the Gulf of Mexico from Florida to southern Texas. (30°N, 90°W) page 38

Gulf of Mexico A part of the Atlantic Ocean in southeast North America. (25°N, 94°W) page 39

Haiti A country of the West Indies. Port-au-Prince is the capital. (18°N, 69°W) page 320

Ireland A country in the northern Atlantic Ocean. It lies west of Great Britain. (53°N, 8°W) page 151

Japan A country off the northeast coast of Asia. Its capital is Tokyo. (37°N, 134°E) page 175

Gazetteer

Korea A peninsula of eastern Asia. It is divided into the countries of South Korea and North Korea. (37°N, 127°E) page 175

Maine A state in the northeastern United States. Its capital is Augusta. (45°N, 70°W) page 40

Massachusetts A state in the northeastern United States. Its capital is Boston. (42°N, 73°W) page 40

Mekong River A river of southeast Asia that flows from China through southern Vietnam. (11°N, 105°E)

Mexico A country in North America, south of the United States. Its capital is Mexico City. (24°N, 104°W) page 54

Mexico City The capital of Mexico. (19°N, 99°W) page 54

Miami A city in southeastern Florida. (26°N, 80°W) page 46

Mississippi River A large river in the United States. It begins in northern Minnesota and flows into the Gulf of Mexico. (32°N, 92°W) page 39

Missouri A state of the central United States. Its capital is Jefferson City. (38°N, 94°W) page 150

Missouri River A river in the United States. It flows from the Rocky Mountains to the Mississippi River. (38°N, 90°W) page 150

Montreal A city in southeastern Canada. It is Canada's largest city. (45°N, 73°W) page 134

Moscow The capital of Russia. It is in the west-central part of the country. (55°N, 37°E) page 326

New England A region of six states of the northeastern United States. (43°N, 71°W) page 119

New Mexico A state in the southwestern United States. Its capital is Santa Fe. (35°N, 107°W) page 74

New York A state in the northeastern United States. Its capital is Albany. (43°N, 78°W) page 101

New York City A city in southern New York State. It is the largest city in the United States. (41°N, 74°W) page 16

Nile River A river of eastern Africa. It is the longest river in the world. (30°N, 31°E) page 29

North America The earth's third-largest continent. (48°N, 97°W) page 110

North Carolina A state in the southeastern United States. Its capital is Raleigh. (36°N, 82°W) page 91

Oklahoma A state in the south-central United States. Its capital is Oklahoma City. (36°N, 98°W) page 90

Oregon A state in the northwestern United States. Its capital is Salem. (44°N, 122°W) page 160

Oroville Dam A dam on the Feather River in California. (39°N, 121°W) page 46

Pacific Ocean The largest ocean in the world. (0°N, 170°W) page 36

Paradise Valley A town in southwest central Arizona. (33°N, 111°W) page 204

Pennsylvania A state in the eastern United States. Its capital is Harrisburg. (41°N, 78°W) page 124

Philadelphia The largest city in the state of Pennsylvania. (40°N, 75°W) page 124

Philippines A country of eastern Asia. Its capital is Manila. (14°N, 125°E) page 175

Plymouth A town on the coast of southern Massachusetts. (42°N, 70°W) page 118

Portugal A country of Europe. Its capital is Lisbon. (38°N, 8°W) page 111

Quebec A province in Canada. (47°N, 71°W) page 113

Rocky Mountains A mountain region in the western United States. (50°N, 114°W) page 37

Russia A country of eastern Europe and northern Asia. Its capital is Moscow. (61°N, 60°E) page 326

San Diego Bay A bay of the Pacific Ocean near the border between Mexico and the United States. (32°N, 117°W) page 112

São Paulo A city in southeast Brazil. It is the largest city in South America. (23°S, 43°W) page 186

Sierra Nevada A mountain range in California east of the Coast Ranges. (39°N, 20°W) page 36

South Africa A country at the southern tip of Africa. (30°S, 26°E) page 250

South America The earth's fourth-largest continent. (14°S, 55°W) page 184

Spain A country in Europe. Its capital is Madrid. (40°N, 5°W) page 55

Sparta A rural community in the state of Georgia. (33°N, 83°W) page 19

St. Louis A city in eastern Missouri. It sits near the Mississippi River. (38°N, 90°W) page 150

St. Petersburg A city in west-central Florida on Tampa Bay. (27°N, 82°W) page 30

Sudan A country of northeast Africa. Khartoum is its capital. (15°N, 30°E) page 320

Syracuse A city of central New York. (43°N, 76°W) page 98

Tenochtitlán An ancient city in Mexico built by the Aztecs. It later became the site of Mexico City. (19°N, 99°W) page 55

Thailand A country in southeast Asia. Its capital is Bangkok. (15°N, 100°E) page 319

United States A country in central and northwestern North America. Its capital is Washington, D.C. (38°N, 110°W) page 8

Washington, D.C. The capital of the United States. It is located on the Potomac River between Virginia and Maryland. (39°N, 77°W) page 240

West Indies A group of islands between southeast North America and northern South America. (19°N, 78°W) page 111

Wisconsin A state in the north-central United States. Its capital is Madison. (44°N, 89°W) page 101

Glossary

adapt (uh DAPT) to change the way you live to fit a new place. (p. 75)

ambassador (am BAS uh dawr) a person who represents his or her government in another country. (p. 248)

ancestor (AN sehs tuhr) a relative who was born long ago. (p. 186)

assembly line (uh SEHM blee lyn) a team of specialized workers. (p. 294)

barter (BAHR tuhr) to trade one item for another. (p. 84)

bay (bay) ocean water that extends into the land. (p. 28)

budget (BUHJ iht) a plan for using money. (p. 268)

canal (kuh NAL) a waterway made by people. (p. 55)

canyon (CAN yuhn) a V-shaped valley made by a river. (p. 37)

capital (KAP iht tl) the city where a state or nation makes its laws. (p. 54)

capital resources (KAP iht tl REE sawrs ehz) things made by people that help workers make goods or provide services. (p. 293)

capitol (KAP iht tl) the building where leaders of government meet to make laws. (p. 234)

cause (kawz) something that makes an event happen. (p. 94)

century (SEHN chuh ree) a period of 100 years. (p. 116)

ceremony (SEHR uh moh nee) a formal act or event that honors a people's beliefs. (p. 77)

citizen (SIHT ih zuhn) an official member of a community, state, or country. (p. 8)

clan (klan) an extended family. (p. 97)

climate (KLY miht) the weather of a place over a long period of time. (p. 30)

climate map (KLY miht map) a map that shows the usual weather of an area. (p. 34)

coast (kohst) the land next to the ocean. (p. 36)

colony (KAHL uh nee) a community belonging to a distant country. (p. 118)

commissioner (kuh MIHSH uh nuhr) a person who runs a government, such as a county, or a government department. (p. 229)

common good (KAHM uhn GUD) whatever helps the most people in a community. (p. 203)

communication (kuh myoon ih KAY shuhn) the ways in which people exchange information. (p. 162)

community (kuh MYOO nih tee) a place where people live, work, and play together. (p. 6)

compass rose (KUHM puhs ROHZ) a symbol that shows the four main directions on a map. (p. 14)

competition (kahm pih TIHSH uhn) the effort sellers make to attract buyers. (p. 275)

compromise (KAHM pruh myz) a plan that everyone agrees on. (p. 210)

conflict (KAHN flihkt) a disagreement. (p. 210)

constitution (kahn stih TOO shuhn) basic laws and ideas that a government and its people follow. (p. 100)

consumer (kuhn SOO muhr) someone who buys goods. (p. 287)

continent (KAHN tuh nuhnt) one of seven huge landmasses of the earth.

costs (kawsts) the money a business pays for workers, machines, and materials. (p. 152)

council (KOWN suhl) a group of officials who make rules or laws. (p. 228)

county (KOWN tee) area of a state that includes several communities. (p. 229)

court (kawrt) a place where questions about the law are answered. (p. 235)

culture (KUHL chuhr) the way of life or beliefs, ideas, and language of a group of people. (p. 76)

custom (KUHS tuhm) something that members of a group usually do. (p. 328)

decade (DEHK ayd) a period of ten years. (p. 116)

decision (dih SIHZH uhn) the act of making up one's mind. (p. 130)

demand (dih MAND) the amount of something consumers are willing to buy for a certain price. (p. 289)

democracy (dih MAHK ruh see) a government in which the people govern themselves. (p. 126)

desert (DEHZ uhrt) a dry area where little rain falls and few plants grow. (p. 37)

diversity (dih VUR sih tee) variety. (p. 172)

economy (ih KAHN uh mee) the way that people make, buy, sell, and use things. (p. 84)

effect (ih FEHKT) what happens as the result of a cause. (p. 94)

election (ih LEHK shuhn) the process by which citizens vote for people to represent them. (p. 225)

entrepreneur (AHN truh pruh nur) a person who takes a risk, or chance, and starts a business. (p. 152)

environment (ehn VY uhrn muhnt) the water, soil, air, and living things around you. (p. 44)

equator (ih KWAY tuhr) a line of latitude that circles the globe exactly halfway between the North and South poles. (p. 332)

erosion (ih ROH zhuhn) the process by which wind or water wear away the land over time. (p. 26)

ethnic group (EHTH nikh groop) people who have their own language and culture. (p. 321)

executive branch (ihg ZEHK yuh tihv branch) the part of national government headed by the President. (p. 241)

explorer (ihk SPLAWR uhr) a person who travels to learn about new places. (p. 111)

export (EHK spawrt) to send goods or services to another country for trade or sale. (p. 301)

fact (fakt) something that can be proven. (p. 358)

factory (FAHK tuh ree) a building where workers make goods. (p. 294)

flow chart (FLOH chahrt) a diagram that shows how something is done. (p. 298)

flow resources (FLOW REE sawrs ehz) renewable resources that cannot be used all the time. (p. 45)

free enterprise (free EHN tuhr pryz) the right people have to make choices to make, sell, or buy, whatever they want and can afford. (p. 288)

freedom of assembly (FREE duhm uhv uh SEHM blee) the right of citizens to meet together whenever they choose. (p. 213)

freedom of religion (FREE duhm uhv rih LIHJ uhn) the right to practice a religion or no religion at all. (p. 213)

generation (jehn uh RAY shuhn) a group of people born and living around the same time. (p. 186)

geography (jee AHG ruh fee) the study of people, places, and the earth. (p. 26)

glossary (GLAW suh ree) an alphabetical list of difficult or special words and their meanings. (p. 60)

goods (gudz) things people buy or sell. (p. 151)

government (GUHV uhrn muhnt) an organization that makes laws and keeps order. (p. 98)

governor (GUHV uhr nuhr) the person elected as head of a state. (p. 235)

gulf (guhlf) a large section of ocean. (p. 28)

hemisphere (HEHM ih sfihr) one half of the earth's surface.

heritage (HEHR ih tihj) the history, ideas, and beliefs that people receive from the past. (p. 134)

history (HIHS tuh ree) the record of past events. (p. 89)

holiday (HAHL ih day) a time to celebrate a special event or person. (p. 338)

honor (AHN uhr) to show great respect. (p. 344)

human resources (HYOO muhn REE sawrs ehz) the skills, knowledge, and hard work that people bring to their jobs. (p. 293)

immigrant (IHM ih gruhnt) someone who leaves one country and moves to another. (p. 174)

Glossary

import (ihm PAWRT) to buy goods or services from sellers in other countries. (p. 301)

income (IHN kuhm) money people earn for work. (p. 268)

independence (IHN dih pehn duhns) freedom. (p. 124)

index (IHN dehks) an alphabetical list at the end of a book. (p. 60)

industry (IHN duh stree) all of the people and companies that sell similar goods or services. (p. 303)

inset map (IHN seht map) a map that gives a close-up view of one part of a map. (p. 246)

interest (IHN trihst) the money a bank pays people for keeping their money there. (p. 269)

Internet (IHN tuhr neht) a large system of computer networks. (p. 80)

interview (IHN tuhr vyoo) a meeting where one person asks another for facts or information. (p. 280)

judicial branch (joo DIHSH uhl branch) the part of government that decides what laws mean and whether laws obey the Constitution. (p. 241)

justice (JUHS tihs) fairness. (p. 353)

lake (layk) large body of standing water, surrounded by land. (p. 28)

landform (LAND fawrm) a shape or feature of the earth's surface. (p. 26)

latitude (LAT ih tood) lines that cross the globe from east to west. (p. 332)

law (law) a rule that tells people how to behave in their communities. (p. 8)

legacy (LEHG uh see) something handed down from the past. (p. 352)

legend (LEHJ UHND) a story passed down form an earlier time. (p. 319)

legislature (LEHJ ih slay chuhr) the lawmaking body of state or national government. (p. 240)

liberty (LIHB uhr tee) freedom. (p. 346)

line graph (lyn graf) a type of graph that uses dots and lines to show how something changes over time. (p. 158)

location (loh KAY shuhn) where a place is on the earth. (p. 36)

longitude (LAHN jih tood) lines that cross the globe from north to south. (p. 332)

map grid (map grihd) a set of straight lines that cross to form squares of equal size. (p. 52)

map key (map kee) the part of a map that explains any symbols or colors on the map. (p. 14)

map scale (map skayl) symbols that help to measure distances on a map. (p. 166)

map title (map TYT l) information that tells what is shown on a map. (p. 14)

market (MAHR kiht) a place where people buy and sell goods. (p. 300)

mayor (MAY uhr) the leader of a city's government. (p. 228)

mission (MISH uhn) a community built around a church. (p. 120)

monument (MAHN yuh mehnt) a building or statue that helps us remember a person or event. (p. 242)

natural resources (NACH ur uhl REE sawrs ehz) things found in nature that are useful to people. (p. 44)

nonrenewable resources (NAHN rih noo uh buhl REE sawrs ehz) resources that cannot be replaced. (p. 45)

opinion (uh PIHN yun) what a person thinks or believes. (p. 358)

opportunity cost (ahp uhr TOO nih tee kawst) the thing that people must give up in order to do what they most want. (p. 275)

participate (pahr TIHS uh payt) to take part in something. (p. 329)

patriotism (PAY tree uh tihz uhm) love for your country. (p. 346)

peninsula (puh NIHN syuh luh) a piece of land nearly surrounded by water. (p. 41)

piedmont (PEED mahnt) gently rolling land at the base of the mountains. (p. 88)

plain (playn) a large area of flat or gently rolling land. (p. 27)

point of view (poynt uhv vyoo) the way someone thinks about an event, an issue, or a person. (p. 232)

pollution (puh LOO shuhn) anything that dirties the air, soil, or water and makes them harmful. (p. 56)

population (pahp yuh LAY shuhn) the number of people who live in an area. (p. 16)

port (pawrt) a place where ships and boats can dock. (p. 29)

primary source (PRY mehr ee sawrs) information from someone who was at an event. (p. 182)

prime meridian (prym muh RIHD ee uhn) a line of longitude that passes through Greenwich, England. (p. 332)

principle (PRIHN suh puhl) a basic truth. (p. 339)

private property (PRY viht PRAHP uhr tee) something that belongs to a person, not the government. (p. 152)

producer (pruh DOO suhr) someone who makes and sells goods. (p. 286)

profit (PRAHF iht) the money a business earns after paying its costs. (p. 152)

railroad (RAYL rohd) a track with two steel rails on which trains move. (p. 161)

recycle (ree SY kuhl) to reuse things that have been thrown away. (p. 47)

reference book (REHF uhr uhns buk) a book that contains facts on many subjects. (p. 80)

region (REE juhn) an area that shares one or more features. (p. 38)

religion (rih LIHJ uhn) the belief in God or gods. (p. 76)

renewable resources (rih NOO uh buhl REE sawrs ehz) resources that can be replaced. (p. 45)

responsibility (rih spahn suh BIHL ih tee) a duty you should do. (p. 214)

right (ryt) a freedom. (p. 212)

river (RIHV uhr) a body of water that flows downhill. (p. 28)

rural area (RUR uhl AIR ee uh) a place far from a city. (p. 19)

scarcity (SKAIR sih tee) a lack of goods or services. (p. 276)

secondary source (SEHK uhn dehr ee sawrs) information from someone who was not at an event. (p. 182)

service (SUR vihs) work that one person does for another. (p. 152)

slavery (SLAY vuh ree) a system under which people have no freedom. (p. 173)

specialize (SPEHSH uh lyz) to do one special kind of work. (p. 287)

steam engine (steem EHN jihn) a machine that turns steam into power. (p. 161)

suburb (SUHB urb) a community next to or close to a city. (p. 18)

supply (suh PLY) the amount producers will make for a certain price. (p. 288)

symbol (SIHM buhl) something that stands for something else. (p. 135)

table of contents (TAY buhl uhv KAHN tehntz) pages that list the sections of a book and tell where they begin. (p. 60)

tax (taks) a fee citizens and others pay to local, state, or national government. (p. 227)

telegraph (TEHL ih graf) a machine that sends signals by electricity. (p. 162)

timeline (TYM lyn) something that shows the dates of events and the order in which they occur. (p. 116)

trade (trayd) to exchange things with someone else. (p. 84)

trade route (trayd root) a road or waterway that people travel to buy, sell, or exchange goods. (p. 110)

tradition (truh DIHSH uhn) a culture's special way of doing something. (p. 91)

transportation (trans puhr TAY shuhn) the way people and things are carried from one place to another. (p. 160)

treaty (TREE tee) an agreement made between nations. (p. 249)

urban area (UR buhn AIR ee uh) city land and spaces. (p. 17)

valley (VAL ee) land between mountains or hills. (p. 27)

volunteer (vahl uhn TIHR) a person who works freely without pay. (p. 203)

vote (voht) to make an official choice. (p. 215)

wampum (WAHM puhm) shell beads. (p. 100)

weather (WEHTH uhr) what the air is like at a certain place and time. (p. 30)

Index

Page numbers with *m* after them refer to maps. Page numbers in italics refer to pictures.

Index

Index

Index

Acknowledgments

Permissioned Literature Selections

Excerpt from *Class President,* by Johanna Hurwitz. Text copyright © 1990 by Johanna Hurwitz. Reprinted by permission of HarperCollins Publishers.

Excerpt from *"Ellis Island,"* from *The World Book Encyclopedia, Vol. 6.* Copyright © 2001 by World Book, Inc. Reprinted by permission of the publisher. www.worldbook.com.

Excerpt from *Eagle Song,* by Joseph Bruchac. Text copyright © 1997 by Joseph Bruchac. Used by permission of Dial Books for Young Readers, a division of Penguin Young Readers Group, a member of Penguin Group (USA) Inc., 345 Hudson Street, New York, NY 10014. All rights reserved.

Excerpt from *Hannah's Journal,* by Marissa Moss. Copyright © 2000 by Marissa Moss. Reprinted by permission of Harcourt, Inc. and the author.

Excerpt from the Speech, *"I Have a Dream,"* by Dr. Martin Luther King Jr. Copyright © 1963 by Dr. Martin Luther King Jr., copyright renewed © 1991 by Coretta Scott King. Reprinted by arrangement with the Estate of Martin Luther King Jr., c/o Writers House as agent for the proprietor New York, NY.

Adapted from *"Johnny Appleseed! Johnny Appleseed!,"* by Marion Vallat Emrich and George Korson in From *Sea To Shining Sea, compiled by Amy L. Cohn.* Copyright © 1993 by Amy L. Cohn. Reprinted by permission of Scholastic Inc.

"Neighborhood of Sun," from *A Movie In My Pillow/ Una película en mi almohada,* by Jorge Argueta. Text copyright © 2001 by Jorge Argueta. Reprinted with the permission of the publisher, Children's Book Press, San Francisco, CA.

Excerpt from *"Searching for Seashells,"* from *Max Malone Makes a Million,* by Charlotte Herman. Text copyright ©1991 by Charlotte Herman. Reprinted by permission of Henry Holt and Company, Inc. and Multimedia Product Development, Inc., Chicago, IL.

"Walking Home From School," by Ann Whitford Paul. Copyright © Ann Whitford Paul. Reprinted by permission of the author.

Photo Credits

COVER (Statue of Liberty) © John Lawrence/Getty Images.(lighthouse) © Stuart Westmorland/CORBIS. (compass) © HMCo./Michael Indresano.(map) Detail illustration on the cover from River Town, by Arthur and Bonnie Geisert. Illustration copyright © 1999 by Arthur Geisert. Reprinted by permission of Houghton Mifflin Company. All rights reserved. (spine Statue of Liberty) © Photodisc/Getty Images. (backcover statue) © Connie Ricca/CORBIS. (backcover nickle) Courtesy of the United States Mint.
i © Michael S. Yamashita/CORBIS.
iii © Michael S. Yamashita/CORBIS.
vi (b) © Myrleen Ferguson Cate/Photo Edit.
vii (t) The Granger Collection. (b) Courtesy of National Constitution Center (Scott Frances, Ltd.).
viii © George H. H. Huey/CORBIS.
ix © Connie Ricca/CORBIS.
xii (t) © Diego Lezama Orezzoli/CORBIS. (b) © David Young-Wolff/Photo Edit.
xiii © Peter Steiner/CORBIS.
xxvi-1 © Ariel Skelley/CORBIS.
2 (l) © Mark Segal/Panoramic Images. (m) © Jose Fuste Raga/CORBIS. (r) © Royalty-Free/CORBIS.
4 (l) © Karl Weatherly/CORBIS. (r) © Jennie Woodcock; Reflections Photolibrary/CORBIS.
5 (l) © Joseph Sohm; Visions of America/CORBIS. (r) © George Lepp/Getty Images.
6 © Yellow Dog Productions/Getty Images.
7(t) © Tom McCarthy/Photo Edit. (b) © Lori Adamski Peek/Getty Images.

8 (t) © Jennie Woodcock; Reflections Photolibrary/CORBIS. (b) © Photodisc/Getty Images.
9 © Sandy Felsenthal/CORBIS.
13 Fachin Fotography.
16 © Ron Sherman Photography.
18 (l) © Joseph Sohm; Visions of America/CORBIS.
20-21 © Mark Segal/Panoramic Images.
21(t) © Jim Cummins/Getty Images.
24 (l) Chris Arend/Alaska Stock. (r) © Royalty-Free/CORBIS.
25 (l) © Royalty-Free/CORBIS. (r) © Ulf Wallin/Getty Images.
26-27 © Reuters NewMedia Inc./CORBIS.
27 (t) © Terry Thompson/Panoramic Images. (m) © Joseph Sohm; ChromoSohm Inc./CORBIS. (b) © Gary Faye/Getty Images.
29 (t) © Ralph White/CORBIS. (b) © Jose Fuste Raga/CORBIS.
30 (l) © Myrleen Ferguson Cate/Photo Edit. (r) Chris Arend/Alaska Stock.
31 © Joe McDonald/CORBIS.
32 (t) © Scoot T. Smith/CORBIS. (b) © Tom Bean/CORBIS.
32-3 © David Muench/CORBIS.
36 © Mark Segal/Getty Images.
38 (l) © Terry Thompson/Panoramic Images. (r) © Robert Holmes/CORBIS.
39 (l) © Grant Heilman/Grant Heilman Photography. (r) © Tom Van Sant/CORBIS.
40(tl) © David Muench/CORBIS. (tr) © Jason Hawkes/CORBIS. (b) © Copyright Dorling Kindersley.
41 © AFP/CORBIS.
42 © CORBIS.
43 © Kevin Fleming/CORBIS.
44-5 © Photodisc/Getty Images.
45 (m) © Owaki – Kulla/CORBIS. (b) © Stephen Frisch/Stock,Boston Inc./ PictureQuest.
46 (t) © Royalty-Free/CORBIS. (b) © JW/Masterfile.
47 (sign) © Jeff Schultz/ Alaskan Express/ PictureQuest.
55 © Schalkwijk/Art Resource, NY.
56 © Danny Lehman/CORBIS.
57 © Macduff Everton/CORBIS.
59 © Robert Frerck/Getty Images.
61 © Jim Cummins/Getty Images.
65 © Russell Curtis/Photo Researchers, Inc.
68-9 © Tom Bean.
70 (l) AKG London. (r) Plimoth Plantation.
71(r)© Rommel/MasterFile.
72 (l) © Ted Spiegel/CORBIS. (r) © Photodisc/Getty Images.
73 (l) Lawrence Migdale. (r) Courtesy of the Woodland Cultural Centre.
74-5 © Gerald French/CORBIS.
76 Marilyn "Angel" Wynn/Nativestock.com.
77 © Ted Spiegel/CORBIS.
78-9 © Ted Spiegel/CORBIS.
78 © Ted Spiegel/CORBIS.
84 Courtesy of the Phoebe Apperson Hearst Museum of Anthropology and the Regents of the University of California 1-1222.
85 © Konrad Wothe/Minden Pictures.
87 (m) Courtesy of the Phoebe Apperson Hearst Museum of Anthropology and the Regents of the University of California 1-1510.
88-9 © Liz Hymans/CORBIS.
89 (l) Marilyn "Angel" Wynn/Nativestock.com. (r) Marilyn "Angel" Wynn/Nativestock.com.
90 Lawrence Migdale.
91 Courtesy of Charlie Soap.
92 National Portrait Gallery, Smithsonian Institution, Washington, DC./Art Resource, NY.
93 (l) Library of Congress. (r) © Greg Probst/Getty Images.
98 The Granger Collection.
99 New York State Museum.

100 (l) Marilyn "Angel" Wynn/Nativestock.com. (r) Courtesy of the Woodland Cultural Centre.
101 Lawrence Migdale.
108 (l) © The Mariners' Museum/CORBIS. (r) Santa Barbara Mission Archive Library.
109 (l) © Kevin Fleming/CORBIS. (r) © Stephen St. John/NGS/Getty Images.
110 AKG London.
112 (l) © Robert Holmes/CORBIS.
112-13 © Bill Ross/CORBIS.
114 (t) © Bettmann/CORBIS. (b) © CORBIS.
114-15 © James P. Blair/CORBIS.
117 AKG London.
119 (t) Plimoth Plantation. (b) © Bettmann/CORBIS.
120 Santa Barbara Mission Archive Library.
122-23 © Burstein Collection/CORBIS.
122 (b) © Larry Williams/CORBIS.
124 Courtesy of National Constitution Center (Scott Frances, Ltd.)
125 Private Collection.
126 (r) National Portrait Gallery, Smithsonian Institution, Washington, DC./Art Resource, NY
128 © North Carolina Museum of Art/CORBIS.
129 (t) © Bettmann/CORBIS. (b) © Bettmann/CORBIS.
131 © Yellow Dog Productions/Getty Images.
132 © Photodisc/Getty Images.
134 (l) © Lee Snider/The Image Works. (r) © Rommel/MasterFile.
136-37 © Royalty-Free/CORBIS.
141 Nebraska State Historical Society.
144-5 © Bettmann/CORBIS.
146(l) Smithsonian American Art Museum, Washington, DC./Art Resource, NY. (r) National Archives.
147 Alcantara/Brazil Photo Bank.
148 (l) The Granger Collection.
149 (l) © Bettmann/CORBIS. (r) The Granger Collection.
150 Smithsonian American Art Museum, Washington, DC./Art Resource, NY.
153 Richard Sisk/Panoramic Images/NGSImages.
159 © Photodisc/Getty Images.
160 Central Pacific Railroad Photographic History Musuem, Photograph by Alfred Hart.
162 (l) Electricity Collections, NMAH, Smithsonian Institution # 74-2491.(r) The Granger Collection.
163 © Craig Aurness/CORBIS.
164 © Connie Ricca/CORBIS.
165 (l) © George H. H. Huey/CORBIS. (r) © George Hall/CORBIS.
170 (l) © Chabruken/Getty Images. (r) Brown Brothers.
171 (r) © Tony Garcia/Getty Images.
172 © Chabruken/Getty Images.
173 (l) © CORBIS. (r) © Bettmann/CORBIS.
174-5 © Greg Probst/CORBIS.
174 (l) California State Library # 912. (r) © CORBIS.
175 (l) National Archives. (r) © Warren Morgan/CORBIS.
176 (l) American Jewish Joint Distribution Committee. (r) V.C.L./Getty Images.
177 © Condé Nast Archive/CORBIS.
183 Brown Brothers.
184-5 © Yann Arthus-Bertrand/CORBIS.
185 Alcantara/Brazil Photo Bank.
186 Miguel Chikaoka/Brazil Photo Bank.
188-9 © Rob Matheson/CORBIS.
188 (b) © Planetary Visions Ltd./Photo Researchers, Inc. (t) Miguel Chikaoka/Brazil Photo Bank.
189 (l) © Tom Brakefield/CORBIS. (r) © ESA/ PLI/CORBIS.
193 Library of Congress.
198 (l) Courtesy Paradise Valley Unified School District, Students Can Build It!/Habitat For Humanity. (r) © Photodisc/Getty Images.
200 (l) Courtesy Paradise Valley Unified School District, Students Can Build It!/Habitat For Humanity. (r) © David Schmidt/Masterfile.

201 (l) © Jeff Greenberg/Photo Edit. (r) © Myrleen Ferguson/Photo Edit.
202 © Myrleen Ferguson/Photo Edit.
203 (l) © David Schmidt/Masterfile. (r) © Myrleen Ferguson/Photo Edit.
204 (t) Courtesy Paradise Valley Unified School District, Students Can Build It!/Habitat For Humanity. (b) © Photodisc/Getty Images.
205 Courtesy Paradise Valley Unified School District, Students Can Build It!/Habitat For Humanity.
213 (tl) © Patrick Ingrand/Getty Images. (tr) © SW productions/Brand X Pictures/Getty Images. (bl) © Jeff Greenberg/PhotoEdit. (br) © Royalty-Free/CORBIS.
222 (l) © Bob Daemmrich/ Stock, Boston Inc./ PictureQuest. (r) AP Photo/Topeka Capital-Journal, Anthony S. Bush.
223 (l) Reuters New Media Inc./CORBIS. (r) AP Wide World Photos.
224 © Gabe Palmer/CORBIS.
225 © Robert Brenner / Photo Edit.
226-7 © Jeff Greenberg / Photo Edit.
228 © Bob Daemmrich/ Stock, Boston Inc./ PictureQuest.
229 (t) © A. Ramey / Photo Edit. (b) © Photodisc/ Getty Images.
231 (t) © Photodisc/Getty Images.
233 © Lynda Richardson/CORBIS.
234 AP Photo/Dan Loh.
236 (t) © David Muench/CORBIS. (b) © Lawrence Migdale/ Stock, Boston Inc./ PictureQuest.
237 © Photodisc/Getty Images.
238 © Royalty-Free/CORBIS.
239 (t) © Lee Snider; Lee Snider/CORBIS. (b) © Joseph Sohm; Visions of America/CORBIS.
240 © Andrea Pistolesi/Getty Images.
241 (t) © Peter Gridley/Getty Images. (b) © Photodisc/ Getty Images.
242 (t) © Theo Allofs/CORBIS. (b) © Arthur Tilley/ i2i Images/PictureQuest.
243 © Walter Bibikow /Getty Images.
248 AP Photo/Ron Edmonds.
249 (l) © Robert Holmes/CORBIS. (r) © Patti McConville/Getty Images.
250 © Louise Gubb/CORBIS SABA.
251 AP Photo/Sasa Kralj.
252-3 © Louise Gubb/CORBIS SABA.
257 © Jeff Greenberg/Photo Edit.
260-1 © Joe McNally.
263 (r) Bill Bachmann/Photo Edit.
264 (l) © David Young-Wolff/Photo Edit.
265 (r) © James Leynse/CORBIS

266 (t) PhotoSpin. (m) PhotoSpin.
284 (l) AP Photo.
284 (r) © Spencer Grant/Photo Edit.
285 (l) © William Taufic/CORBIS.
285 (r) © Jeff Zaruba/Getty Images.
286 AP Photo.
287 (t) © Mark Gibson.
288 © Robert Landau/CORBIS.
294 (t) © Michael S. Yamashita/CORBIS.(m) © Roger Ball/ CORBIS. (b) © William Taufic/CORBIS.
296 © AFP/CORBIS.
297 The Granger Collection.
302-3 © Liu Liqun/CORBIS.
303 © Earl & Nazima Kowall/CORBIS.
309 © David Young-Wolff/Photo Edit.
312-13 © Ariel Skelley/CORBIS.
314 © Peter Hince/Getty Images.
315 (r) © Syracuse Newspapers/Dick Blume/The Image Works.
316 (l) © Donna Day/Getty Images.
317 (r) © Robert Brenner/PhotoEdit.
318 © A. Ramey/Photo Edit.
320 (t) © Dan Connell//The Image Works. (b) © Michael S. Yamashita/CORBIS.
321 © Donna Day/Getty Images.
326 © Diego Lezama Orezzoli/CORBIS.
327 © TASS/Sovfoto.
328 (l) © TASS/Sovfoto.
329 © Peter Hince/Getty Images.
330 (t) © Photodisc/Getty Images. (b) © TASS/Sovfoto.
336 (l) © Michael Newman/Photo Edit. (r) © Mark Reinstein/Getty Images.
337 (l) © Bettmann/CORBIS. (r) © Bettman/CORBIS.
338 Lawrence Migdale.
339 © David Young-Wolff/Photo Edit.
340 (t) © Michael Newman/Photo Edit. (b) © Arthur Tilley/Getty Images.
341 © Annie Griffiths Belt/CORBIS.
342 © Norbert von der Groeben/The Image Works.
343 (t) © Bill Aron/Photo Edit. (b) AP Photo.
344 © Joe Sohm/ Stock, Boston Inc./ PictureQuest.
345 © Bettmann/CORBIS.
346 (l) © Jan Butchofsky-Houser/CORBIS. (r) © Ariel Skelley/CORBIS.
347 (l) © Pete Saloutos/CORBIS. (r) © Photodisc/Getty Images.
348 (l) © David Young-Wolff/Photo Edit. (r) AP Photo.
349 © Royalty-Free/CORBIS.
350-1 © David Young-Wolff/Photo Edit.
350(b) © Bettmann/CORBIS.

351 AP Photo/U.S. Postal Service Handout.
352 © Syracuse Newspapers/Dick Blume/The Image Works.
353 (l) Library of Congress. (r) © Oscar White/CORBIS.
354 (t) The Granger Collection. (b) © CORBIS.
355 © Richard Howard/ Black Star Publishing/ PictureQuest.
356 © STONE LES/CORBIS SYGMA.
357 (t) AP Photo/Danny Wilcox Frazier. (b) © The Nobel Foundation.
359 © Bettmann/CORBIS.
363 © A. Ramey/Photo Edit.
R1 (bl) Johnny Johnson/Photographer's Choice/Getty Images. (bkgd) Paul A. Souders/CORBIS. (tr) Photo Library International/CORBIS.
R2-R3 (inset) Chip Henderson/Index Stock Imagery. (bkgd) CORBIS.
R4-R5 Richard T. Nowitz/CORBIS.
R6-R7 Liz Hymans/CORBIS.
R8 (cl) CORBIS. (frame) Image Farm/HMCo. (br) Bettmann/CORBIS.
R14 Art Wolfe/Stone/Getty Images.
R15 (tl) Michael T. Sedam/CORBIS. (br) D. Rose/Zefa/Masterfile.

Assignment Photo Credits

292, 295 © HMCo./Joel Benjamin. v, 14, 17, 47, 64-65, 81, 95, 131, 140-1, 144-5, 155-7, 192-3, 206-9, 211, 215, 230-1, 244-5, 256-7, 262 (l), 264 (r), 265 (l), 267, 268, 269, 272, 273, 274, 275, 278, 279, 289, 300, 308-9, 317(l), 319, 362-3 © HMCo./Angela Coppola. xxiv-xxv © HMCo./Ken Karp. 214, 281 © HMCo./Michael Indresano. 45 (t) © HMCo./Carol Kaplan. 18 (m) (b), 19 © HMCo./Ken Krakow Photography.

Illustrations

xxiv-xxv © Sally Vitsky. 10-11 Diane Greenseid. 28-29 International Mapping Associates. 58-59 Will Williams. 82-83,86-87 Inklink. 96-97 Francis Back. 103-104 Bill Farnsworth. 152 Steve McEntee. 154-157 Nenad Jakesevic. 161 Patrick Gnan. 188-189 Ken Batelman. 217 Eric Velasquez. 226-227, 235, 254 Andy Levine. 271-273 Rich Harrington. 290-291 Ruth Flanigan. 292-293 Luigi Galante. 298-299 Steve McEntee. 301 Andy Levine. 304-305 Annette Cable. 310 Rob Schuster. 322-324 Phil Boatwright. All charts and graphs by Pronk & Associates. R14-R15 International Mapping Associates.

Maps

All maps by MapQuest. All atlas cartographic maps done by Ortellios Design.

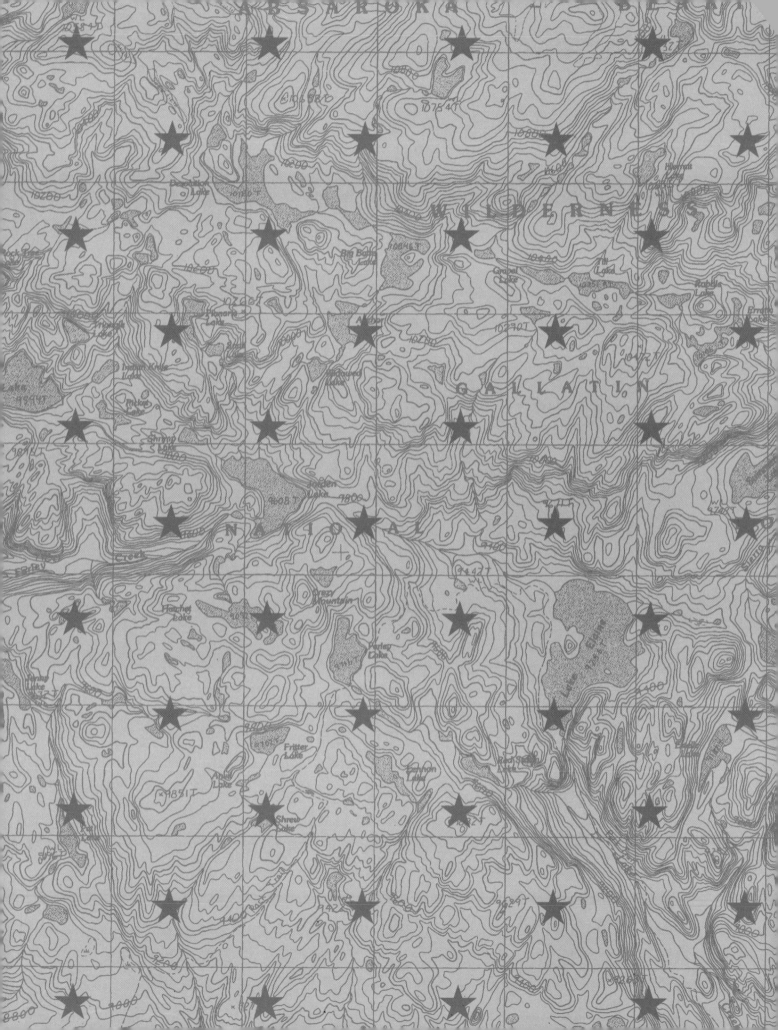

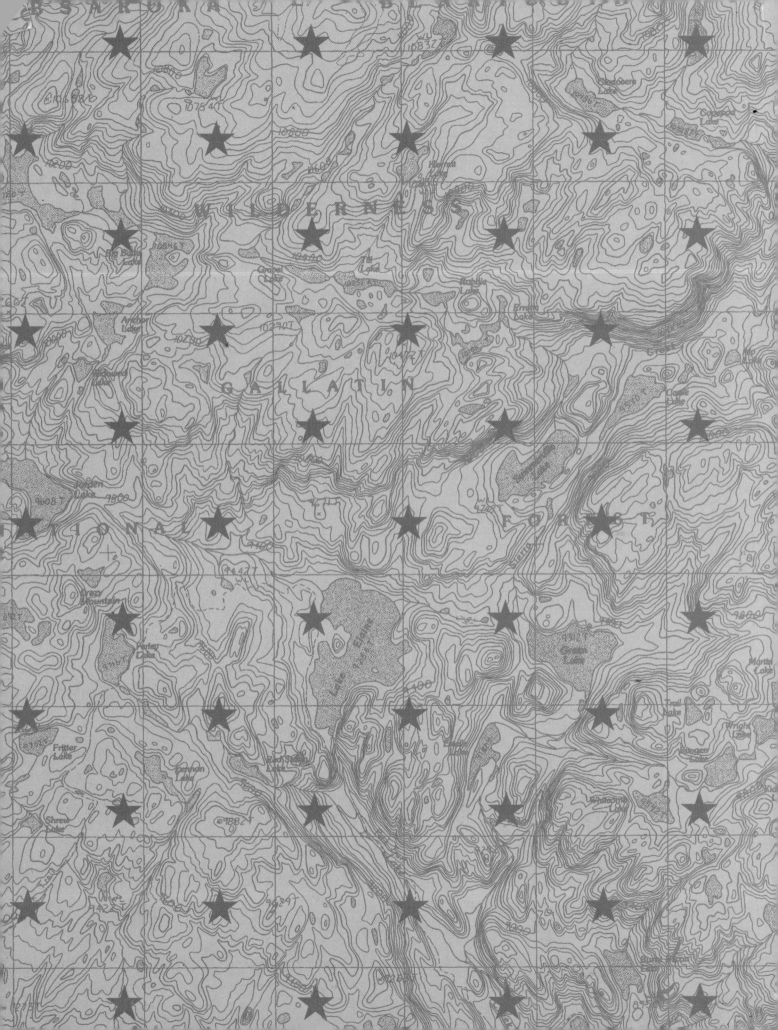